Somehow I am Different

NARRATIVES
OF SEARCHING AND BELONGING
IN JEWISH BUDAPEST

ALYSSA PETERSEL

If you enjoy this book, please leave a review on Amazon or via social media. You can connect with Alyssa at @apetersel on Twitter or Instagram, or visit www.somehowiamdifferent.com for more information.

Interior design by Alyssa Petersel and Jessica Therrien
Cover Graffiti by Zsili and Ebook Cover Design by www.ebooklaunch.com

ISBN: 978-0692584118
First Edition: March 2016
10 9 8 7 6 5 4 3 2 1

Praise for *Somehow I Am Different*

"The quality and care in the writing and Alyssa's human sensitivity have really helped her to capture the richness and reality of life among those who trusted her with their stories. This achievement is remarkable, especially in such a young writer."

Alex Russell, Rocín Publishing

"Alyssa Petersel's first book is a tour de force narrative and a compelling exploration of contemporary Jewish life in Budapest. In bringing together twenty-one different voices of men and women, and highlighting important topics such as tradition, rebellion, memory, belief, and leadership, she offers the reader a unique glimpse into a little known but robust and dynamic community of Jewish seekers and strivers. This book is well worth reading for anyone interested in matters of identity and community."

Niles Goldstein, founding rabbi of The New Shul and award-winning author of ten books, most recently Eight Questions of Faith: Biblical Challenges That Guide and Ground Our Lives

"You will become engrossed in these captivating stories. Alyssa Petersel's clean, elegant prose will take you on a journey to discover the beauty and resilience of Budapest's young Jews. Moving and full of charm, this book is a meditation on belonging and what it means to be human."

Simon Goldberg, PhD candidate at Strassler Center for Holocaust and Genocide Studies, former Director of Education at Hong Kong Holocaust and Tolerance Centre, former Executive Director at Triangles of Truth

For a full list of reviews for *Somehow I Am Different*, please visit www.somehowiamdifferent.com/praise

For Rozália Berman

and all the searchers out there.

AUTHOR'S NOTE

To support *Somehow I Am Different*, I raised $12,085 through Kickstarter (kickstarter.com). You may learn more about the invaluable individuals who donated to make this project possible in *Acknowledgments*.

From June 6, 2014 to January 13, 2015, I immersed myself as best I could into the routines, adventures, and culture of contemporary Jewish life in Budapest. I conducted over fifty interviews. The twenty-one interviewees presented here illustrate a range of perspectives and experiences that represent my understanding of modern Jewish life in Budapest. I say life because life is what strikes me in Budapest – life, not death.

I have intentionally included twenty-one, or three times seven, interviews in this book. Seven is the most sacred number in Judaism. Rabbi Yaakov Salomon said that, "For reasons unknown to us, G-d seemed to have a special affinity for the number seven." Seven centers us; it gives us direction and a foundation on which to stand and to build. Seven inspires us to create, to learn, and to innovate. I believe that my interviewees are recreating what it means to be Jewish and to live a life of purpose. These individuals set an example for others who are searching for meaning. As seven is also a symbol of continuity, this text is a call for action. With this book I ask you to redefine your wholeness. Unveil what you are yearning for and commit to its completion.

October 2015

CONTENTS

SOMEHOW I AM DIFFERENT

(Lech-Lecha, Lekh-Lekha, or Lech-L'cha) לֶךְ-לְךָ
Hebrew for "Go!" or "Leave!"
Literally "Go for you," or "Go to yourself."

"Get you (לֶךְ-לְךָ) out of your country, and from your kindred ...
to the land that I will show you."

Genesis 12:1

INTRODUCTION

"If we could see the miracle of a single flower clearly,
our whole life would change." - Buddha

"WHY ARE YOU HERE?" MY HUNGARIAN PEERS ASKED.

Two years ago, I ventured to Budapest for my interviewees to help me find the answer to their very question. Why are we here? How do we come to find meaning and purpose that drives us?

In 1944, the Holocaust began for Hungary. Prior to 1944, despite mounting anti-Semitism politically and socially, Hungary was immune to the darkest depths of the Holocaust due to its strong alliance with Nazi Germany. Following suspicion of betrayal, Germany invaded Hungary in March 1944. By May 8, 1945, The Nazi Party and its Hungarian accomplices had murdered nearly 500,000 Jews and other minorities in forced labor and concentration camps.

For the few survivors, their return home to Hungary was deeply challenging. In contrast to their high hopes, they arrived to discover their property and possessions were stolen; their friends, families and acquaintances either abandoned them or were killed; and their country, the only place they knew to be home, deemed them as less human than their non-Jewish peers and equals.

Consequently, a majority of Hungarian Jews swore off their Judaism. They yearned to protect their family from a feared repetition of the ominous past. For those that maintained their Judaism, they kept their faith a secret, especially during the Hungarian Communist Era. Accordingly, children and grandchildren of Holocaust survivors with Jewish roots were left not only without faith, but also without an awareness that faith was once prominently woven into their families' identity.

Not until this generation – *my* generation – has Judaism again become a topic of conversation.

Upon the fall of the Hungarian Communist Regime in 1989, religious doors flew open. Young Hungarians opened community centers and schools, launched exploratory programs and initiated pub-crawls and spirituality hunts. The drive to define and connect with spirituality flourished throughout the city.

In March 2013, I benefited from the privilege of participating in a Jewish service trip to Budapest, Hungary organized by two Northwestern students and supported by the Fiedler Hillel on Northwestern University's campus. The unique opportunity to interact with young Jewish Budapest face-to-face told me a story I would not have encountered elsewhere.

Today, Hungarian young adults discover their religious roots in a host of unexpected places. A grandmother on her deathbed may confess her Judaism to her granddaughter because she does not want to die without sharing her *real* identity. A grandson may notice his grandmother's matzah ball soup for sale at the newest and hippest Jewish deli in the center of town. A daughter may feel mysteriously drawn to the Jewish community center down the block as an opportunity to find a sense of belonging.

What I find most inspiring about these stories is not that older generations are suddenly feeling comfortable enough to share with their children and grandchildren. What is most compelling for me is the reaction of those receiving the information. In spite of chronic anti-semitism in Hungary and living successfully for sixteen to thirty years with no awareness of their Jewish roots, more often than not, these individuals with newfound knowledge are moved to do something with it. These young adults become the focal points of their spiritual communities. They ignite an unprecedented creativity through their religious expression and the expression of their peers. These individuals are the educators, the storytellers, the change makers and the leaders. These are the voices we ought to be listening to.

Though I originally traveled to Budapest with the intention of giving something to the community on the ground, the reverse came to be true. International news and media outlets paint frightening circumstances inside and out of Jewish Hungary. Jewish Budapest, however, filled me with light, opportunity, and hope.

For other struggling communities or individuals, Jewish Budapest has the capacity to illustrate how to capitalize on strengths in order to not only survive, but to thrive beautifully. The individuals that make up Jewish Budapest mark a search for identity that individuals across the globe can relate to.

Somehow I Am Different is a case study of how we can come to better understand ourselves by better understanding others. I hope that after reading this book, you are more understanding of the tremendous diversity and life of Jewish Budapest. I also hope that after reading this book, you are more likely to relate to your neighbor, whether he or she is the neighbor next-door, the neighbor on the train on the commute to work, or the neighbor in a foreign country.

Regardless of our differences, we have a lot in common.

If we are able to understand this notion, we can look past headlines that bleed blood, violence, and hatred. Instead, we can believe in the strength, potential, and humanity of our fellow people. Once we have faith in each other, we can explore and reinvent the ways in which we respond to atrocities like the Holocaust and present-day oppression and marginalization.

This generation holds the responsibility to make a difference. We, as an international community, can create a platform to unveil a brighter future despite past periods of darkness. We have to step up.

These individual stories have changed my life. I believe that they can change yours, too.

ZSUZSANNA FRITZ

"Everybody around me was Jewish: my grandparents, my parents, friends, relatives, everybody… but I had no idea."

THE HIGH-PITCHED WAIL OF MY ALARM jolted me awake. Rolling onto my back, I peered at the ceiling to find a smooth white coat of paint that I did not recognize. I sat up and looked across the room to find my pocket-sized purple alarm clock, the same clock that had made it through a variety of week and month-long trips, stuffed into the side pouch of my oversized tattered backpack. I sighed a long, meditated exhale. I was not at home. I was in Budapest, in my new apartment, in my new bed, awaiting my new shower. Reality rushed through me – my alarm rang at precisely 8:32am. I had an interview downtown in one hour.

I tossed the sheets to the side and leapt into the bathroom. I pulled back the shower curtain to find my shower had only a hand-held spout. For the next eight months, my thick, brown hair would win the fight against the showerhead to retain most of its shampoo and conditioner.

Nearly fifteen minutes later, I peered into the only floor-length mirror in the apartment. Tilting my head to the left, I took a deep breath and gathered my pack of equipment: my miniature recorder, an iPad to hold the recordings, my cell phone to direct me to where I needed to go, my wallet to purchase my first latte, my journal containing quotes of encouragement, and a pen for everything else.

I stepped one foot after the other out the kitchen door. Natural light shined through the open ceiling and plants overflowed their pots lining the perimeter of the building's shared courtyard. I hurried down three sets of wide, marble stairs when *smack*! I ran straight into the door.

It wouldn't budge. Stepping back to massage my palms, one of my neighbors approached me with narrow eyes and a cunning smile. He pushed a white button that resembled a light switch. A buzzer sounded as he gracefully exited the building. "Aha," I thought to myself, "the exit button."

The brightness of the day burned the corners of my eyes. The streets appeared deserted - no people, no cars. Google maps predicted a forty-five-minute walk to Bálint Ház, the Jewish Community Center in the heart of the Seventh District of Budapest.

Twenty-three districts make up the two sides of Budapest, Buda and Pest, divided by the Danube River. I had settled in the Seventh District in Pest, colloquially nicknamed "The Jewish District" because of its notable collection of Jewish pubs, cafés, community centers, and social activism hubs.

Directly across from my apartment sat a charming hole-in-the-wall café and bakery. I entered and found myself nose-to-nose with who I presumed to be the owner, an elderly woman in a salmon pink long-sleeved t-shirt. Her short, silver curls framed her rosy cheeks. She spoke to me in Hungarian. I requested a latte in English. She furrowed her eyebrows and watched as I exited her shop. I stood on the street, face lifted toward the sky, hoping the sunlight would miraculously install fluent Hungarian into my system.

As I continued my walk, I admired the magnificent streets and colors of the Seventh District of Budapest. The closer I got to Bálint Ház, the more people, cafés, and shops seemed to inundate the streets. I slid my back against the wall of a building to allow a group of young men to pass. A mural painted on the opposite street caught my attention. Above the circular abstract image of a girl with a rainbow arching away from her heart was a quote that read in English, "Is this just a dream?" While the sunlight originally stunted my vision, the mural fed my motivation to pursue.

I glanced at my map. It appeared I had arrived, though I was still lost. I circled the block, taking in smells of pizza by the slice and sights of gyros for 200 forints (about one U.S. dollar). Finally, my eyes settled on a familiar multi-colored logo composed of seven *mezuzot*.

A *mezuzah*, Hebrew for doorpost, is a piece of parchment—often enclosed in a decorative rectangular case—inscribed with particular Hebrew verses from the Torah (Deuteronomy 6:4-9 and 11:13-21) that comprise the Jewish prayer *Shema Yisrael*. According to Jewish law, the act of posting a mezuzah on the doorposts of a home fulfills a mitzvah, or Biblical commandment. Spiritually, the mezuzah protects the home and those within it. Practically speaking, today, the logo represented my destination: Bálint Ház.

I tugged at my dress, hoping to smooth out its kinks, and walked into the building. Security stopped me at the door. After answering their questions unsatisfactorily, I found myself in a waiting room decorated with pictures of smiling faces and Jewish-holiday-themed cartoon posters. Picking at my fingernails, I repeatedly crossed and uncrossed my legs.

Zsuzsa, a woman with over thirty years of experience in building and renovating Jewish Budapest, bounced into the room. The Hungarian "zs" is pronounced close to the French 'j' as in "Jacques" or the consonant in the middle of the English word "measure."

Bright orange curls branched away from her face. Though nearly twenty-five years my senior, Zsuzsa's vivid dress and flowery hand gestures welcomed me as an equal and a friend. We hugged. I sat back in my chair, took a deep breath and placed my hands comfortably in my lap.

While I was still in the U.S., Zsuzsa responded to my countless emails, questions, and needs throughout every stage of the endless process of drafting a project proposal, applying for grants, being rejected from grants, creating a Kickstarter, and being funded successfully enough to land square in the middle of this booming town and bellowing Jewish culture.

Zsuzsa was born in Budapest in 1966 and has lived in the city ever since. She grew up in the very center between the Hungarian Academy of Sciences and the House of Parliament. She said, "My grandma was taking me in the... what do you call it..." She wafted her hand and closed her eyes. "*Stroller!* In front of the Parliament in the stroller. I have pictures of that."

Three generations of Zsuzsa's family lived together: her maternal grandparents, her parents, and her. She said, "Everybody around me was Jewish: my grandparents, my parents, friends, relatives, everybody... but I had no idea."

When Zsuzsa was in elementary school, she remembered whispering between two of her best friends who asked each other, "What religion are you?" Zsuzsa said to herself,

"Okay, what am I, what am I? What should I answer?" She had no idea. She somehow understood at the age of eight that she was not Catholic because there were no crosses in her apartment. "So, I said I was Protestant, because that seemed like, I don't know what that is, but probably I am that."

In the 1960s and 70s, Hungary was a communist country and religion was not a topic to discuss. Zsuzsa said, "Religion was something if you wanted individually to live it, you could, mostly. Not secretly, but very low profile because if you were religious, it meant that you were probably watched, or definitely you were not going to advance in your career. Your child may have difficulty in getting into universities. Even people for whom it was really important, they tried to really keep a low profile. So, there was almost nothing happening Jewishly as well. You know, if five Jews came together, that was Zionist activity, which was forbidden."

Zsuzsa did not know of her Jewish roots until she was sixteen years old. She realized because her father's funeral was a Jewish funeral with a rabbi, Hebrew gravestones, *tefillin*, which are two small black boxes containing scrolls of parchment inscribed with verses from the Torah that observant men strap to their head and arm each weekday morning to pray, and *kepot*, or small round caps worn by Jewish men to fulfill the requirement that a man's head be covered at all times.

"I wouldn't say suddenly, but I realized that I somehow am different from most of my classmates," she said. "As it later on turned out, not all of my classmates." Many years later, Zsuzsa reconnected with friends and classmates who learned long after high school that they were Jewish. They were all relieved to learn they were not as alone as they thought.

Zsuzsa said, "At first, it didn't really mean much. It was more like these puzzle pieces coming to their places. People always ask me, 'So what did you do?' It wasn't a big shock; I didn't know what Jewish meant."

Nothing in Zsuzsa's apartment or lifestyle helped her to define what being Jewish was. "No mezuzot, no menorahs," she said. "Maybe there were a couple of books about Judaism, or something, that I of course didn't notice as a child."

Select phrases or expressions that Zsuzsa frequently heard her grandparents say helped her later on to define her Jewish identity. "For example," she said, "if on TV there was somebody Jewish, my grandparents would say, *'Izere'*, or, 'Also a musician' in Hungarian, meaning 'Also one of us.' Of course, because I didn't know, I didn't know."

A few months after her father's death, Zsuzsa's mother told her that her best friend's daughter went to the rabbinical seminary and met a boy. "She said maybe I should go, too. So, I went."

The rabbinical seminary was one of the only Jewish institutions operating during the communist regime. Professor Sándor Schrieber was the director and rabbi of the seminary at the time, who Zsuzsa remembers to be a great rabbi, man, scholar, and personality. She explained, "He would gather around himself a lot of young people. Every Friday night there was a Kabbalat Shabbat in the synagogue of the rabbinical seminary in the Eighth District of the city. Then, after the Kabbalat Shabbat, all the people from the service and all these young people would go upstairs for Kiddush. Then he would speak something interesting and there was hot chocolate and *challah*, braided bread traditionally eaten on Shabbat. There were like thirty- forty- fifty- young people standing in the back of the room listening to him."

"I suddenly got dropped into this thing," Zsuzsa said. "I went with this guy, and then we met all these new people. The only thing that connected us basically was that they were also Jewish."

Zsuzsa paused.

"I fell in love," she said. "I suddenly had this community. That's how I started learning what Judaism really means, or what Jewish means. That's where I started somehow forming my Jewish identity."

Zsuzsa and her community talked through big debates about whether they were more Hungarian Jews or Jewish Hungarians. With her peers, she spent Friday evenings discussing not just Jewish issues, but literature, politics, Hungarianisms, and "all this thing." She said, "It was the 1980s... everybody thought the regime will end, so it was much more *free*. All these young people were more and more active in Jewish life and more and more there were possibilities."

Gradually, Zsuzsa surrounded herself with friends she met and connected with through Judaism. "I was sixteen," she said. "It was exactly the time when you look for people."

The more excited Zsuzsa got telling me her story, the heavier her Hungarian accent became. She nearly stood from her seat as she explained that when the Iron Curtain fell, suddenly, there was a possibility to make official Jewish organizations again. Jewish schools and youth movements were established.

"We were very active and involved in all of them because it was this big energy," she said. "It was kept in ourselves during the time that it was not possible to raise your voice as a Jew. We had to whisper Judaism. Then suddenly everyone is active and involved. I really loved it. This is the core of my personality."

In 1989, Zsuzsa went to Israel for the first time as a *madricha*, a youth counselor. At that time, she was an English teacher and participated in a program that enabled her to spend three weeks in a camp in Israel and then travel for one extra week around the country. She met people in Israel who would come to the Jewish Agency in Hungary the following year as *shluchim*, or Jewish messengers dedicated to the growth and strength of Judaism. When they arrived and established their grounding, they frequently contacted Zsuzsa for help with youth programming. She became more and more involved.

In 1990, Zsuzsa received a job offer to be a Jewish educator at the American Joint, which would open its office in Hungary in July 1990. The American Jewish Joint Distribution Committee, more informally nicknamed the Joint or JDC, identifies as the world's leading Jewish humanitarian assistance organization. According to its website, since

1914, the Joint has stood by a philosophy that all Jews are responsible for one another. Today, as an action-oriented organization, JDC works in over seventy countries worldwide to "alleviate hunger and hardship, rescue Jews in danger, create lasting connections to Jewish life, and provide immediate relief and long-term development support for victims of natural and man-made disasters."

Zsuzsa said, "This offer was very funny because I was a teacher of English and Russian. I had some ideas about education, but I had no ideas about *Jewish* education. They said, 'No worry, we gonna teach you.' I said, 'Okay, fine.'"

Zsuzsa began working for the Joint in 1990 and continues to work for the Joint today. 2014 was her twenty-fifth year. The summer of 1990 was the first year of Szarvas, a Jewish international youth summer camp. Zsuzsa said, "I went there, and I have been there ever since. I got stuck. I get stuck in these things."

As a result of her limited Jewish upbringing and education, Zsuzsa felt she knew very little at the beginning of her career at the Joint. "I learned the day before a holiday what that holiday really means," she said. "Everybody was like that. Nobody had real knowledge. When we started the camp, every song was new. Every Jewish dance was new. It was also a big euphoria because of like, 'Wow, a new morsel of knowledge.'"

Zsuzsa glanced around the room at the smiling faces in the hanging photographs. She turned back in my direction and mirrored the children's smiles in her eyes.

"People really wanted to be in it," she said. "People really wanted to form their identity, to learn about what Jewish really means. There were a lot of people who discovered, through the freedom, the possibility of belonging to this community. Us, who were involved a few years before, we were basically the keys to the community."

In 1994, the Joint opened the Jewish Community Center (JCC) in Budapest called *Bálint Ház* where Zsuzsa and I now sat. Zsuzsa moved to the JCC and her role became to run youth programming in Budapest. Her mission was to create an ongoing Szarvas camp in Budapest all year long.

"This didn't happen," she said.

"First of all, if it's a community center, it's not just youth who use it. Youth decide where they want to go and it's not necessarily a community building where there are also elderly and adults."

When the JCC first opened, many people visited, utilized its programming and were excited about their new discoveries. After a few years, the commotion died down.

"The excited period expired in a way," Zsuzsa said. "Democracy showed people you really have to work to make a living. There was also way more things the city was offering culturally, so there was a lot of competition going on."

Zsuzsa's voice grew hoarse. Between us sat a pile of colorful square and circle-shaped toys. Zsuzsa reached for a small, orange ball and squeezed it in her right hand.

"All of the Jewish organizations didn't open up and say, 'Okay, let's cooperate,'" she said. "So all these Jewish organizations were working side by side, not together. There came a period when a huge disappointment replaced the renaissance and the euphoria of the first years."

In 2005, Zsuzsa became the director of the JCC. "First, I refused. Then, I refused, then refused, then refused. Then, I said, 'Yes.'"

Zsuzsa's began to think about, "Okay, what is a Jewish community center? What is the role in this period of time? What can we do? What *should* we do?"

As Zsuzsa said "should," she nearly threw the orange ball across the room.

One of the major goals that came out of her brainstorming was to cooperate with other organizations. "It took a few years," she said, "but now, the Jewish organizations really understand that we really mean it." Many Hungarian organizations look to the JCC for partnership in a variety of projects. The JCC is also increasingly becoming involved in projects with non-Jewish organizations that are involved in the betterment of society. "That's also something important for us to do as Jews," Zszusa said.

Zsuzsa explained that by principle, the JCC charges for almost everything, with the exception of a handful of free outreach programs. She said, "Still, today, the community basically lives on outside money. We want to teach people to contribute. Even if it's a contribution of your entrance fee, you need to understand that whatever we are creating is a value, and if you want this to continue, then you will have to start contributing."

Zsuzsa's Jewish identity was formed around a sense of community. "That was Judaism for me," she said. "That is

16

one of the things we needed to create. You could hardly find positive and happy in Budapest or in the everyday community of Hungarian Jewry. So, we decided that we could create a positive Jewish identification. We created an open door and said whoever wants to come, we are happy to receive you."

Zsuzsa feels a commitment to staying in Budapest despite ominous political and economic changes in the country. "I feel there is a need for community life here and we have a task in that," she said. "I never really felt the need to leave. It is a very deep pit right now in Hungary…it's very difficult to stay positive about a lot of things. But I really feel that there is a value that this community created in this country and it should be kept on going. So yes, I am committed to staying."

Jewish life is not what worries Zsuzsa in her day-to-day routine. She said, "Right now in Hungary, Jewish life continues. Many times I feel that if I read the articles and comments, I think the situation is horrible. But if I don't read these things, it's like you live in a bubble and Jewish life is growing. At the same time, the political moves are undercutting democratic liabilities and that is much more depressing than anti-Semitism. Because okay, we know anti-Semitism. We know that. That's there."

Zsuzsa's posture stiffened. She leaned forward on the edge of her seat. "Most of the time, I think the negative attitude, it doesn't really come from the outside threat," she said. "It comes from the traumas that we are carrying for generations. From our great-grandfathers who survived, or didn't survive, the Holocaust. These are the traumas that we are carrying and the hidden stories that are not spoken about. That's what creates ambivalence about identity. Everything is fearful because you didn't really work through it."

Zsuzsa had the chance to understand her roots at a time when it was encouraging to do so. She could experience community as an optimistic thing. "I am lucky in that sense," she said. Among her friends, there are a number of people for whom Judaism is something that they are not entirely sure about. They suffer from past traumas that have not yet been digested.

Zsuzsa credits her positivity to her family. She said, "I really think that what I received from my parents and grandparents is a lot of love and joy and humor. That gives me energy." She grew up in a safe and secure environment with a lot of laughing and singing, hikes and travels, and love. "I am sure that is what gives me positive energy," she said. "And when I work with youth and children, that gives me energy, too."

In reference to her Judaism, intermittently throughout our conversation Zszusa said, "It is just me." Her Judaism is not something she switches on or off depending on where she is or who she is talking to. It is not something she pulls out of her pocket when she is going through a particularly blissful or challenging situation. It is just her, as integral to who she is as her family name or eye color.

Zsuzsa placed the orange ball on the surface of the table between us. She stood from her chair, wrapped me in a firm embrace, insisted we meet again soon and excused herself to tend to a community gathering in the room next door.

One kiss on each cheek later, she walked toward those who were patiently waiting.

MÁRK SÜVEG

*"Hip hop and rap helped me a lot. So, what it gave me,
I have to give back."*

"LEATHER JACKET AND HELMET, leather jacket and helmet..." I reminded myself of how Márk said I would
recognize him. A mid-autumn crisp morning, the sun
peered through Jelen's tall windows, highlighting artwork
sketched across its four interior walls. Jelen, pronounced
yell-en, which means *present* in Hungarian, was covered in
posters for music and documentary film festivals. Beneath a
wide, high ceiling, Jelen boasted two stages for live music
and an eclectic collection of mismatched chairs and wooden
tables of varying heights. I turned the corner and walked
headfirst into a man smoking a cigarette in the doorway. I
slowly lifted my gaze from toe to head. He was wearing a
leather jacket. He was not wearing or holding a helmet.
When I reached his face, I was struck to find he was staring
at me, too. Our eyes met. I bowed my head in greeting. He
pointed to the table to his left. On it, a helmet.

"Márk?"
"*Szia!*"

He stood tall, thin, and pale, with a close-shaven head
and a dark goatee shaped like an anchor rooted around his
chin. I followed as he walked through the doorpost entrance
of Jelen and sat across from him at a low-top wooden table.
He began, "I don't really have much to say, I mean..." he
removed his leather jacket and draped it around the back of
his chair.

Márk Süveg (Mah-rk Shuh-veg), a thirty-four-year-old man born and raised in Budapest, is a performer. He is the owner of hiphop.hu and the lead rapper in his group A.K.K.E.Z.D.E.T.P.H.I.A.I. Though he has never lived outside of Budapest, traveling around Hungary and traveling internationally to perform rap music for over fifteen years and slam poetry for eight has allowed Márk the opportunity to say with confidence that living in the capital of Budapest is different than living elsewhere in Hungary, or living elsewhere in the world.

The son of a Jewish mother, a Christian father, and the grandson of an activist who feigned loyalty to the Nazi Party during WWII in order to distribute stolen documents and stamps to endangered people, Márk will tell you that he has a "crazy, crazy family story." His mother's mother was the only member of his family to survive the concentration camps. The psychological damage of the camps remained with her for the rest of her life. She was pregnant with Márk's mother while hiding in the streets of Budapest, making Márk's mother a "Holocaust child." Márk cringed, elevating wrinkles above the arch of his nose, as he explained that the psychological trauma that affected his grandmother also affected the baby being born.

Without hesitation, Márk ordered a draft beer from a tall waitress with a platinum blonde pixie cut, sleeve tattoos and a septum nose ring. From that moment on, he needed no probing or assistance. He lifted his right hand from the table and circled it in the air with his pointer finger extended as though he were painting an image. I mustered, *"Kérek szépen egy lattét,"* or "May I please have a latte," one of the handful of Hungarian phrases I'd adopted.

Upon her return to Hungary, Márk's grandmother never failed to wear long sleeves in order to conceal the tattoo she was given on her forearm of her identification number in the concentration camps. She especially did not want Márk or Márk's brother to see it and ask about its origin.

Márk shook his head as he described, "There are two types of people. One wants to really forget it and the other wants everybody to not forget it." His grandmother was the first. She dropped religion and wanted her family to have nothing to do with the risks associated with being a Jewish Hungarian, or just a Jew in Hungary.

Consequently, Márk's mother chose a similar route. Márk was brought up without any religious awareness or awareness that he himself was Jewish.

When Márk was around six years old, he noticed his grandmother's tattoo for the first time. As expected, he began to ask questions. Márk's mother cooed, "I will tell you later when you grow up."

The first time Márk talked about Judaism seriously with his mother was when he was in elementary school, sometime around the fifth grade. He said, "I knew about Nazi stuff, like swastika, but not too much." Márk had a friend who went to the market and returned with Nazi paraphernalia, like badges, helmets, and memoirs of the war. Márk didn't entirely understand why someone would want those things, but he felt a stirring sense of trouble, and asked his mother what he should do. She said he shouldn't be friends with this person. Márk loved this friend, and they had been friends for quite some time; however, he conceded. Later on, this friend became a leader in an underground anti-Semitic movement in Budapest. He made speeches in basements draped with Nazi flags, coached marches, and saluted to pictures of Hitler. Márk smirked, "The funniest part was that he was twenty-one at the time. Then he found out that he was a Jew so we became friends again. It was crazy."

At the time that Márk began discussing Judaism with his mother, communism was still in effect and socially, Jews and Gypsies were not heavily ostracized. After the fall of the regime in 1989, Hungarian society was excited to adopt democracy. People were eager to embrace a positive change. Within two years, however, many Hungarians felt democracy had failed them. They hadn't received the jobs they were promised. The schools that would educate their children hadn't improved or received more funding. Much of the frustration with the political system led individuals to either search for alternative methods of governance or seek a group to blame, such as minority groups like the Jews or Roma.

Márk saw the gentrification of the city of Budapest and the draw of the city, bringing in youth from the surrounding areas otherwise plagued with a less fortunate and less optimistic culture. Softening his voice, Márk empathized with his friends who wanted to leave Hungary. He said, "They gave up. They didn't have a chance; that's what they think."

Márk's voice escalated as he said, "Young people are leaving." High percentages of young Hungarian adults are increasingly either moving to a different country because of the current Hungarian government, or moving to Budapest from other Hungarian cities in the hope of achieving a more optimistic future with more personal, professional, and cultural options. While there are more opportunities in Budapest than in the surrounding areas of Hungary, young adults often continue to feel unfulfilled and they often move further away. Approximately 600,000 Hungarians live in London as of 2015, and another 400,000 in Berlin. That totals to one million people—ten percent of the Hungarian population.

Márk can not imagine living elsewhere. His first reason is because he is in love with the Hungarian language. Márk raps and writes poetry in Hungarian. Despite traveling worldwide to perform, he confessed that the longest time he has been away from Budapest was two months. After two months, he wanted to hear people speaking in Hungarian.

More intrinsic than his love for the Hungarian language, Márk's love for music has driven his professional and personal relationships for as long as he can remember. He met his rap group through music. He said, "My partner was the only person I ever met who knew Wu Tang Klan and the *lyrics*, not just the group. He understood the Wu Tang. I met him and it was love at first sight."

For Márk, music is about more than rhythm, or the number of beats per verse. Márk confided that a part of him is due to a lot of the "conscious" rap he listened to growing up. He believes, "those lyrics developed my personality."

For a young adult or child, rap music, like the supportive embrace of a mentor or encouraging adult, can serve as a protective factor against the many obstacles of growing up. As rap was developing rapidly in the United States and other cities in Europe, in Hungary, Márk explained that there was only one "gangster" rap group and one other group performing comical music and routines. Though the music satisfied a certain level of entertainment, Márk noticed a void in wit and intellectual charm. Márk saw opportunities for movement and impact within the Hungarian language that others not only didn't utilize, but also didn't understand.

When he was seventeen, Márk began his rap career writing in English. He thought there was no Hungarian rap because the Hungarian language was not suited for rap. It wasn't until two years later, when his brother teased him for mimicking the art of the States, that he realized he had an advantage to do something new and to become really successful at it. He then switched from English to Hungarian.

Now, Márk and his group write their own lyrics and frequently make use of word play. Márk explained that the Hungarian language is perfect for this because "For instance, when you take French or Spanish, it's a flowing language. If you take the Slovak languages, those are harsh. This language can be both in the same sentence. It's really special." Touring through Europe, Márk learned that though English speakers rarely understood what Hungarian meant, they enjoyed the sounds and spirits of the language and the culture.

Both personal experiences and social factors influence the content of Márk's music. His group has been performing two albums for fifteen years. Their first album is a rebellious expression of youth angst while the second begins to integrate each individul's frustration with politics and government. Márk said that at seventeen, "the political part wasn't emphasized because we didn't see any problems with the politics. We were just rebels without a cause." After six years, Márk and his group began to see patterns they didn't like and they felt mobilized to do something about it, or to say something about it.

Today, Márk is working on his group's third album. As the group has evolved, their focus has grown from rapping for fun to a mature call to action. This new album will emphasize a political stance beyond personal experiences.

Márk said, "Kids listen to us now. There's a lot of responsibility and we have to use that. Every single time, even if it's about a personal thing, there's at least two or four lines mentioning something about the government or politics or social stuff. We mention racism and anti-Semitism all the time."

Márk's fans and friends know him to be a proud Jewish Hungarian rapper. It wasn't always this way. Márk explained that when he started rapping, no one knew that he, his partner or his DJ were Jewish. As the news became more widely known, Márk felt targeted as a "Jewish group." He defended that he and his partners were childhood friends who came together for the sake of rap not for the sake of promoting Jewish causes.

Márk's defensiveness struck a chord regarding the deep shame associated with being Jewish in Hungary. As a result of Holocaust survivors returning from the war and either swearing off Judaism or becoming committed Jewish activists, many young Hungarian adults either don't know about their Jewish roots or do not feel strongly enough about them to commit to any particular cause. Moreover, anti-Semitism in Hungary never has and never will fully die. This fact poses danger to young Jews and begs a sacrifice for those so daring as to openly identify.

Initially, Márk did not want to spread awareness of his Jewish roots. He sat up straight and placed his palms firmly on the surface of the table as he said, "We started talking about it because some people started talking bullshit about us. So, you have to react."

Others pieced Márk's story together when his group began performing in a number of Jewish-themed events organized by Jewish organizations to promote Jewish pride and culture.

Márk's pivotal moment of Jewish identification came when his group was faced with the challenge of creating a new logo. He knew that he needed something that included an "A," a "K," a "P," and an "H" because the group name consisted of those letters. However, Márk didn't want to overcomplicate the graphic. He wanted to make it compact and simple.

Márk reflected, "I was thinking for days and days, drawing and everything. And then I suddenly realized that I have the perfect thing for the logo: One third of the Star of David. There is the 'A,' the 'K,' the 'P,' and the 'H,' just like that."

Márk slid back his shoulder blades to protrude his chest, sporting his band's logo in a bright white embroidered fashion against an ominous black cotton backdrop. He looked up at me and slouched his shoulders, pride draining from his face. "That's when things started getting a little bad."

Márk's partner acknowledged that the logo was really nice but feared that Márk had gone too far and was taking too many risks. Márk worked his magic to convince his partner otherwise.

Upon the release of their new logo, competing groups and media outlets reported Márk's group as "Jews who were too proud." Márk repeated under his breath a memory of what he thought they really meant, which was, *"They shouldn't be that proud."* His gaze lifted and his eye contact grew more piercing. He whispered, "Then we started talking about it."

Márk talked with fans when they recognized him on the street, in a club, or at a pub. Sooner or later, he knew the subject of being Jewish would always arise. Fans would begin by saying, "I love your music, I have the album, I love the lyrics..." or so Márk says, "normal stuff." After some time, they would appreciate that Márk and his group were friendly, open-minded, and approachable, and the flow to the conversation would abruptly stop. They would begin with, "Don't get offended, but..." and Márk would calmly reply, "I know what you are going to ask." With many, Márk then engaged in meaningful, impactful conversation.

Despite not growing up with especially close ties to the Jewish culture or a Jewish identity, Márk chooses to highlight his Jewish roots rather than to diminish them. He chooses to remain prideful about his Jewish background in the midst of an increasingly anti-Semitic Hungarian culture.

Márk has won two national poetry slams in his career. His second winning performance was about the experience of Jews being taken from their homes and forced onto train cars to concentration or forced labor camps. He wrote the poem in memory of his grandmother because she was the only person he personally knew who was taken. Márk said, "You know how the train sound goes *too-too, too-too*? That's how I recited the poem. It was like that." He started with candles and a prayer for Shabbat. Then, knocking on the door. *Too-too, too-too.* Then, the family being taken. Finally, the train.

Driven by an internal need to recite this poem, Márk didn't care whether he would win or lose the competition. He knew that his mother and father would be watching and that he would never say the poem again in his life.

Márk was in a trance. After twenty-five other performers, Márk was the final slot. He waited, and waited, and waited. The tension built until two minutes before the performance when all that tension dissipated. "I went up there and I did it," he said. "It was the weirdest experience of my life."

In Hungarian, *"ma"* means *"today"* and *"mama"* means *"grandma"* or *"mother."* In the rhythm of the poem, Márk recited, *"Ma-ma," "ma-ma,"* weaving his Hungarian word play into the sound of the train removing his family from their home. When he said "Ma-ma" for the first time, he almost cried, knowing that his mother was in the crowd and that her heart was likely breaking. He knew, though, that she was really very proud. Márk's poem ends with, *"Today is Saturday and I am not leaving. I am staying here."*

"Then, it was 500 people, and dead silence," said Márk. "That was the biggest experience of my life. I am really glad it is connected with being a Jew." His cheeks grew wide with his smile.

Márk tilted his head back to take a long sip of his drink. He looked back in my direction and the corners of his lips quivered as he swallowed.

"Then, reality came in," he said.

After his win, Márk walked with an intimate group of friends to a pub nearby the venue. As he approached the bar, he noticed eight or nine large men huddled outside. He stepped around them, entered the bar, and ordered a round of drinks.

One friend went outside for a smoke. He returned to say, "They talking about you. They gonna beat you up when you come out."

Originally, Márk was unfazed. Riding the high of defending his title, he "didn't give a fuck about them." Two more

31

friends entered the bar and warned Márk of the men outside.

Márk had enough. He marched outside to confront the situation. "They were huge guys," he said. "The one in the middle started talking to me. The others were behind him, waiting for me to say something or move. I didn't say anything and I didn't move."

Márk remembered the man in the middle shouting, "You fucking Jew, I am going to cut you up." He said, "Stuff like that, usual shit." Márk didn't say a word and didn't move. He knew that if he moved or spoke, he would get hit. So, he waited.

"The guy's friends started laughing at him because he was screaming at me. Loud, really loud. I kept smiling," Márk said. The man's friends were teasing him. Then, the man in the middle said something about Márk's mother.

"That's when my friend raised an arm," Márk said. "He wanted to say you shouldn't talk like that, but he just said, 'You shouldn-' and he was hit right in that moment. I was right. They just wanted one word or move."

Márk's friend was knocked out. When Márk turned to pick him up from the ground, he was hit, too.

Márk swung his arm in the air and squeezed his eyes shut as he described the hit. Squinting one eye open, he explained that he was hit from the side but he didn't lose balance. "He hit me really hard, but I wasn't knocked out." He pulled his friend up and encouraged him to walk away. "It really hurt like hell," he said. "My luck was that they were martial art people and not just street fighters. They appreciated in a fighter mentality that he was twice my size and I wasn't knocked out. So, they stopped him. They said to let him go." Márk and his friend escaped.

Márk knew that his mother would worry if she learned of this event, so he made a point to protect her from the information. He held his right hand in the air and dropped it in rhythm with his words. "No worries, no plans," he said. "I just say, if there is a problem, solve it. Boom. That's it."

He remembered a phrase that he grew up with that he hasn't heard anywhere outside of Jewish Hungarian communities. "My mom told me this," he said. "A phrase called *Kepura*. When anything bad happens and someone starts to worry about that thing, someone from the family or the community or whoever is there would say, 'Kepura,' which means that whatever bad thing happened, only happened because it protected you from something bigger. You should be glad that this happened. Real simple, really wise, typical Jewish thinking. I love that. I live by that. Kepura."

Márk looked at the table for a moment, then tapped the left pocket of his pants and slid a pack of Marlboro reds onto the table. He placed a cigarette in his mouth and lit the tip. Exhaling a cloud of smoke, he said, "I became a person, who I am right now, because of rap."

As an otherwise highly introverted person, Márk credits conscious rap with the development of the strong, hard, independent sides of his personality. "The kids motivate me," he said as he inhaled another breath of smoke, igniting the tip of the cigarette into a sparkling orange circle of light.

"Hip-hop and rap helped me a lot. What it gave me, I have to give back to other kids."

Márk does not yet have kids, but worries that the darkening environment in Budapest would push him outside of the city if he does have children. "I love this country and I love this city," Márk said, "but the other part of my mind says that my kids shouldn't grow up here…that's what I'm afraid of."

He doesn't worry too much, but now, Márk is worried about what he sees in the media and what is going on with the Hungarian government. "It's really saddening, and almost frightening," he said. "I am not afraid of being bullied or being beat up, or my fans leaving us, but I am afraid for the kids."

For the first time since we sat down, Márk looked up at me, patiently waiting for guidance. He told one final story.

When Márk was a young man, living with his mother, he put on a suit in preparation for a job interview. As he approached the door, he looked over his shoulder into the mirror. He looked back at his mother. He saw how proud she looked. He held her gaze and said, "I'm not going."

Márk didn't recognize himself in the mirror. He described that to disappoint his mother pained him more than anything else ever would. After he won the slam-poetry championship the second time for his moving performance, he looked back at his mother again. She beamed with pride and fulfillment. Márk knew then that he had made the right choice.

TAMÁS BÜCHLER

"Instead of emphasizing our victimhood like a parrot, we should really tell another story."

MY THIRD DAY IN BUDAPEST was also day one of the Me2We Conference, sponsored by the Schusterman Foundation to unite a passionate group of professionals and entrepreneurs to discuss the meaning of faith, what it means to be Jewish and how Jews can better engage in repairing the world. In an oversized T-shirt and a pair of checkered boxer shorts, I sat at the broad, wooden desk in my room and typed the address of the *Le Meridien Hotel* into Google maps. The hotel was a forty-minute walk from my apartment.

I packed my most elegant gear for the three-day-and-night stay at the hotel, quickly showered and dressed in my nicest baby blue button-down shirt and black knee-length elastic skirt. I perched my hiker's backpack on the couch and squatted with my back against the pack. Filled to the brim, I weaved my arms awkwardly through the straps and shakily straightened my legs. The bag crankily settled into the small of my back. *Forty minutes. I could walk like this for forty minutes.*

I made it to the hotel in one hour. I was just in time for registration. Out of breath, I unbuckled my backpack, dropping it onto a nearby couch in the lobby and catching my reflection in the mirror above the couch. The bag left sweat marks in the shape of its straps across my chest, outlining both armpits and hugging my waist. The elegance of the hotel sharply contrasted my shabby appearance. I marveled at the crystal chandelier above me, hanging just tall enough to avoid grazing the heads of passerbys. At reception, two young men wore satin black suits and red bowties. To my right, sixty-nine fellow social justice activists gathered at the welcoming reception of the Me2We Conference. Gliding along spotless white carpeting, parading champagne glasses filled with lemon and cucumber water, my colleagues rocked colorful summer dresses, blazers, light beige suits and pale green and yellow ties. I rushed to the bathroom in desperate search of a hand dryer that could possibly resolve my sweaty situation.

After about half an hour of small talk and nametags, the group walked together through an all-white hallway to our first conference room. At last, my eyes settled on a nametag that I recognized: Tamás (Tomi) Büchler (Ta-maash (Toe-me) Buke-lare), the conference organizer who I had been communicating with via email for weeks. A tall, blond man in his thirties wearing a bright blue plaid button-down shirt and black slacks, Tomi beamed with optimism and determination as he walked to the front of the room to greet his audience. Formally the director of MiNYanim, a two-year learning and entrepreneurship fellowship for Jewish leaders, Tomi also serves informally as a grounding pillar of stability and support for Jewish Budapest. He spoke with an all-consuming Hungarian accent, emphasizing the first syllable of each English word and escalating his tone at the end as though each sentence were a question. The minute he began talking he won me over.

For three full days, we woke at 7am and laid to rest at 2am. Between riveting spiritual and activist debates, the group utilized every minute of every coffee break to get to know neighbors and fellow changemakers. We became a small family in those three days, with help from the love and encouragement of Tomi.

After our original meeting at the Me2We Conference, Tomi and I traveled together to Bánkitó, a Jewish music festival in Bánk, a small town in Hungary. A few weeks later, I participated in the Budapest portion of Tomi's international MiNYanim initiative to deepen spiritual knowledge and initiate authentic cultural exchange. Beyond MiNYanim, we met frequently for coffee, updating each other on the ins and outs of our work and perspectives.

Nearly five months after Tomi welcomed me to Budapest, Tomi and I met at My Little Melbourne, a small café in the center of the Seventh District rumored to brew Budapest's best coffee. The intimate coffee shop hosted a total of five tables with mismatched brightly colored chairs on a miniature loft above the baristas. While I waited for Tomi to arrive, I gazed at the Australian flags and pictures of kangaroos, koalas, and beautiful coastlines around me. Fellow patrons murmured in Hungarian behind me, anchoring me back to reality.

Within minutes, Tomi broke my gaze as he approached the table. Finishing a conversation on the phone, he smiled through his fast-paced Hungarian. Hanging up the phone, Tomi extended his arms in a hug, bending down to meet me at my significantly shorter level. I sat down and cupped my chai-coffee-latte (a My Little Melbourne specialty) close to my face, relishing in scents of green tea, chai, and espresso. As Tomi and I caught up, the door to the café swung open and closed, welcoming and sending off new customers and regulars alike. The coffee grinder whined as the barista tapped its switch one- two- three- four- times to gather espresso grinds for each order. Wafts of freshly baked brownies drifted upstairs. Tomi offered to begin sharing his story only after buying us a treat to share. He walked downstairs and returned with a golden croissant flaking around its edges. He tore a piece off the corner and chuckled, "Yeah, so... birth." He sat up straight, crossed his legs and put his hands in his lap.

Born and raised in Budapest, Tomi feels very connected to the city, especially the story of Jewish Budapest. A couple of years ago, researchers found various documents from Tomi's family that date back to 18th century Hungary, proving Tomi to be a tenth generation Hungarian Jew on his father's side. Both grandparents on Tomi's father's side were raised as orthodox Hungarian Jews, an already rare occurrence in 19th and 20th century Hungary and an almost unheard of identity in Hungary following World War II and the Holocaust.

On his mother's side, Tomi's grandfather is from an intimate town on the Austrian border of Hungary where only two Jewish families lived – one of which was his mother's. Tomi laughed, "They were six brothers and sisters, and this was pretty much the Jewish population of the town."

When his grandfather was a teenager, for financial reasons he moved closer to Budapest to one of the most Jewish neighborhoods in Hungary. Nearly forty percent of the neighborhood residents were Jewish. Tomi said, "This is where my grandfather became a young adult. Then he was taken to a forced labor camp."

Forced labor began in 1939 as civil service for Jews in the Hungarian army. It became a tool for discrimination in 1941 when Jews were labeled as "untrustworthy" soliders. Jews were then forced from their homes to perform manual labor toward the German war effort in civilian clothing with no access to or possession of weapons. Depending on the commander of the forced labor camp, their treatment ranged from relatively humane to mass extermination. Labor camps differed from concentration camps, or sites operated by the Nazi Party to exterminate Jews and minorities, though some locations hosted both.

While Budapest was relatively protected from German invasions until the very end of World War II because of its allied relationship with Nazi Germany, the neighborhood where Tomi's grandfather grew up was not technically included in the borders of Budapest at the time, so it was not protected in the same way. Tomi reflected, "My grandfather's family was almost entirely killed during the Holocaust in Auschwitz." Unlike forced labor camps, Auschwitz-Birkenau was a network of Nazi German concentration camps and extermination camps operated by the Third Reich in Polish areas annexed by Nazi Germany during World War II to exterminate its inmates as efficiently as possible. Most individuals sent to Auschwitz were not sent to perform a task but were sent to their death.

For Jewish individuals and families living in Eastern Europe at the time of World War II, being Jewish brought injustice, isolation, and death. Tomi's grandmother survived partly in the Budapest ghetto, where Jewish families and individuals were forced to live, and partly hiding with families with forged documents.

The apartment where Tomi lives now was once the apartment of his grandmother on his mother's side. She and her family did not come from much money; anything they did have they lost during the war. Tomi said, "I know from their stories that when they were living here, there were seven of them in a flat that I live in alone since I left college. It's not a very big flat."

Tomi said, "My grandparents' stories are pretty average when it comes to the Hungarian Jewish narrative, but my parents' stories are a bit different."

Compared to many children of Holocaust survivors, who chose to abandon their spiritual roots, Tomi's parents chose to embrace them.

Tomi's mother and father were born and raised after the war in Budapest in the early 50s. They both knew, even as children, that they were Jewish. Much unlike their peers, their parents from both sides – though not especially out-spoken about being Jewish, which may have resulted in unequal treatment in school, limited professional opport-unities, or safety risks for the famiy – never celebrated Chri-stmas, never lied that they were not Jewish, and never made any attempts to hide.

"So, this is how my parents grew up," Tomi said.

Tomi's mother frequently told him that in the 70s in Hungary, you couldn't ask someone if they were Jewish. Tomi wondered, then, how his parents knew that they were both Jewish. On one of their first dates, his mother shared, they went to see a cabaret set during World War II in Berlin. During a scene where Jewish people were being attacked, Tomi's mother felt his father holding her hand just a little bit tighter. Then, she understood. He may be very sensitive to this topic, so he may be Jewish.

Tomi pinched the croissant with wide eyes and a huge grin. He laughed, "Today, for me, it's ridiculous, because my parents have very Jewish last names, and, you know, every-thing about them is so Jewish that I wouldn't think twice that they might not be Jewish. But, they didn't know."

Tomi's parents had an orthodox Jewish wedding, which was also very rare in Hungary in the 70s. Though they were practicing within the Neolog sect of Judaism, which is a sect that exists only in Hungary as an in-between to reform and orthodox traditions, they had an ultra orthodox rabbi perform the wedding ceremony. As the Neolog leadership was formally connected to the Hungarian government, Tomi's parents feared the rabbis from the Neolog community would report them. Not only was a religious wedding forbidden, but if it were discovered that such a wedding was occurring, the families involved would be punished socially, politically, and financially. One could lose his or her job, be kicked out of the Communist Party, and "they could make your life hell if they wanted to," Tomi explained.

In order to keep their wedding a secret, Tomi's parents got married at home. Tomi said, "They closed all the curtains, closed the doors, and invited only close family because even friends were reporting each other. You did not know who you could trust. Everyone was an agent in one way or another. Everybody was forced to report on somebody."

Tomi and his brother were born in the 80s. Though at the time of their birth, Hungary was still part of the communist regime, from their first days, Tomi's parents made being Jewish a priority at home.

Tomi remembers being told they were "a bit different from others." He recalled, "Kindergarten teachers called my parents when I was three because I was telling other kids that we were not celebrating Christmas at home because we were Jewish. In the 80s, in Budapest, it was a big 'No.' It's not something you are *supposed* to do, even if you are three."

Often, when we are deemed different than the majority of our neighbors, we internalize that there is something wrong with us. However, Tomi didn't question his Judaism,

43

his family, or his culture. The system was a mystery, but his self-esteem remained in tact.

He tore away the opposite corner of the croissant and turned it over in his fingers as he explained, "After the fall of the regime, of course, everything changed."

Tomi thought his family was fairly assimilated. From the beginning, his parents took him to synagogue and his family celebrated holidays like *Hanukkah*, the eight-day festival of light, and *Pesach*, the eight-day celebration of the Jews' emancipation from slavery in Egypt. Upon the collapse of the Communist Regime, Tomi abruptly realized that he was one of the only families in Budapest keeping traditions. He said, "There were no more than one hundred families in the entire country, for sure. All of a sudden, we were hosting Israeli guests, discussing Jewish food, and my parents were both reading Jewish books all the time and watching all kinds of movies. *Fiddler on the Roof* was all over our apartment."

Though his family had a very strong Jewish identity, Tomi explained that his parents did not receive a formal Jewish education. He found them confused by basic questions about Judaism because they never went to Sunday school, participated in a Jewish youth movement, or played in a Jewish camp with Jewish friends. Anything they knew came from Jewish literature. For example, before their wedding, the ultra orthodox rabbi asked Tomi's mother if she had been to the *mikvah*. According to Jewish tradition and ritual, a mikvah purifies a woman. Orthodox women bathe in mikvahs after every menstrual cycle and before every large life event, including their wedding.

Tomi dropped the corner of croissant onto the white ceramic plate between us and flew his hands in the air. "My mom had no idea what a mikvah was, but she didn't want to say so, so instead, she said, 'Yes, I've been there many, many times…' and the rabbi was like, 'Why would an unmarried young girl go to the mikvah very many times?' Mom just left the question there, but she really had no clue." Ultimately, Tomi's parents understood that if they wanted their children to have a stronger Jewish identity and stronger Jewish education, then they would have to send them to places where they could learn.

First, Tomi and his brother went to *Talmud Torah*, classes on Judaism for children. Tomi said, "When I say classes, you know, it was really just a rabbi sitting in front of us and talking." Tomi wasn't especially impressed.

Then, Tomi's parents discovered *Szarvas*, an international Jewish youth camp. They sent Tomi and his brother there, too. Tomi laughed again, "Not immediately, but after my mom understood that we might survive a night without her, which wasn't that early, maybe I was nine or ten, we spent our summers away."

Tomi elaborated that at Szarvas, even if the Jewish knowledge wasn't especially sophisticated, it was extremely charged emotionally. He said, "The emotional and community experience that you go through at Szarvas is so strong that it stays with you for your whole life. I remember as a child, or a small teenager, I enjoyed it so much. The activities… we were hiking in the forest during the night pretending that we were fighting the Nazis, or we were on a boat in the river pretending that it would take us to Israel, and... you know, when you are young, these memories are fantastic. I think that was the first time that I consciously understood that Judaism is a part of me and it's something that I should care about."

From a very early age, Tomi understood that Judaism was "something cool." He said, "It's something that really brings richness to my life. Of course, I didn't articulate it this way when I was nine, but I think as a child, I felt it as joy."

Tomi recognized that he, his brother, his parents, and his grandparents triggered each other's connections to Judaism in different ways. As he and his brother became more involved in Jewish life, his grandmother began to light candles on Shabbat again. His other grandmother began attending synagogue regularly. By the time Tomi was in high school, not only was Jewish life prominent in his home, but many of his friends surrounding him were Jewish friends he met in Szarvas or at school, which built an increasingly stronger bond between Tomi and his Judaism.

After high school, Tomi started law school. In Hungary, students begin professional studies right after high school. Tomi remembered, "I liked law school, but I also felt that it was very boring, very dry, not very exciting. I already had a passion for everything Jewish."

Soon thereafter, Tomi transitioned into rabbinical school at the Jewish Theological Seminary, the only Neolog Jewish university in Budapest and in the region. He cringed as he said, "The whole thing was a bit, I don't know, tired, dusty, and sleepy." After a few years, Tomi had no intention of becoming a rabbi. He just wanted the knowledge. All his life, he was learning about Judaism in different spheres and from different angles. Here, he said, "was the place where everything came together. I had a structure and I could put each book on its shelf."

After rabbinical school, Tomi moved to Israel for a volunteering scholarship. "In Haifa," he said, "I became, you know, as cliché as it sounds, like a man." As the first experience away from home, Tomi grew independently from his safe, protected Jewish bubble. He said, "I really understood what was going on outside."

After Tomi returned home to Budapest, he began working with Birthright. Also known as Taglit-Birthright or Birthright Israel, Birthright is a non-profit educational organization founded in 1999 that sponsors an entirely expenses-paid ten-day trip to Israel for any Jewish individual between the ages of eighteen and twenty-six. *Taglit* (תגלית) is the Hebrew word for *discovery*; accordingly, participants, mostly visiting Israel for the first time, are encouraged to discover new meaning in their personal Jewish identity and connection to Jewish history and culture. For Hungarian Jews, though originally approached as merely a free vacation, Birthright often opens a brand new door to one's relationship with Judaism, sparking a hunger to learn more and to engage further.

Tomi said, "I think this is where my story gets to a second chapter."

The first time Tomi accompanied a Birthright group to Israel as a *madrich*, or youth counselor, he had a very strong experience. On the first day of the trip, Tomi gathered the group of madrichim in the hotel in Jerusalem. He asked the counselors to put on their *kippah* (head cover for men) because they were going to the *kotel* (The Western Wall, or the holiest site in Jerusalem, toward which Jews turn during prayer). Tomi said, "I can still recall the blank stares on their faces, like, 'Okay, what is kippah, and what is kotel, and what is Tomi talking about, and what is this whole thing about?' This was a really transformative experience for me. I understood then that I really grew up in a bubble. My Jewish story, and my Jewish upbringing, might refer to, let's say, five percent of the Jewish community of Budapest. It's not the typical story."

Throughout the years, Tomi thought that the average Jewish male his age had two Jewish parents, just like his. He imagined their grandparents telling them about the Holocaust, just like his grandparents had told him about the Holocaust. He felt sure that Jewish youth camp and Jewish youth movement were the normal Jewish upbringing. He said, "I was already in my early twenties when I understood that I am in the five percent. Also, I understood that it's just wrong as it is."

Tomi saw a challenge and understood that this challenge was one he had to take because of all that Judaism gave to him. He explained, "Judaism made my life so much richer. I really want this experience to be the experience for others."

As I played with the croissant crumbs left scattered across our ceramic plate, my mind marinated in the realization that somewhere in our early adulthood, we start to discover that our upbringing was not as normal or as average as we thought. We start to realize that we are unique. There really isn't a normal or average; if we are lucky, we have been blessed in certain ways. In other ways, we recognize how our lives might have been richer. Moreover, we start to feel grateful for the advantages we have enjoyed and we are regretful of the opportunities we have missed. If we are like Tomi, we seize opportunities to increase advantages and decrease regrets for others.

Upon his return from Israel, Tomi started working for the Jewish Agency to create post-Birthright activities. He illustrated that, at the time, the Israeli leadership at the Jewish Agency had the approach of being "here to learn and here to help." He described his experience as one of empowerment. Encouraged to do what he wanted while guided by consistent consultation and advisement, Tomi, as a young Jew in his twenties, was coached through spearheading a brand new industry. He said, "We didn't have Masters in Community Development or Jewish Leadership." Laughing, he admitted, "Obviously, we made a lot of mistakes. Every year, we made an effort, and we changed what needed to be changed. We tried to make every mistake just once and to learn from it."

Tomi impacted not just the Jewish Agency, but also participated in the growth of other organizations, like the Jewish Community Center in Budapest, Jewish charities, and various foundations. He said, "I have a lot of friends and people I know that have had the same experience."

For Tomi, his inexperience was an advantage. His blank slate at his beginning drove his determination to learn what *does* work.

While his passion and idealism enable Tomi to envision a life for Jews in Budapest that he may one day help to make a reality, a handful of difficulties stand in Tomi's way. Tomi described that within the Jewish revival scene in Budapest, there are so many exciting Jewish programs, initiatives, and amazing new ideas. Unfortunately, currently, the most successful programs, or the programs that attract the most people, are the programs that come without commitment or responsibility. Tomi said, "You cannot build a community without commitment and responsibility. So, if you take a Jewish festival, which is brilliant, and fun, and brings in new Jewish faces, and really shakes the young Jewish scene, it might be a great first step. It might be a door opener for a young Jew, but it's just an initial step. It is always very important to remind ourselves that it is just the beginning, not the end."

Tomi squinted his eyes, unveiling creases between his eyebrows. "You know, we had these posters for the Bánkitó Festival for years that said, 'Being Jewish is sexy,'" he said. "It *is* sexy, but it's not *just* sexy. That's the thing. Being Jewish also comes with heavy baggage. If you want to have a real community of people - and everyone can define community however he or she wishes - the way I see a community, community is definitely not just about fun."

Tomi insisted that it is crucial to see the bigger picture, and the bigger picture right now for Jewish Budapest is that large Jewish American organizations that are currently supporting a large percentage of Jewish Hungarian programs are going to pull out soon. He said, "We know it. We are going to lose most of our funds. We are going to need to change everything if this generation doesn't understand that without its own contribution and commitment everything is going to fall into pieces. This keeps me awake in the night. Maybe not next year, maybe not in three years, but in less than twenty years, everything will change."

While Tomi understands that people otherwise unaffiliated with Judaism may originally only be attracted to free festivals and parties, like his group of campers in Jerusalem, he encourages that once those people arrive, it is crucial to paint the whole picture. He said, "Once they are there, once they understand the values, the knowledge, and the understanding of the importance of Judaism, we can suggest that if you like it, then it's yours. But it comes with a responsibility."

Despite international focus on rising anti-Semitism in Europe, Tomi believes the issues of financial sustainability and outreach are ten times more important than the anti-Semitism discourse. He said, "I'm not saying that anti-Semitism doesn't exist or it's not unpleasant or it's not ugly, because it is, and it's there. But I don't see it as an existential threat. If ninety percent of the funding of the Jewish community is cut, that is an existential threat." Tomi explained, "I also think that anti-Semitism is a problem, but it's not a Jewish problem. It is a problem of the Hungarian society. It's not a disease, it's a symptom of something really bad, and just one symptom." Since the economic crisis in 2008, hatred has grown stronger in Hungarian social, political, and economic environments. Tomi said, "Not just the Jews, but the Roma minority, the LGBT community, and women. Basically, anyone who could be a threat is under attack."

Tomi glared ahead. He said, "I am not scared, I am not frightened. Not because I am so brave, but simply because I just can't see it as a threat. One of the dangers of bringing up anti-Semitism again and again and again is exactly strengthening the kind of victim identity that we want to avoid when we reach out to real people. We want to show them that Judaism is more than being a victim. It's more than the stories of persecution of their grandparents. So, instead of emphasizing our victimhood like a parrot, we should really tell another story." He shook his head and looked at the floor.

"You don't need to be a psychologist to know that victim identity is not a healthy identity," he said. "It's not something you can base your life on."

Tomi sighed. He described that once you are so involved with your community professionally, and that involvement begins to fulfill your life, then the lines between your private life and your professional life are blurred. He said, "You don't know anymore which belongs to where." Tomi questioned, "When I am in MiNYanim in a Kabbalat Shabbat on a Friday night, am I there for my own spiritual experience, am

I there because my friends are there, or am I there because I am the director of the project? Or all of them?" One of the biggest challenges in Tomi's life is to sort out a healthy division between work and private life.

Tomi glanced around at the other four tables, crowded with students, plugged into headphones, typing at their computers. I wondered whether Tomi's perspective could be taught, or whether it had to be learned through experience - through days upon nights of parenting, socializing, traveling, and quite possibly, struggling.

Pushing his chair out from under him, Tomi stood and walked downstairs to pay for his coffee. As many young Hungarian Jewish activists would say, anti-Semitism does exist and it is ugly. Challenges do exist. Funding is an issue. However, somehow, individuals fighting to find solutions continue to fight. With people like Tomi at the front of the line, young individuals will increasingly learn the value of community in Jewish Budapest. More than that, Tomi and other leaders hope that more and more individuals will come to see their participation and support as necessities to keep their communities alive.

ANDRÁS MAYER

"It's an age-old question: What is Jewish? Who is Jewish? Nobody could really ever answer that question properly."

I DUG INSIDE MY BLACK MESSENGER BAG in search of my miniature recorder. My pointer finger grazed the thin rubber wire wrapped in a tight cylinder. I tugged on the wire and placed the recorder in my pocket. I shuffled past the front door and knocked on the kitchen window of Rabbi Hurwitz' apartment. His dear friend András (An-drash) saw me and summoned for me to come in. He yelled, "The door's open!" I tip-toed into the apartment and quietly removed my shoes.

The flat was larger than I expected. Ahead of me laid a living room with a high ceiling and a long, wide wooden table covered with stacks of religious texts and youth programming papers. Children's toys splayed across the floor while two young boys sat at the far left side of the room practicing magic tricks. I moseyed aimlessly past the laundry room and bathroom and stumbled into the kitchen, where András was brewing homemade *pálinka*.

Pálinka is Hungarian schnapps that packs both a stronger punch than your average liquor and a concentrated Hungarian history. While it used to be the "poor man's drink"—made from fruit that was discarded as inedible and unlikely to be found in any establishment that people were proud to frequent—pálinka has evolved to become the hip drink for Hungarians of all ages and can now be found in any bar in Hungary in a variety of fruit options.

András, one of the two Mayer brothers who run the Teleki Tér shtiebel, a small apartment-style prayer house in the Eighth District of Budapest, introduced me to pálinka at one of Teleki's regular community celebrations. He is a tall, extroverted man who rocks a pronounced five o'clock shadow. András talks quickly and muddles stories together. After many weeks of attending Saturday Shabbat services and lunch at Teleki, he invited me to join him in his next brewing adventure.

We agreed to meet at the Hurwitz apartment where the Teleki rabbi and his family live. The pálinka brewing consistently took place there in order to ensure that it was *kosher*, or brewed according to Jewish dietary law. With each phase of the brewing process came more storytelling and enthusiasm from András, with snippets like "I remember our first time brewing when..." and "Do you know why we do it this way?"

Like a child baking cupcakes with his mother for the first time, energetically licking frosting off his fingers only to cover them with frosting again, András continuously dipped his fingers into a small cup of warm pálinka to see how it was coming along. "Smells like *barack* (peach) but tastes like alcohol!"

"It's an age old question," he said. "What is Jewish? Who is Jewish? Nobody could really ever answer that question properly. In Hungary, it's even more of a mess than in other places."

András grew up with his mother in the Jewish District of Budapest, a nickname for the Seventh District, where Jews have historically lived since the late 19th century. The district now proudly exhibits trendy Jewish cafes, pubs, synagogues and museums.

András' family was communist. His grandfather was killed during World War II for his political views. His grandmother was an "internationalist," which meant that she wanted to do away with distinctions across race, religion and language. "To her, we were all one, united as Hungarians," András said. "The two of them considered themselves Hungarians with a communist ideology with a Jewish background, in that order. They thought 'Jewish' as an identity was something that would disappear because we were all equal."

András found out that he was Jewish when he was eight years old. "We were not particularly Jewish, you know?" He remembered, "I used to think that 'Jewish' meant religious because my mom's mom, unlike my paternal grandparents, was very religious. So when it turned out that I am Jewish though I am not religious, it was a bit like a revelation."

When András was ten, he fell in love. He told his father's mother, "There is this girl in my class, she is also ten, and uh... I am in love with her." András laughed. "My grandma asked me if she was Jewish. Even the Hungarian-communist-non-Jewish-grandmother asked me that. So, Judaism, even though it was number three in the list of priorities, was more important than I thought."

András attended a regular non-Jewish primary and secondary school. "I never really fit in, but I didn't attribute it to being Jewish," he said. "Only later, when I became a photographer, I realized the similarity between Jews and journalists—it's a marginal experience. You're never really *in* it, but always on the edge of an event, a party, a political movement, or society itself. Always on the move, growing shallow roots, never really settling in."

In secondary school, Judaism wasn't a topic that András talked about, but it wasn't a topic he specifically avoided either. "It was a non-issue," he said. "I knew, more or less, who was Jewish in my class. I say 'more or less' because since it wasn't really an issue, I often wasn't really sure."

András poured a dash of pálinka into a clear shot glass. The skin around his eyes remained wrinkled as he focused with a grin splashed across his face. "My mom always knew," he said. "She looked at this very good friend of mine and said, 'He is Jewish.' I was dumbfounded when I asked, 'How did you know?' She replied, 'Have you seen his mother? Look at her!'"

András never knew. "He was my very, very good friend for a long time, and I never knew."

Though András expressed being relatively disconnected from Jewish history, tradition and culture, he did feel a connection to Israel. In the 1980s, Hungary practiced "soft communism." Hungarians could travel but traveling was not the norm. However, András and his family traveled to Israel every third year. András remembered, "When I was fourteen, a very good friend of mine told me that when he met me, he thought that I was a superhero. 'It was 1986,' he says, 'and you're this guy who says he has been to Israel—four times!' He says, 'You could have said you were on the moon and back four times!'"

András knelt down to the large metal barrel of hot brewing pálinka and replaced the full plastic container underneath the spout with a small, empty ceramic bowl. He held the fresh pálinka to his nose. He said he became more interested in Judaism in high school. A friend of his convinced him to attend regular Friday evening speeches hosted by their local rabbi. All he needed was food and friends. "A lot of young people went there just to be there," he said. "It still exists and the rabbi is still there. He is very old now, but he is very cute. That is how my foray into Judaism really started."

Still, throughout high school and university, his friends didn't talk much about religion. Then, he went to Teleki for the first time when he was twenty years old. He remembered, "At first, I would go once a year when they really needed a *minyan* for Yom Kippur. I didn't love to go, but I went. I was there."

In Judaism, congregations need at least ten men, a *minyan*, to pray. Post-World War II, many congregations in Hungary and Eastern Europe more broadly failed to reach minyan because the majority of practicing Jewish communities was exterminated. *Yom Kippur*, also known as the Day of Atonement, is one of the holiest Jewish holidays during which Jews fast for twenty-five hours and pray for forgiveness for that year's wrongdoings. As one of Judaism's holiest holidays, congregations prioritize reaching minyan for at least that one occassion every year. Many Jews who do not attend synagogue regularly will go to synagogue for *Rosh Hashanah*, the Jewish New Year, and Yom Kippur.

A chain of lucky coincidences led to Teleki's continued existence after the war. Tamás Raj, the rabbi at Teleki during the Communist Regime, and Gláser, an elderly man who ran Teleki, endearingly nagged others to join the congregation. Gláser brought András and András brought his younger brother Gábor. András said, "If any of these chain links were missing, I don't know what would have happened. Most probably, the place would have closed down ages ago."

At first, the crew just wanted to have a minyan. András went once a year. Then twice. Then every other month. "There was always Gláser nagging me," he said. "Then, I was nagging other people." András remembered Gláser calling him every Tuesday morning at 7:30am. "I remember his voice distinctly. 'András, come, *szombaton* (Saturday).' He actually sounded like a woman with a high-pitched nasal voice." András grinned. "I would say, 'Come *on*, it's 7:30 on a Tuesday,' and he'd respond, 'Oh, you weren't sleeping, were you?'"

He said that Gláser was a *nudnik*, a nag, but that was his way of keeping the place alive. András went every Saturday. After services, András and Gábor went with Gláser to a café nearby where Gláser shared stories. When they entered, the servers had already prepared cappuccinos the way they liked. András said, "Gláser was drinking tea or a cappuccino with five or six sugars and he was telling stories about the war and about when he was young."

He held a shot glass out toward me and asked me to smell it. "*Barack*," I said. It smelled like peaches.

I thought about how every Tuesday for as long as I can remember, my father took his mother to Ben's Kosher Deli in Flushing, New York, a short drive from my grandmother's apartment. He would listen to stories of her youth and of her journey to the United States from Hungary. Before

long, my father knew the staff by first name. Shortly thereafter, my father and his mother would find their favorite
booth already set up for them with a fresh, steaming cup of
chicken noodle soup just the way they liked. My father knew
that my grandmother would add pepper to her soup until it
was so peppery that she would sneeze after each sip.

András' eyes curved with admiration and pain as he remembered Gláser. He explained that in its transition days,
Teleki wasn't very strict about religious rules. He said,
"Gláser was very, very flexible because he had to be. There
were no Jews around. The choice was: be flexible or close
down."

The risk of closing down after World War II forced a
number of Jewish communities in Hungary to reinterpret
the rules of Judaism. One traditional custom is that if there
are ten men praying and one has to step out to go to the
bathroom, the others shouldn't stop the Torah reading.
Instead, they should open the ark and count the unopened
Torahs in the ark as another person temporarily. András
said, "In Hungary, it was fairly common to look around the
room and say, 'Oh, there are...one-two-three...nine? Okay,
so we'll open the ark...' It was necessary to keep the place
alive."

Gláser passed away in 2006. The fate of Teleki hinged on
one meeting in Szóda, a bar in the heart of the Jewish
District, where a small group of Teleki's most regular
community members met to determine its future. András
said, "My stance was that the memory of a charismatic old
man would not keep the place running. It was already in

survival mode for some twenty years before we got there. It was a ton of work for Gláser. So, I voted to shut the community down."

He looked up from the barrel. "As fate would have it, I was voted against. So I said, Okay. Let's do it. Let's go on."

From 2006 to 2009, they opened the doors and let people in, but the place was in need of large renovations. A substantial deterrent for new guests was its bathroom. "You couldn't fathom the situation in there," András said. "Whatever you imagine, it was worse." His theory was that if the team managed to repair the toilet, then girls would be willing to come, and if girls were willing to come, then boys would be willing to come. "If there are guys, then more girls come, and if more girls come, then more guys come...and we need a *minyan*!"

In 2009 they started to renovate. That's when it all began to change. More and more people joined the community. András, his brother Gábor, and a handful of other close community members emailed people, called people, hosted events and festivals. "Now, we have more girls than we had and we are very happy about it," András said.

Toward the end of the 1930s, Teleki had boasted a strong female presence. "They say on a festival you couldn't get a place in the women's section," András said. "You had to pay and *still* you couldn't find a seat!"

Frequently at other orthodox synagogues, the women's prayer section is smaller than the men's, outside, upstairs, or excluded. At Teleki, however, women were very involved. Teleki was a family-oriented community. While elsewhere, women may have stayed at home while their husbands prayed, at Teleki, women joined the service, then ran home before their husbands to put the cake and pálinka on the table.

András waddled from one side of the kitchen to the other, imitating elderly women running home and rushing around cake and libations. "They were singing," he said. "They were very knowledgeable women. They were correcting men's Torah reading."

In the time of Gláser, there was no food at Teleki. Everybody went home when András and Gábor went with Gláser to the café. András said, "We always wanted to have Teleki Tér in the Guinness Book of Records for fastest Saturday morning service because we started at nine and at ten we were already sitting at the café."

Sometimes after prayer the group would have *pálinka* to celebrate an anniversary or a special event. Since the renovation, however, the Teleki community began to enjoy *cholent*. "This is what we have now," András said.

Cholent is a traditional Jewish stew. It usually simmers for twelve hours or more before Saturday lunch in order to conform with Jewish law that prohibits cooking on Shabbat. Every week at Teleki, one of the regular members of the community, most often the rabbi's wife, Devora, prepares cholent for the entire congregation. The cholent at Teleki generally consists of beans, potatoes, meat on special occasions, and a thick gravy made of paprika and other spices. After a few weeks at Teleki, my Saturdays wouldn't feel complete without piling into a small kitchen with twenty or thirty Jewish Hungarians to lean over piping containers of stew, ladling gravy atop of piles of potatoes and meat.

András' eyes widened as though he'd reached a realization. He leaned against the ledge of the counter and took a long sip of pálinka. He smiled gently as he said, "A few weeks ago, I was in the courtyard with a cup of tea when a friend asked me why I looked so happy. I've told this story one hundred times since then because that's when I realized... *We made it.* I couldn't have looked very good that day because I didn't sleep very much. I was happy, though, because I could have tea with her in the courtyard. In other words, they didn't need me in the service! We had more than ten men! They were praying there, and they were not missing me, because there were thirteen of them. It only took us ten years! This is where we are now."

Teleki has reached a comfortable size. András said, "The right size is that we have a strong minyan but we can still fit into the kitchen for lunch. We have always said that all we need is a minyan plus one."

The rabbi's youngest daughter peered mischievously into the kitchen. Upon noticing András, she galloped into his arms, nearly toppling him over. He laughed through his words and continued, "Every time I would buy a new bike or a buy a new basket for my bike, first I fit the cholent pot because I biked the pot to Teleki. Priorities! Now, we have a kitchen and can leave the pot there, but I still carry the cholent to the shul every week in boxes."

András sat on the floor with his legs crossed, the young girl in his lap. He said, "Now, we have cholent every week and on special occasions, we have pálinka. It was my idea to make our own pálinka. Everybody has projects. Pálinka is my project. I am responsible for it. I am running it. I am enthusiastic about it."

About five years ago, the Hungarian government legalized brewing pálinka at home. András said, "People were making pálinka at home forever, it was just totally illegal." András said that while he was growing up, pálinka smelt and tasted terribly. Traditionally, it was made from the rotten inedible fruit. Eventually, the prestige of good pálinka began to grow.

András said, "Fifteen years ago, maybe there were three kinds and two of them were crap. Now, they say the good pálinka must be made out of perfect fruits. If you go in any bar in the neighborhood, you have a big variety of pálinkas." In 2002, Hungary patented the word *pálinka* internationally so the word couldn't be used unless the drink was made in Hungary and made specifically from Hungarian fruit.

András never thought of making it, but one night at a friend's place they thought they ought to give it a shot. The following week, they went apple picking and bought the brewing barrels on the way. They bought new knives as well to make sure they were kosher.

"We were all over the place," András said. "The tree branches were breaking with the weight of the apples. We had so many big, beautiful yellow apples. You really saw them for making pálinka."

András and his team received instructions over the phone from a friend who had experience with brewing—what to do, how to do it, how much to do, what to add, what not to add and so on. His first pálinka, he said, was, "like the Hannukah miracle."

During the time of the Second Temple, between 530 BC and 70 AD, Greek leaders ruled the Holy Land, robbed Jews of their property, banned Torah learning, outlawed Jewish holidays and Jewish marriage ceremonies and set up idols, which were illegal according to Jewish law. Additionally, the Greeks made all oil impure. Miraculously, the Maccabees found one jar that had been overlooked, but it only had enough oil for one day. They had so much faith that they lit it anyway. Hannukah celebrates two miracles. One is that the Maccabees, a small band of Jews, defeated the mighty Greek armies in the Maccabean Revolt of 167 BC. The second is that the oil that was supposed to last one day actually lasted eight. The miracles of Hannukah occurred in a dark time when Jews were inhibited from practicing their faith. Hannukah celebrations highlight that joy has the power to overcome darkness and break any evil decree.

The *tzefre*, or mashed fruit used to make pálinka, is generally best if it is distilled after one month. It can spoil any time before or after that. András marveled at the fact that for his first batch, the tzefre "didn't go moldy, it didn't lose taste, it didn't lose alcohol, it didn't rot, and it didn't go vinegar. For months! Magic."

In order to make the pálinka kosher, Teleki's Rabbi Sholom Hurwitz hosts the brewing in his flat and oversees its ingredients and procedure. Extending a shot glass half-filled with clear peach pálinka, András said, "So, this is Sholom Hurwitz kosher pálinka. The next batch should be done very soon. This is going to be the fourth. I am very proud of it. This is how we are doing things at Teleki. We go ahead with an idea and then we'll see what happens. We learn how to do it. We make it work. My brother says the place has a sort of something that attracts the right people. We have been pretty lucky with this."

András explained that one of the most important aspects of Teleki is that people can contribute. "Only in a small community can you see that your contribution actually does something. In a big community, you don't see it."

András' friend Peller used to come to Teleki for years. He consistently donated a bottle of grape juice and equally consistently apologized that he couldn't contribute something more. András said, "It matters whether you have grape juice or you don't have grape juice. You can't drink 1400 forints. So, it does make a difference. A lot of small contributions like that make the difference. Small things keep the whole place running. This gives a feeling of community."

András believes that people need more small places like Teleki. "People have their global Facebook experience, but they need a real small community and they won't find it in big synagogues. It's in small communities, that's what I think. This is not only for Jewish communities. For example, 'grow local vegetables,' 'buy local stuff' exists. I think these movements are a good thing. There is a need for us, and people and places like us."

Accordingly, Teleki is growing. There are the regulars, who used to be three or four people but who are now closer to ten or fifteen people who come every week no matter the season or time of year. There is another handful of people who come regularly but do not come every week. There is a larger group of fifty or sixty people who come once a month, or come for a few consecutive months, and there are even more people who may come just once a year. "These four different groups, they make a minyan," András said. "And now, there are kids."

Teleki today is rejuvenating the Teleki that once was. In the 1930s, four or five extended families filled Teleki week to week. "This is what is happening now," András said. "It's becoming something similar to what it used to be."

András isn't exactly sure the best way for Teleki to grow, but imagines that the best thing for the community and surrounding Jewish life in Eastern Europe would be to initiate a handful of other small, apartment-style synagogues in the neighborhood. "To revive them," András said.

When he and Gábor began to travel on behalf of Teleki, to spread word about their projects and to mobilize other struggling communities to empower themselves, he realized that other places were starting from where Teleki was twenty years ago. "I wish that when we first started, we knew that someone else was in a similar place and had gotten past it. I feel energized to tell those places that they are not alone."

As I imagined this future for Teleki and for András, I realized that my attraction to Teleki was not necessarily rooted in the shtiebel's practice of Jewish ritual or the particular taste of cholent. Rather, Teleki and the people within it reminded me that despite my nationality, which was different than theirs, and my Jewish identity, which was also different than theirs, I was not alone.

András endearingly eyed the massive metal pálinka pots beside him. My own experience with pálinka was mostly connected to my experience with Teleki and closely tied to the cheers, *"L'Chaim!"* which means "To life!" in Hebrew. When any friend of Teleki experienced a birthday, a raise, a birth of a child, a return from a vacation or any form of good news, the Teleki community celebrated with pálinka. Whenever I saw someone preparing the tray of shot glasses after lunch, I interrupted the Hungarian conversations around me to ask in English what the celebration was to address the proper congratulations to the deserving friend. If not for pálinka, Teleki would still survive, but for me, the celebrations demonstrate that a thriving community is about more than coming together in hard times. It is about supporting each other in good times and celebrating the small beauties of life.

Before my return to the United States, receiving a patented bottle of "T22"—named after Teleki's location at 22 Teleki Tér—was the best gift I could have asked for.

DEVORA HURWITZ

"I am I. Maybe I'm not perfect. Maybe I'm not gorgeous. Maybe I'm not skinny, or fancy, or rich. But I'm me. At least I am me."

THE WOMAN. THE WIFE. The perceived-to-be-inferior by observers of Hasidic Judaism. The lover. The caretaker. The magician. The smart, beautiful, brilliant role model for her children.

I stood outside Devora Hurwitz's front door on *Wesselényi utca* in the heart of the Seventh District, twirling a silver ring shaped like two birds kissing on my right middle finger. I rang the buzzer with no answer. I waited another three minutes before ringing it again. I glanced at my watch. The door to the building swung open as a young man left the flat. An opportunity. I dashed inside.

I heard the echo of Devora calling my name from upstairs. She must have heard the buzzer the first time. "You know where we are - on the second floor!"

I walked one by one up the wide, winding stairs to Devora's front door. I pulled open the iron gate and twisted the brass door knob. Before both my feet had a chance to step inside, Devora spun past me in a contagious burst of energy and said we are going out for coffee. "The house is such a mess!"

Devora does not lead the easiest life. She is an observant Jewish woman and the wife of an observant Jewish rabbi in the Eighth District of Budapest. Devora's pious life poses challenges in a nationalistic country with rising anti-Semitic political parties. While the average Jewish individual can roam the streets of Budapest without much threat of verbal or physical harm, visible Jewish dress and practice present unique risks of harassment or abuse.

I met Devora my second week in Budapest. It was a Saturday. I sat with my legs twisted around each other in the back row of the women's section of the *Teleki Tér shtiebel.* I held a prayer book written half in Hebrew and half in Hungarian in my hands. Peering through the white lace curtain separating me from the Torah, I observed the dark silhouette of an elderly man hovering around the Torah and the whisks of his long grey beard.

I stood when I was supposed to. I thumbed through the heavy black book in my hands yearning to stumble upon a Hebrew word that I recognized. I struggled to understand the accent of the chanting men on the other side of the curtain. Picking the skin around the edges of my fingernails, I quietly stood and waited for lunch.

Within seconds, Devora noticed me standing near the door. Her long, elastic black skirt swept against the floor and accented the black long-sleeve T-shirt underneath her white short-sleeved blouse. She wore a shimmering dark black wig that graced her shoulders. She approached me and said, "Hi, how are you?" in English.

This time, my lack of response was not because I did not understand the question but because I couldn't believe someone else's first language was English.

Devora quickly introduced me to her life highlights. She grew up in England and met her husband, Sholom, Teleki's rabbi, in New York where he studied at rabbinical school and she earned a teaching degree in Judaics. Upon graduation, they married and vacationed in London for five days before returning to New York. For the following two and a half years, Sholom and Devora worked in Calgary. "Middle of nowhere," she said. "Who else would go where there is no kosher meat and no kosher milk? No problem! We'll figure it out!"

Devora insisted that I sit next to her during lunch. She inquired about my life, my journey and my spirituality. We discussed a wide spectrum of philosophy, politics and recipes. A mere two hours later, she squeezed me into a tight embrace and promised she would bake something special for the following week's dessert.

Four months later, we walked a few blocks from her apartment to *Carimama*, the nearby kosher *pizzéria* & *pékség* (pizzeria and bakery) located on the renown *Kazinczy utca* with other kosher eateries, orthodox synagogues and Jewish-themed restaurants and bars in the Seventh District. We stepped along the wide cobblestone street and curved into the entrance. Fresh scents of baked bread and newly frosted pastries met us at the door. The chef stood behind the glass display case slathering red sauce onto pizza dough. We walked upstairs and found a table for two tucked between the staircase and a booth for four.

Underneath a poster of an orthodox man with a long beard and a pastry in hand, Devora placed her hand on mine on the surface of the table. She suggested that we order a *lángos*, the Hungarian specialty of deep-fried dough traditionally topped with sour cream and Trappista cheese, with whatever coffee we like.

I leaned forward, prepared to ask my first question, when she began reflecting unprompted. "The Rebbe had this incredible drive."

In 1950, Rabbi Menachem Mendel Schneerson, known to many as "The Rebbe," became the seventh and last Rebbe of Chabad-Lubavitch. Chabad is a Hebrew acronym for *"Chochmah, Binah, Da'at* (חכמה, בינה, דעת), or "wisdom, understanding, and knowledge." It was founded in 1755 by Rabbi Schneur Zalman of Liadi and is now one of the world's best-known Hasidic movements, especially known for its outreach. Rabbi Israel Baal Shem Tov founded Hasidic Judaism in 18th-century Eastern Europe as a branch of Orthodox Judaism that promotes spirituality through the popularization and internalization of Jewish mysticism as the fundamental aspect of the faith.

After World War II, most European Jewish families had either been killed during the Holocaust or had abandoned their Jewish faith as a result of the Holocaust. The Rebbe was responsible for transforming a nearly extinct Holocaust-affected Hasidic community into one of the most influential forces in world Jewry.

Devora looked up and smiled as she said, "The Rebbe was really approachable. You could go, even if you were in jeans, or you weren't wearing anything. He talked to you. This was *radical* for a Hasidic Rebbe and for Hasidic philosophy."

She said the Rebbe's philosophy was: Let's get Judaism back together again. Let's get past the trauma. "That absolute, unconditional acceptance is very therapeutic. People felt wicked or 'I'm a bad Jew,' you know, 'cause their grand-parents were all more religious once, even though it sent them to Auschwitz or through the chimneys. The next generation felt guilty for not being so religious. The Rebbe said, 'There's no such thing as a bad Jew. You're a Jew. You're good, and you're okay.' That was massive."

Devora insisted, "Every single person has a job. Every person, no matter who, is a soldier." She lifted her hand in the air and wafted in circles as she said that as long as you are doing something positive, you are doing a good thing. She said, "So do good then. Make the world a better place."

She scanned the room and wondered aloud where our waiter was. She said, "If you are a police officer in New York City and you are stopping crime, you are doing a good job, making the world a better place. If you are a veterinarian and fighting for dolphins, you are doing a good thing, making the world a better place. It is good if you are sitting in the prayer hall learning Torah. That is amazingly good. If you are helping dolphins, that is amazingly good, too."

Devora tapped my hand as she stood from the table to retrieve our waiter from downstairs. When she returned, the waiter followed her. She ordered two lattes and one lángos with two forks. The waiter—a tall, slender man in a black button-down shirt and black slacks—disappeared down the stairs.

Devora siad, "I think the biggest success of Chabad is the flexibility. If it's fashionable to eat *palacsinta*," a beloved Hungarian pancake similar to a French crêpe, "then let's cook palacsinta. If it's fashionable to drink soup, let's make soup.

76

Why not? If that's what everyone wants and that's the need at the time, then make soup. That was very much the Rebbe. His philosophy is the philosophy we take."

In Hungary, Devora does not see that there is *one* Jewish community, but rather, a collection of smaller Jewish communities. She identifies with the Chabad community and the Teleki community and visits a number of synagogues regularly.

Devora was brought up Chabad. Both of her parents, on the other hand, were not. Both sets of Devora's grandparents walked away from the Holocaust severely traumatized thinking, "How could this happen?" They did not want their children to be Jewish, and certainly did not want their children to be religious. They thought, "Let them just live and be happy."

As the children of Holocaust survivors, Devora's parents were unexposed to the meaning of Judaism and its rich culture. They were also removed from the trauma and risk. They found themselves questioning, "What is all this fear about? What is all this 'be careful?' Be careful of what?" So, they started searching.

Their generation found Chabad. They embraced the new tradition because they felt it was open, creative and would fill whatever need they were experiencing. As followers of Chabad, they understood their job as not to become rich or famous, but to spread Judaism, the awareness of Judaism, and the joy of Judaism. Their resounding foundational belief was that to be Jewish was something to be proud of, not something to fear.

Abruptly, Devora started singing, "I am a Jew and I am proud, and I'll sing it out loud, 'cause forever that's what I'll be. Oh yeah!"

I jumped at the unexpected volume and flickering pitch. Devora smiled and explained, "Those kinds of camp songs were created about forty years ago. We translated them into Hungarian and they are very powerful. It would be nice if the Jewish communities in Budapest worked together and people could get past this shame and vulnerability of being Jewish. Deep, deep, deep shame. I only know it because I work with kids and they don't pretend. They don't put on masks. When I take the kids to camp we sing songs and then we come to Budapest and there's no way, even in their own synagogue, that they'll sing those songs. They feel very, very embarrassed and shameful. That is something that blows my mind. I am determined to change it."

Devora has lived and worked in Budapest for nearly two decades. She looked at me as though words would never do her thoughts and experiences justice when she said, "It takes a long time to describe the philosophy of Chabad, but from it is built *shluchim*, which is what we are one of."

Shaliach (plural: *shluchim*) means "messenger" in Hebrew. In the case of Chabad, shluchim missions are built upon strong Jewish values and ideologies.

"Each messenger is as if he or she is the Rebbe himself," Devora said. "We are brought up by the concept in the *Gemara,* the component of the Torah comprising rabbinical analysis and commentary on the Mishnah, the first major written redaction of the Jewish oral traditions known as the

'Oral Torah,' that my message is your message and we are in the same boat. It is as if the Rebbe thought he was everywhere, and his message was everywhere, which is really what it is, because his message is so strong."

Massaging a packet of sugar in her hand, Devora said, "People who don't know Chabad very well say, 'Okay so, being a shaliach is a life sentence?" She laughed, "Yeah, maybe, okay, but only because I feel committed to something I have dedicated myself to. Listen. We could leave anytime. We could say goodbye, this is over, this was nice, we did our job, I'm done. However, it's a choice to stay here, and it's a choice I make everyday."

In Hungary, Chabad supports eleven shluchim. Eleven translates to twenty-two individual messengers because most often shluchim work as married couples. Each shaliach works with a different synagogue, performs a different job, and serves different needs. As followers of Chabad—also known as *Chabadniks, Chasids, Hasids, Lubavitchers,* or *Chabadskers*—their philosophy is that so long as they are doing good work, they should keep doing it. "You never know why G-d sends you where he sends you," Devora said. "Do what you need to do."

Devora realized that in Hungary, many individuals and families avoid Judaism because of fear and stigma. This realization led her to step out and go directly to the people. She started Alef Kids, a Budapest-based Jewish organization for children to discover and embrace their culture and identity. Devora explained that just the week before, almost three hundred people attended the Alef Kids carnival hosted by the Óbuda synagogue. The carnival provided a way for children to have spiritual fun. On one side of the park, children decorated paper hats with sparkling Stars of Davids and multi-colored stickers. On the other side, a magician performed tricks and called on children in the audience to participate in his show.

Devora said that one challenge most Hungarian communities face is a financial one. "So many young people are leaving," she said. As of November 2014, the Central Statistics Office (KSH) found an 8.8 percent unemployment rate in Hungary. The average monthly salary was 176,514.10 Ft or about $627.99. An average one-bedroom apartment in the city center costs about 88,367.35 Ft per month, or $314.39, and utilities (electricity, heating, water and garbage) cost about 47,870.33 Ft, or $170.31. That leaves only $143.29 per month for food (a meal for two costs about $26.68 at an average restaurant), transportation ($33.80 for a monthly pass), Internet ($13.68 per month), and clothes (one pair of Levi jeans costs $63.95 on average). If these were the only expenditures, the average Hungarian would have only $5.18 to spare, but many more expenses contribute to day-to-day life.

Devora found the high number of attendees at the Alef Kids festival surprising because attendees had to pay an entrance fee. The fee was not to cover the cost of putting on the carnival, which was otherwise subsidized, but to reinforce the idea that Jewish events like the carnival are worth paying for. The community showed up, which illustrated that Devora, Alef Kids, and the Óbuda synagogue were on a valuable track.

Devora is the mother of two daughters and four sons. Her children range in age from seven to sixteen. They would like to continue to live in Hungary if Hungary continues to have a place for them. "If the country goes all the way down and they can't sustain themselves, then it's not going to work," Devora said. "However, if they can sustain themselves, I think my children would like to live here. Not because they love Hungary so much, but because they are inspired by the work. They are very proud and they feel purposeful."

Part of their pride, Devora said, stems from their role models treating them as equals. They sit with the adults at Shabbat lunch in synagogue. People speak with them as they would speak with their peers. Devora emphasized, "It's important that they feel empowered because they are the future. They are what's next. They have invested in the language, in the roots, and in understanding the city. They gave up the opportunity to be in a community with hundreds of religious children like themselves to be here to make a difference in the world."

Devora's voice cracked. She cleared her throat and unfolded her hands on the surface of the table. "When things become hard, the purpose and the mission keep me going," she said. "It's the job. I could leave, but then what? Then my life is easy. And what's happened? I haven't changed a thing. You know what I mean?" She took a sip of water and coughed on some liquid flowing down the wrong tube.

Despite her visible religious background and minority status, Devora said the hardest thing for her in Hungary is not being Jewish. Devora struggles most with the culture of victimization. She finds it difficult to cope with Hungarian individuals "finding drugs of all forms to escape from a victimized identity that hasn't healed."

"It's like anti-Semitism," she said. "You think anti-Semitism is anything about the Jews? It's not about the Jews, come on. People need to let out their anger somewhere. I have a theory. Obviously, they are hurting. They need to hurt others in order to release the hurt. Why the Jews? There are two things I think. First, people feel the Jews are strong enough. The other extreme is that people feel the Jews have no defenses. Preying on the defenseless victim makes the bully feel more powerful. That's what I've seen in children who bully in schools. Children only play the same games adults play."

Devora put her right palm against her forehead as she said, "So many Hungarian people walking on the street would prefer that there would be no Jews in Hungary. I mean, you have lots of Jews in Budapest."

Eighty percent of Hungarian Jews live in Budapest. Those individuals account for nearly 6.4 percent of Budapest's population. Though observant Jews in Budapest still face discrimination and isolation, their circumstances are far safer and more accepted than in surrounding areas of Hungary where Jewish populations are negligible. "That helps," Devora said, "At least you have the Jews who aren't anti-Semitic."

Devora's laugh could not mask her self-protective insecurity. She looked at the floor as she whispered, "My children ask where Aushwitz was. The first time they asked me was on the train about nine years ago. I think it was my son, Levy. He must have been three and a half. 'Mommy, where is the Auschwitz? Is it far away? Why do we need to go there? Is it a nice place?' I turned around to look at the man behind my son and he carried on. 'The Arabs should finish you off with one big bomb. You'll be gone, it'll be good for you, then we'll have peace in this world, you gobbling suckers.'"

For a moment we sat in silence.

Raising her gaze, Devora said, "Hasidic philosophy that I have studied for years has come to help me understand one thing. If I wake up in the morning, there is a reason I wake up. I believe in G-d and I believe He made me wake up. So, if I wake up in Hungary with my six children still alive and my husband still alive and everything still happening, there is a reason. There is something I need to do. So when I go into the street and find this and this, there's a reason. Everything has a purpose."

Devora's belief that Hungary is a wonderful place overrides her negative experiences. Consistently, she is amazed by the surviving Hungarian spirit. She explained, "Hungarians are struggling. They have a government against them, they have history against them, they have neighbors against them. It's not easy. Still, they are plodding on."

Devora's smile returned. She told me about the amazing people in Hungary, specifically in Budapest. A woman named Judit, for example, a friend of hers who attends the same synagogue in Teleki square, teaches belly dancing to help women feel more comfortable with themselves. Devora exclaimed Judit's passionate motto, *"Be proud! We are women! It is just us!"*

Judit highlights one of Devora's most inherent life philosophies: instead of finding yourself when someone tells you that you are good enough, you ought to build power within yourself.

She said, "I focus on the individuals who are making a difference. In Hungary, in my community, and in my work, I don't look at the larger picture, I look at the individuals."

Devora understands the most important rule of life to be sharing your light with others. Some amazing people do things because they understand the darkness and they want to spread their light. "If you feel the light," she said, "you have to spread that. Teach the world that."

People are frequently wrapped up in questions like, *Why? What am I? Who am I? How do I respond to the world?* and *What do I want to do?* Devora said, "These questions will only go around and around and around and around until we fix that. We fix it one person at a time."

Devora savored a mouthful of lángos with her eyes closed. She opened her eyes and said, "Every time I get a microphone, this is what I say. Follow it carefully, because it gets confusing. 'If I am I because you are you and you are you because I am I, then I am not, and you are not. So who are we? Nothing. But if I am I because I am I, and you are you because you are you, then I am and you are. Then we have two people.'"

She understands this to mean that we cannot base who we are on the needs, expectations, and affirmations of others. This underscores that every individual needs to first understand for themselves who they are and who they want to be. Before doing so, a person is standing on weak ground that can easily crumble. After doing so, a person can withstand anything.

Her voice grew stronger as she said, "Because I am I. Maybe I'm not perfect. Maybe I'm not gorgeous. Maybe I'm not skinny, or fancy, or rich. But I'm me. At least I am me. If not, I am trying to be you, but then I'm nothing, and so what have we got? Nothing."

Devora's excitement was infectious. I asked her simply, "How do we fix it?"

She smiled as though I had finally asked the right question. "What happens when you turn on the light?" She asked. "It spreads."

She continued, "The point is - do you want to beat vulnerability? Be vulnerable. Accept vulnerability. It's okay to not be perfect. It's okay to look like an idiot and be embarrassed about looking like an idiot, and say, 'It's okay.' That's vulnerability. When you embrace vulnerability, you build a strong enough armor internally, a real armor, to bear it. For Jews, vulnerable and strong is not a contradiction. It is actually a balancer. If you are strong enough, you can manage the vulnerability, and if you can manage the vulnerability, you become even stronger."

To be afraid, she said, is to hide. To hide is to sacrifice centuries of tradition, culture, and life. We must not allow fear to paralyze us in the past. Instead, we should enable our communities to renovate, create and change in order to initiate a brighter, lighter tomorrow.

I took the final sip of my latte and stood to put on my coat. I distantly whispered, "It always amazes me how international Jewish communities seem to be simultaneously the strongest and the most vulnerable."

Devora smirked, "Well, that's just it. To be vulnerable is to be strong. You cannot have one without the other."

I slipped my arms through the sleeves of my white and black plaid wool coat. Devora and I linked elbows and climbed down the stairs of the bakery together. Arm in arm, we walked the cobblestone street back to her apartment, prepared to take on whatever the day had to offer.

ÁDÁM SCHRÖDL

Photograph by Lili Vékássy Photography

"I think if you feel something, do it. Never make compromises."

MY FIRST WEEK IN BUDAPEST ended with my first Hungarian Shabbat, the Jewish day of rest that falls every Friday at sunset to Saturday at sunset. The only place I knew to go was *Mózes Ház*, or Moishe House. During my first trip to Budapest the previous year, I attended a Passover Seder at Moishe House, from which I maintained a few friendships and connections.

As the sun set, the night grew cool. I was dressed for the hot summer day in a cotton floral dress that fell just below my knees and barely covered my shoulders. A breeze brushed against my face, raising hairs on my arms. I paced down *Király utca* (King Street) in the Seventh District, past endless rows of restaurants and pubs, my eyes glued to the numbers on the buildings. Each building I passed—beautiful, authentic and eroding—was equally capable of housing the young passionate Jews I so desperately sought. I power-walked up and down the entirety of the street two times. No Mózes Ház.

Pivoting my right foot on the pavement, I prepared to turn around and return home when I noticed a young woman standing on the street corner. Another young woman was locking her bike across the street beneath a mural of a baby blue sky blanketed with stark white and grey clouds. The bike-rider approached her friend, kissed her once on each cheek, and together they punched in a code at the front door of the building directly to my right.

I approached them hesitantly and said, "S-szia... do you speak English?" They smiled. Someone upstairs released the lock to the door, and the three of us walked together into Mózes Ház.

We climbed two levels of wide, white marble stairs and the two girls dashed inside. I peered through the doorway with caution. The lights were out. I wondered if we were the first to arrive. Somewhere in the distance, I heard a soft plucking of a guitar and a man's voice humming a familiar tune. I stood in the entryway of the apartment and looked in. To my right was the kitchen; a stack of dirty pots piled in the pint-sized sink and glasses half-filled with wine and soda dispersed haphazardly across the counter. To my left, coats were laid atop a table with a poster above it that read *Mózes Ház* in neon block letters. Straight ahead, a room full of people surrounded round quarter-sized candles on the living room floor.

A young man sat on the floor with his eyes closed and his legs crossed, singing. He wore a tight red t-shirt and jeans. His dark blond hair was short on the sides but long on the top, flipped across the front of his forehead. He wore a round, hand-woven multi-colored cap on his head in place of a *kippah,* or traditional Jewish head cover. I crept into the living room and sat down, hugging my knees to my chest. I joined the service, humming ceremonial Shabbat tunes that ignited memories from my childhood. My mind danced around the notion that I had never met these people before yet we had these songs in common.

As the service came to a close, the young singer closed his eyes and sat in silence for a brief meditation. Opening his eyes, he blessed the wine and the challah, as is custom before meals in the Jewish tradition. Finally, he stood, smiled, motioned toward the kitchen and encouraged his guests to eat.

Towering what seemed like two feet above me, he introduced himself as Ádám. As he welcomed me to Moishe House, his home and the heart of his community, he bent to meet me at my level and offered me a plate of pasta with garlic parmesan sauce. After ensuring that I had everything I needed, Ádám buzzed around the room, checking in and chatting with every single guest.

A few weeks after that first Shabbat together, Ádám and I met for a drink on a weekday evening in the Seventh District at a pub called *Fekete Kutya*, or Black Dog – one of our mutual favorites. Fekete Kutya is known for its local regulars, wooden stools, dark lighting, and craft Belgian and Czech beers on draft. Our ears were bombarded with neighboring laughter and shouts of *egészségedre* (egg-eh-shegg-eh-dreh), or "cheers" in Hungarian.

Ádám wore a black baseball cap and a fitted black t-shirt under a grey unzipped hoodie. He sat across from me, shoulders hugging the air around his drink, clasping his right hand around the stein and slapping his left hand against his knee as he laughed. I asked Ádám to tell me a little background about his family. He said, "My name is Ádám Schrödl. Schrödl, actually, is a German name, which is a good starting point for the story."

He smiled widely, but his smile faded as he continued, "Before I borned, my parents just divorced. My father left us and never visited me. Never visited us, actually, although he lived just couple of blocks from our apartment."

Ádám said his father's side of his family was always more interesting for him because he knew little about it. He knew they were German settlers from the 18th or 19th century, but that was common in Hungary at the time. He knew there were also some mixed marriages between his father's family and Jewish families. This was the only thing he knew.

Ádám's eyes darted along the surface of the table. He said he only knew one of his grandparents: his grandmother on his mother's side. All of his other grandparents died before he was born. His mother's mother was a "very, very Catholic person, but in a liberal way." Ádám found Catholics in Hungary to be very open minded. He said, "Actually, I think my grandmother was more empathizing than my mother with my new and, let's say, *progressive* ideas about identity. She was more accepting."

Ádám was born in 1987 and raised a Calvinist. A glimpse of mischief grew in his eyes as he said, "My mother was a very strict Calvinist person. The very, very strict kind. It was always hard for my mother." For a woman who loved and embraced a strict, specific, regulated spiritual tradition, a rebellious, free-thinking son would be quite a challenge.

Following his mother's tradition, Ádám had his confirmation as a child and was very active in the Calvinist youth club. He was a top member of his church and volunteered often with children of his neighborhood. "I believed in it," he said. "Still, some core things remained in me."

Ádám shook his head and said, "I remember though, when it hit me that something wasn't right."

When Ádám was in primary school, his pastor told him and a group of his peers to put their words in light of the Bible. When Ádám heard that, he thought that judging his behavior by a book did not account for the particularities of different people in various circumstances. At a young age, Ádám recognized the gray area. He wanted to be more in tune with his feelings and intuition. He saw countless people arguing with each other in the church. "Different groups understood the same Bible words quite different," he said. Ádám emphasized, "It made me think, 'How does this pastor mean this thing, to put everything in light of the Bible?' If I put everything into the light of the Bible, then my understanding is equal to others, but my understanding wasn't equal to others. So, I started to think different."

When Ádám thought about the Trinity, again he felt different than the others. He speculated it may have been because he never knew his father. As he grew into a teenager, he began arguing about the Trinity in youth camp. His group leader said, "Oh, don't think about it. It will make you crazy," to which Ádám replied, "Then maybe I want to be crazy." He needed answers.

Ádám attended a Calvinist high school. "I think I was always a black sheep there," he said. "I did not know it, I just felt it."

At the time, Ádám was conservative. He was known to say a few anti-Semitic things when he was fifteen. "I am not proud of that," he said. "I didn't say much, but I really thought that maybe the country was bad because of Jews. It was hard for me even then, but I tried to believe it, because to believe it would put me into the group."

Later in high school, Ádám started to have incidents. He listened to punk rock music and yearned to be "liberated." One day, he went to a memorial to the Peace Treaty of Trianon and the Revolution of 1956 wearing a handkerchief with Che Guevara on it. Ádám remembers that one of his teachers told him to take off the handkerchief because Che Guevara was "a genocider." Ádám replied, "Yeah, who cares?" To me, he shrugged and said, "It was harsh, but I did it."

Ádám's first acquaintance with Judaism happened during his final year of high school. He went to his youth group and suggested to the leader and to his peers that the group incorporate a series about Judaism into their studies. He thought that Judaism was in the core of Christianity.

"There was a big silence after that," Ádám said. "After no support, I felt like, 'What the fuck, man? What are we talking about? I mean Jesus was Jewish, right?' Then I realized for sure, like, fuck, something was wrong here."

Ádám's next encounter with Judaism came while he was attending university. He majored in Hungarian literature. When he was confronted with choosing a minor, he was torn between Arabic and Hebrew. Originally, he wanted to choose Arabic because he thought it would help him in business. For one reason or another, Arabic conflicted with his schedule and goals at that time, so Ádám enrolled in Hebrew for the next semester.

"That made me think a lot about myself," Ádám said. He started to learn Hebrew and met his first Jewish friends in his Hebrew classes. Ádám explained, "I had a girlfriend at the time whose family was Holocaust survivors. She was Jewish. That changed me." He said it wasn't only his girlfriend that changed him, but also his studies and the whole of the academic environment caused Ádám to rethink his previous understandings.

Reflecting on his childhood relationships, particularly with his friends from school and church who Ádám later discovered to be Jewish, he said, "Even before I knew, I liked that they were different. I did not know how they were different, but I liked the difference in them."

Ádám's introduction to Judaism and Jewish culture sparked his transformation. One day, the girl sitting next to Ádám in one of his university classes learned that he was studying Hebrew and started a conversation with him. "What is special in *me?*" Ádám wondered. He told her that he really wanted to experience a Jewish community. She painted a picture of a new informal community that she and her friends were trying to build up in Budapest. She offered Ádám to visit with her one day. Then, for the first time, Ádám visited Moishe House.

On the night of his first visit, Ádám was almost late. He was used to being late, but the reaction by those he met at Moishe House was different than the reaction he was expecting. "The event just did not start," he said. "Even if it was time to start, they did not start it. People were just hanging around. It was great! I was like, 'This is awesome. I want this!'" Ádám craved a similarly relaxed, community-oriented experience in church but his church community was quite strict. He explained, "I always thought that wasn't the point. People just wanted to hang out. That's why they were there."

Beyond the relaxed timeline of the evening at Moishe House, Ádám was surprised by the open nature of the conversation. He said, "They were talking about politics – even openly! They were talking about taboos like gay people, transsexuals…it was great. I felt like *anarchism is here,* it's real here! Even if I am in the ghetto, I am more free than outside of it."

From that moment on, Ádám visited Moishe House every Friday evening. He learned Hebrew liturgy. He met rabbis and had the chance to talk with rabbis about differences and similarities between a variety of spiritual traditions and spiritual paths. He also met Protestants and Christians who also thought that Judaism was an integral aspect of Christianity. He remembered, "I felt like, great, I'm not that creepy asshole anymore. What I say is valid."

Two and a half years later, Ádám received his degree and went on to receive a Masters in History of Religion paired with a Masters in Literature. At that time, one of the girls living in Moishe House announced that she was moving out. The other roommates told Ádám that they felt he would be a great person to take her place. Ádám remembered his reaction. He said, "No way. I am not Jewish, I cannot represent the community. I cannot be a leader. I can do whatever you want, I can help you, but not in this way." The others told Ádám that it didn't matter what his religious label was. They encouraged him by saying he was already a hugely helpful member of the community. They insisted he join the apartment. "So, after about a month, I moved in," Ádám said. "I was really, really in. I felt much more in than in any other community."

Ádám brushed a long piece of hair across his face and admitted that before Moishe House, he struggled to fit in. Sometimes, he felt that even if he identified with a principle, he felt frustrated by how the principle was overlooked in practice. When he visited Moishe House, however, he felt that not only did people talk about theories, but they also practiced those theories, which was more important for Ádám. "I came here and I learned," he said.

Ádám has since lived in Moishe House for five years. For the first three years, Ádám wanted to formally convert to Judaism. He explained, "Whether or not to formally convert was a big decision inside me."

Much of Ádám's hesitation came from the notion that the Jewish tradition does not encourage conversion, which Ádám believed was more often than not a positive practice. After discussing with a series of rabbis the intricate details of his belief, Ádám decided that he did not need to convert to feel as passionately as he did about Jewish culture, tradition and people.

Around March of 2013, Ádám decided he would not convert. "But *then* who am I?" he questioned. Ádám looped his right hand around his stein and took a long sip of beer. He put his stein back on the table with a loud clank and said, "So, I started to search."

For two years, Ádám visited a variety of churches to find a tradition that was right for him. He felt the Moishe House community was on the right track, but he needed something that was *him*.

Somehow, on the Internet, Ádám found Unitarianism. "That is the first thing I read that I said, 'Yeah, I can believe this,'" Ádám said. "Even if it is a liberal, very ongoing thing, and most of the Christians think, 'Unitaristic go to hell,' maybe, if that's how I go, I'd rather go to hell."

Ádám swirled the inch of beer left in his stein around on the table. As the bubbles settled on the surface, he said, "Finally, I started to form my personality and identity." He felt like he did not have to decide between what he had to practice. Ádám practices many aspects of Jewish tradition. Sometimes, he prays because he feels he needs to. Other times, he doesn't because he isn't in the mood. He feels no shame. He explained, "Sometimes I just do it. Sometimes I feel that I am very Jewish. Sometimes I feel I am Protestant. That's me. It's great."

Ádám laughed. "A Judaist Unitariast, or something like that. That can fit with me. This is what I am."

In an even tone, Ádám said that in one week he would move out of Moishe House in order to move into a larger home with his girlfriend. He tapped the palm of his hand on the surface of the table and sighed. "I am going to miss this place. Many of my friends are at Moishe House. I don't want to separate myself from it. I am a person who needs Jews around him. I think I will always go to synagogue on Friday night."

Though Ádám feels comfortable identifying himself as a non-Jew, he maintains passion and commitment to Judaism and Jewish culture. After his final sip of beer, he described his admiration that Jewish people "are always trying to step over themselves."

He elaborated that Judaism is unique in the way that it values debate and proving or disproving multiple perspectives and interpretations of a similar text or circumstance. He said, "Hungarians and Hungarian culture have a huge capacity to step over borderlines, but people are afraid to do it. I don't know why. I never felt it. I did it. Just do it. Just choose wisely and never make prejudice. Just do it."

As Ádám stood to retrieve another round from the bar, he joked, "If I could speak with Moses, I think I would have some very good ideas." He returned holding two tall glass steins tight by their thick rectangular handles. He said, "I think if you feel something, you gotta do it. Never make compromises. If you feel you are not comfortable with something, don't do it. Just don't. It doesn't matter if your parents say that it's right. Maybe it's not. You should question that."

Ádám placed one of the two beers in front of me. The small, circular stage light perched above the bar shined into the glass, turning what otherwise looked like a dark brown beer an illuminated bronze color.

A group of three young men burst through the wooden door of the pub with their arms around each other's shoulders. Ádám recognized the man in the middle as a friend of his who had recently gotten married. He stood from his stool, hugged the man in the middle and handed him his beer. Ádám pointed in my direction, guiding the group to our table as he returned into the darkness to replace his drink.

ANDRÁS RÉNYI

"Remembering, real remembering, means you are telling your stories. You are repeating your stories…a kind of discussing and discovering and dialogue. Not just erecting a monument."

SHARP WINDS WHIPPED MY HAIR ACROSS my face. I stood in front of *Szabadság Tér* (Liberty Square) where the Fidesz government, currently in power in Hungary, erected a monument for the victims of the Nazi Occupation. Across from me, Archangel Gabriel—who the government built to represent Hungary—gazed above my head with outstretched arms. Hovering above Gabriel was a dark silver eagle, built to represent Nazi Germany. Jagged cement pillars formed a semicircle around Gabriel and the eagle, leaving an eery sensation of something unfinished. My eyes scanned the scene for more information and settled on a number in the far right corner: 1944.

Nazi Germany invaded Hungary in March 1944. Until that point in World War II, Hungary was a German ally. That year was one of the most brutal of the Holocaust, a genocide in which approximately six million Jews were mass murdered by the Nazi regime and its collaborators.

The Liberty Square monument represents the Hungarian government's official stance on history. A group of mostly

Jewish Hungarian civilians created *Eleven emlékmű*, a Living Memorial, as a protest against the Fidesz government erecting something so significant without consulting the public. The protest began as a flashmob, then graduated to a Facebook group and now constitutes a passionate, committed group that continues to meet frequently and organize programs in person.

I knelt at the base of the statue to grasp a wrinkled black-and-white photograph between my fingers. At my feet, fresh fluorescent pinks, reds, and oranges replaced the dried and deteriorating petals of flowers past. Candles, burnt to the glass, sat adjacent to roaring flames. Handwritten letters, stained and torn, rustled in the wind. Real people. Real faces. Real trauma.

Behind me, a playful fountain shot explosions of water into the air, spigots alternating left and right, like manmade volcanoes. Children, screeching with laughter, ran about the water that unexpectedly turned on and off, testing whether they could make it through unscathed. The children did not seem to notice Gabriel and the eagle. They skipped past the personal monument in front of Gabriel, seemingly unaffected by the photographs' intent to bring a traumatized past back to life.

Standing in the middle of all three – children, suffering, and government – time stood still, paralyzed by the tense standstill of Hungarian ground-level politics. A recently published poll evidenced that about a third of the Hungarian public was in support of this monument, about a third of the Hungarian public was against this monument, and about a third was unsure or had no opinion. I turned my back against the two monuments, envying the children's ignorant bliss.

Two weeks later, I swung open the door to Massolit, a bookstore-turned-coffee-shop in the heart of the Seventh District. I clung to the only information I had about the appearance of the man I was looking for, which I gathered from his Facebook picture: he could be my father's age.

I slid into a wooden booth that hit hard against my sit bones and spine. A tall man in a worn t-shirt and ripped jeans entered and greeted the barista behind the counter with a kiss on each cheek and a few phrases in Hungarian. His protruding collar bone suggested he was a man who ate to satisfy a need rather than to fuel a desire. He turned 360 degrees in place and made eye contact with me, flashing a smile. András.

András Rényi (Reh-ñi) is an art historian who heads the Institute for Art History at Eötvös Loránd Science University (ELTE) in Budapest. He is a main player in the coordination of *Eleven emlékmű*. Based on the work he does and the advocacy he supports, I imagined a man with a fierce glare and an intimidating stance. Yet András seemed as approachable as a small town butcher who knew each of his customers by first name. I clumsily offered András his side of the booth. He peered at the stiff, wooden bench, glanced at the cushioned chairs adjacent to neighboring tables, and sat with me.

"I am sorry, my English is not very good," he said.

I smiled. "Already it is better than my Hungarian."

As András smiled back at me, the wrinkles that formed around his eyes unveiled a wisdom that age alone could not. He explained to me that his son, an English language student of mine, had briefly described to him my project to document Jewish identity in Hungary. He asked what I needed *him* for. I laughed to myself that the most influential individuals often happen to be the humblest.

"I should tell you that I don't have anything like a Jewish identity," he explained. "I don't identify myself with the Jewish tradition. Not me. That's quite typical for many Budapest Jews. So my story…well, can be seen as a typical one."

Though both of András' parents were Jewish, they lived without any connection to Judaism. András said that even though his grandparents lived with Jewish last names, his mother and father were "Christianized". They changed their names to dismiss any religious affiliation. Both sides of András' family were not religious but they were leftist. Some of his family joined the communist movement very early on.

András and his parents moved to Hamburg, Germany from Hungary when he was just under three years old. His family had to leave Hungary after 1920 during the White Terror, a period of repressive violence that led to the imprisonment, torture and execution of communists, socialists, Jews, leftist intellectuals and others deemed to threaten the traditional Hungarian political order that the militantly anti-communist government sought to reestablish. András was fifteen years old when Hitler came to power in 1933, at which point, he and his family returned to Budapest.

"They came back for the same reason they left," András said. "This was the pattern of history."

The first anti-Jewish law in Hungary, passed in 1920, surfaced as a reaction to severe trauma and loss of terrority following World War I. Later during Hitler's leadership in Germany, Hungary enacted many laws that hindered educational and professional opportunities for Jewish citizens. For example, the first of this series of laws passed in 1938 and restricted the ratio of Jews in intellectual professions to twenty percent. The following year, the twenty percent was restricted further to six percent.

András' father attended a German secondary school in Budapest just before the onset of World War II. His school was liberal in that it allowed him to take his final exams despite his Jewish background. His younger sister was even allowed to finish her exams in 1944. However, when András' father graduated secondary school, he was not allowed to attend university because, according to Hungarian law, only up to fifteen percent of university students could be of

Jewish origin. After 1939, no Jewish students were allowed to attend.

Instead, András' father went to a small town in southern Hungary to work at an internationally renowned printing house. He learned there that he was quite talented.

"It was enough for him," András said. "He was absolutely not interested in going to university and learning philosophy."

András closed his eyes and allowed the steam from his mug of tea to moisten his face. In meditated words he said, "In this way, he got the skill to make false papers, which became very important during wartime. With this skill, he helped people to escape. This was the link that got him close to the underground. He became a member of the illegal party."

The 1944 Nazi Occupation of Hungary declared the *Szociáldemokrata Párt,* or Social Democratic Party, illegal. The leadership was executed, imprisoned, or driven underground. After the war, as a member of the Communist Party, András' father became an activist. András said, "From this time on, this was his main activity. It was more…it was kind of an obsession."

András shifted his weight on the bench, swallowed hard and gazed ahead. He told me his parents met in the Communist Movement, which they had joined from very different backgrounds and for very different reasons.

"My father's identity was the identity of a German intellectual," he said. "My mother… she had a very tough childhood with no family. With nobody."

András' mother came from an impoverished family in East Hungary. She became an orphan at the age of three and was raised in a variety of Jewish orphanages.

"She hated it," András said. "You can imagine. She hated the rightist, fascist system, and she was against this Jewishness as a mark that she would wear on her forehead."

In 1949, András' parents had his eldest brother. Four years later, in 1953, András was born. Two years later, András' younger sister was born. "We were born during the Communist times in a Communist family with parents with no Jewish identity, and yet, the whole family was Jewish," he said.

András is sure that his role in the Living Monument has nothing to do with his being Jewish. "It's *my* generation. Not your generation," he said. He explained that while being Jewish doesn't cause any problem for my generation, it does cause pause and risk for his.

He whispered, "My story of learning I was Jewish was a trauma for me."

When András was fifteen, he was learning German in school as an extra language. His father grew up in Germany; he sometimes spoke better German than Hungarian. Most of the children in András' family decided to learn German in school for this reason. It was their own familial tradition.

One day, András' teacher gave a lecture on a well-known Lessing drama, *Nathan der Weise,* or Nathan the Wise. The drama was written about religious tolerance in the late 18th Century during the Enlightenment. "It is a kind of Enlightenment fairytale," András said. "The Jewish rabbi, Nathan the Wise, made peace between the nations and between the religions."

András was quite good at German. He always did his classwork. One of his classmates wanted to copy his work for this lesson. He wrote on the back of András' paper, "Rényi the Wise."

András' paper landed in the hands of András' teacher. She asked him who wrote it and András told her. She asked, "What do you think about this?" András replied, "What's the problem? It's a joke." András teacher told him to ask his mother for her opinion on the matter.

At home, András explained what happened. His mother told him, "It means that you are Jewish."

András' eyes pulsed, briefly widening before narrowing and coming to a close. He remembered shouting, "What?! What do you say? How is it possible that my classmate knows something about me that I do not know about myself?"

"It was a real trauma," he said.

At our table, András bit the skin around the nail of his right pointer finger. "My mother told me there are some basic features on my face. From then on, for about ten years, I was always fantasizing of operating on my face. As a young guy, I had long, curly hair. It was the beat times, very fashionable. From then on, I was always thinking about how can I make my hair straight. I did not want to identify myself as a Jew. I never asked for it. I wasn't interested in knowing who was this or who was that."

At a time when most Hungarians could not travel, And-rás' family had the opportunity to travel to Israel because of their well-respected status and relatives living in Israel. Still, "I didn't want to," András said. He wasn't ready.

It wasn't until 1989 when András was just over forty-years-old that he first went to Israel. "That was the first time I *dared* to go," he said. "I felt, okay, this might be interesting."

Today, András is a leading scholar on the representation of religion in art. His main research questions surround monuments, the cult of memory and how visual arts and plastic arts were originally meant to secure memories of people or events that would otherwise disappear.

He wrote a number of articles about different monument case studies and the problem of memory. He said, "Man very deeply and anthropologically needs those signs left behind. This is one of the main motives for taking pictures. It's important to understand what happened. When you see a painting, or a monument, or a statue, what is going on in you? How do you understand what this is for? These kinds of questions are very much my interest."

With one hand, András held his tea bag by the string, dipping it in and out of the mug held in his other hand. "My interest and my personal, emotional presence in this matter has nothing to do with my Jewish identity. Nothing to do with this. I still do not have this."

It was in the early 90s that András realized pictures are an exciting issue within the Jewish tradition. He has always been interested in how Christian art uses pictures to illustrate stories. According to the Ten Commandments in the Jewish tradition, creating pictures of holy figures and erecting monuments is prohibited. Following his trauma around his discovery of his Jewish roots, András found himself immersed in the intensive study of a form of art that the Jewish world seemingly did not accept.

András explained that the Hungarian Constitution states that both the historical lack of serenity in Hungary and the reattainment of serenity need to be commemorated by monuments or physical reminders to mark those periods of time. The Hungarian government prioritizes categorizing history into distinct periods of loss and victory.

Unfortunately, history is not always so black-and-white. András admitted that Hungary has a way of rewriting history into clear periods with "a sign, a statue or a square." He stressed that this way of making monumental gestures really upset him.

As András grew into his sense of self, took ownership of his expertise and acted on behalf of his identified sense of right and wrong, András spearheaded a movement against a Hungarian monument that he found to be falsifying history. Somehow, he aligned with the Jewish Commandments he had originally rejected.

"Memorials work against forgetting," he said. "This is the opposite of the way in which these Hungarian memorials work. These national monuments are trying to implement, create, or indoctrinate ideas."

András gripped his hands firmly around his mug. He said that what is happening in Szabadság Tér with the erection of the national monument of Gabriel and the eagle is Hungary's opinion about "how history *should* be seen" or "how it *should* be understood." Against it, the Living Monument erected by the people is a personalized suggestion about how to personally remember history. "This is fascinating for me as a professional," he said, "these two facing each other."

András described how the Szabadság Tér monument came to be. On December 31, 2013, the Hungarian government decided to erect a very significant monument. They announced they would dedicate a large sum of money to it by March 19 the following year without any public debate.

When the plan leaked, Hungarian Jewish communities and organizations and a slew of Hungarian historians and intellectuals raised an outcry because they saw this as a falsification of history. Hungary's Prime Minister Viktor Orbán wrote a response to criticism in a letter to *Mazsihisz*, The Federation of Jewish Communities. He cited Hungary's constitution to argue that Hungary was stripped of sovereignty when Germany occupied it in 1944. This implied an unmistakable lack of culpability for the ensuing genocide.

András said that as a result of the controversy, the government changed its stance regarding the monument. "They said, 'Okay, this monument is just about the German occupation, but it is in honor of the victims.' This was even worse." The monument posed all Hungarians as equal, innocent victims, which was not the case, and shifted blame away from Hungary and onto Germany.

The Hungarian government, however, was not innocent. For most of WWII, Hungary was an ally of Germany. In early 1944, Germany realized Hungary was conducting secret negotiations with the United States and United Kingdom. Germany invaded Hungary in March. By July, Hungary appointed a government sympathetic to Nazis that deported over 450,000 Jews and Roma to concentration camps.

Even before 1944, Hungary was no paradise for Jews. Anti-Semitism was a significant part of political and intellectual life, especially in the late 1930s. Hungarian authorities passed more than one hundred laws discriminating against Jews that restricted their professional, educational and cultural lives. Before 1944, Hungarian authorities deported thousands of Jews, many of whom met their death in pogroms, mass murders and government-sanctioned forced labor camps.

András said that the Szabadság Tér monument traumatized Hungarian Jews. They considered it a resurgence of disrespect. They felt they needed to rebel.

2014 was the 70th anniversary of the Holocaust and the Hungarian government allotted a significant amount of money for Jewish NGOs to hold momentous commemorative events. As a result of the controversy surrounding the monument, the Hungarian Jewish organizations refused this money.

A fight ensued. Hungarian artists organized a flashmob – which drew a crowd of four hundred people – to intervene. András said, "We asked people to bring stones and candles and photos and personal things and books and all sorts of objects of personal remembrance to put on the site."

András sat with proud broad shoulders. "This monument is above a garage ramp. From an artistic, sculptural point of view, it's nonsense. We speculated about why that location was chosen and there is only one reason, which is that in the same square there is another monument that was erected in 1945 for the Soviet army soldiers. Having a monument for the German occupation and another for the Soviet occupation is in accordance with the new constitution. The forty-six years of Hungarian loss of serenity are a result of the two occupations."

In response to that realization, András, his colleagues and his fellow activists said, "Okay, then what if *we* make a site?" It was their logic that if they put masses of personal objects there, the government would not dare to move them, which would prevent the monument from being built.

András sat back on the bench and crossed his arms across his chest. "They didn't dare," he declared.

At first, the government announced that they would postpone the monument. András speculated that this was because general elections were approaching. He said, "Everything is politicized and disguised in a normal way as if they actually wanted to discuss the issue."

Fidesz, the majority party, won the election. "The *second day* after," András said, "they begin the building activities. This means they never wanted to discuss anything."

András looked at the floor and shook his head. "For the next two or three weeks, every time the officials came to clear the area and put a barrier, the people returned with more belongings and more protests. Take away, bring them back. Take away, bring them back."

He smiled for a moment, but his expression soon turned into deeper disappointment. "They erected the monument. Overnight," he said. "Since then, the two monuments are standing against each other, continuing to challenge each other."

The monument was erected in July, five months before this conversation in Massolit. András twiddled his mug around his thumb. He said, "People are coming now twice a week. It's winter, it's cold, and still, twice a week, people come together. In small groups they are discussing important topics. Remembering, *real* remembering, means you are telling your stories. You are repeating your stories. You can hope that remembering is a collective remembering, a kind of discussing and discovering and dialogue. Not just erecting a monument."

András continued, "This is something we are missing in this society: dialogue. Asking, answering, telling every side. What we are saying is that a community needs to reflect upon its own responsibilities. The main idea behind the Living Monument is that we want Hungarian society to reflect on its own role. Some Hungarians did not care about the Jewish Hungarians. Some of them were very keen on getting those material things they left behind. Others were interested in losing their concurrence in the business life. Others were not interested and were just ignoring. This mix led to this national tragedy. What we have to do is think about what we *would* do, what we would have done, and what are we actually doing now."

András said, "I would say Budapest Jews are otherwise very right in feeling hurt by anti-Semitism, but are they just as sensitive for other minorities? These kinds of questions should be discussed. Self-reflection and self-criticism - *this* is the Living Monument. Remember things because you are interested in understanding better for your personal situation here and now. That's what's moving me."

András and the Living Monument group are thinking now about how to make the discussions something stable and continuous. He said, "One way would be if it could become more of a movement. Different people coming together in different places, not only one group, not always the same people, same place. Until now, this group has not moved away from the site. It's a site-specific project."

Another challenge, he said, is that there is no money in it, but that once money is introduced there begins a kind of institutionalization. "There is a leader, someone is deciding, others are not allowed to decide. The Living Memorial has no single leaders. There is no hierarchy. This is living only as long as it is not a society or a party because then personal interest, and other interest, are the driving factors, and that's the end of it."

András explained that this kind of civilian movement, with no intention of achieving power or money, is rare. "There is no guidebook for how to do it," he said. "We are just learning this, how to do this, now. This movement can be, or *should* be, to make people understand what they need in order to get a better life. They need to learn. We do not know how to remember. We do not know how to live as independent citizens in an independent city. What does it mean? Every citizen must be responsible for the whole."

Though he wished things were different, András said he did not believe that every citizen in Hungary felt responsible for the whole of Hungary. Not yet.

"If I were ten years younger, you might convince me to leave because of it," he said, "but I cannot leave because I love this city. Budapest is a fantastic city."

András sighed, "Sometimes, I envy the tourists. They can so freely experience and freely enjoy. A little bit more freedom would help us."

He laughed, "I never, never would have thought myself being an activist. I am a university man; I belong in a library. It will change, I am absolutely sure. I don't know what, and I don't know how. Maybe it will be worse."

"Hopefully not," I teased.

He smiled. "Hopefully not."

GÁBOR MAYER

Photograph by András Mayer Photography

"I don't know who they are - they might not even be born yet - but we need the next generation to care."

I WAS TOLD PRIOR TO LEAVING for Budapest that I should look out for him. On day three, I recognized his name at the Me2We Conference. Energetically introducing myself, I extended my hand. Wearing a fitted grey suit and tie, he shook it with maintained vacant, professional eye contact. We exchanged names. For some time, this was our only interaction.

Throughout the conference, Gábor (Gah-bore) struck me as a businessman, angular in his body language and precise in his words. His long, bushy mustache and beard rarely parted to reveal a smile or opinion.

On the final day of the conference, Gábor led an optional tour to his *shtiebel*, or small apartment-style synagogue, Teleki Tér. With a group of seven, I stood in the courtyard outside of Teleki. The cobblestone courtyard, walled in by four five-story apartment buildings, absorbed shreds of early evening light. Windows and doors guarded by black iron vertical bars stood protectively between us and the life inside. I looked up to find the silhouette of a black bird with its wings spread wide, circling above us against a backdrop of open sky.

Gábor asked us to guess which door was the entrance to the shtiebel. We gazed with blank stares, eyes welling with anticipation. He slowly gravitated toward the door in the far right corner and pointed to the iron bars above the door. He asked, "Notice anything?"

The vertically positioned iron bars above every other door around the courtyard were systematically separated by a few inches each. Bar after bar, perfectly parallel. The iron bars above this particular door were bent, colliding into one another at the bottom and branching out in opposite directions at the top like a flower. I gasped as I realized the symbol was not a flower, but a *menorah*, or a nine-pronged candelabrum also known as a *chanukiah* lit during the eight-night celebration of the Jewish holiday of Hannukah.

The Eighth District of Budapest, the neighborhood surrounding Teleki Tér, hosted various shtiebels before WWII. Teleki uniquely continued to draw a minyan even during communism when, technically, it was illegal to do so. Accordingly, there was no neon sign encouraging Jews to "Come pray here!" Instead, the shtiebel had a secret message to incoming Jews: follow the menorah.

Today, there is only Teleki. Gábor fiddled with the lock and opened the door. As though there were an invisible force guarding the premises, upon entering Teleki, Gábor's face melted into a wonderfully warm welcome. As he explained the history of Teleki and the work gone into renovating and maintaining it, the pride in his eyes grew deeper and even more sincere.

After a lesson in contemporary life at Teleki, Gábor hurried to lay out cookies, coffee, tea, pastries, chips, pretzels, napkins, spoons and small plates decorated with blue and white ceramic Stars of David on the coffee table in the small kitchen area adjacent to the prayer hall. We sat, reminisced, and laughed, floating around the snacks. From that moment forward, I attended Shabbat lunch in that very room every Saturday.

Three months into my stay in Budapest, I entered Gábor's office first thing Monday morning. I felt as though I had entered a different sphere of his world entirely. Amidst sounds of fingers hitting keyboards and drips of coffee rippling into an empty coffee pot, I found Gábor sitting at a long black desk in front of a desktop computer, surrounded by disheveled stacks of paper across from co-workers whose faces shined with the reflected light of their respective computer screens.

I introduced myself to a variety of Gábor's co-workers and followed him into the office kitchen. We sat across from one another at a quaint plastic fold-up table next to a cracked window. On the other side of the window, paint bubbled and peeled off the surface of the building opposite us. Gábor stood to fix more coffee.

Gábor was born in the Seventh District of Budapest on August 5, 1981. When he was two, he and his family moved to the Eighth District where he attended primary and high school. In 2006, Gábor returned to the Seventh District and has lived there until very recently, when he moved in with his new wife in the First District.

"I really like where I grew up," Gábor said. "A lot of friends live there, our rabbi lives there, I know a few of the shop owners. I always have one or two places where I can go in, eat, drink, and leave without paying."

Gábor winked as though he were kidding, but I knew from mutual friends, he really did have many connections across the Seventh District that would happily feed him in exchange for his hard work and friendship. He asked whether I would like milk or sugar in my coffee.

Pouring a few drops of reduced fat milk into his own mug, he explained that the Eighth District used to be the worst area in town. "Parts of it still are," he said.

Gábor grew up during the Communist Era. "The town was grey," he said. "You know, the exhaust of car, and everything, just stuck on buildings. If you go to old descriptions of Budapest, it was described as a very colorful city. When I was growing up, everything had bullet holes on it, and it was grey and black and dark. You felt decay everywhere."

He grew accustomed to the look. "I really like it, actually," he said. "I prefer a view with decaying houses than with brand new things. For me, it's much more homey, more cozy. Much more detail."

Gábor handed me a mug of steaming coffee with a touch of milk painting clouds along the surface. He sat back down across from me. Traffic buzzed beneath the window beside us as we sipped our caffeine.

Growing up, being Jewish wasn't an issue for Gábor. "It wasn't talked about at all," he said. "I know people who are blond and blue eyes, and no one would guess they are Jewish, but with me...it was kind of obvious."

Gábor sports a short, dark buzz cut and a fit but stout build. His fair skin sharply contrasts his long, dark beard covering the lower half of his face. His nose boasts a pronounced arch precisely between his nostrils and his eyebrows.

"I was told in kindergarten that I was Jewish," he said. "The other children would tease me saying, 'My parents told me!' I didn't know what they were talking about. I went home and asked, 'Somebody told me I am Jewish. What is that?' My parents told me that the Jews are the people that used to live in Israel a few thousand years ago." Gábor returned to the children at school and told them that his ancestors used to live in Israel thousands of years ago. He asked, "Where were your ancestors a thousand years ago?" When they didn't know, Gábor felt proud that at least he knew more about his roots than his peers.

For many years, Gábor knew that he was Jewish but nothing else. "We always had a Christmas tree," he said. "Christmas was normal for everybody. It wasn't about the little Jesus or about being Christian. In Budapest, people have Christmas trees. That's it."

When Gábor was in his twenties, for the first time, he met people who did not have Christmas trees. "Now, I have quite a few friends who do not," he said.

A young, blonde co-worker of Gábor's peered into the room and asked in Hungarian if she could talk with Gábor for a moment. He rendered an apologetic grin and followed her outside. Once the whispering outside the door ceased, Gábor returned and took a long sip of coffee.

Gábor's first real Jewish experience was Teleki. He said, "I started going around '98 and then I stuck to it." His brother András was going for a while before him. "We started going there as a handful of youngsters, talking in the back, not knowing what was happening. We were just there so the place could go on praying. Sometimes we stood up, or didn't talk, or did whatever we needed to do. We didn't know why we needed to do those things. The others didn't care that we didn't know. They could go on praying and that was enough."

Gláser, the elderly, charismatic man running Teleki at the time, had a great sense of people. Gábor said, "Even though he was about ninety, he made it possible for Teleki to survive many, many years because of the kind of person he was. He told us all the time these stories of how he almost died, and how he could read people. If there was someone new in the shul, in an hour, he would know what they do, who they were friends with, what their parents do, everything. Gláser had a different relationship with every single person. He could remember every person from all his life. In the 80s or 90s, he ran into a guy in the streets who used to be a superior in the army in the 30s, and he remembered him!"

Gláser trusted Gábor. "Somehow, I started helping him," Gábor said. First, he asked small favors. "I was there, and I helped," Gábor said.

This evolved into Gábor replacing Gláser as the leader of Teleki when Gláser was in the hospital. Then, a small group of loyal congregants decided they would continue to operate Teleki when Gláser was gone.

As the group ran things on their own, they began to realize that there were things that needed to be done apart from just opening the door. "It was uncomfortable for us to be there," Gábor said. "There was no proper toilet, it was too early in the morning, and there was no coffee." So, the team started to renovate.

"This has been evolving ever since," he said. "This is where we are now."

When visitors return to Teleki after some time, they don't recognize the shul. Gábor remembered, "One man came back after decades and stared at the walls and said, 'It's not the same.' Of course it's not the same! When he was coming here, it was just people in their 80s. Now, there are younger people, too."

Gábor stirred a small spoon around the inner lining of his coffee mug. "It's interesting to think about what you were and how you were," he said. "When I started, Judaism was new for me. It was more about seeing what was there and protecting what we were not allowed to give up. For my generation, now, our relationship with Judaism is more about...I think we are the bridge. I feel now that I am trying to do as much as possible to take from the past and to bring it into the future so we will have a lot to embrace from the old times. This is our last chance to do that."

This is a large responsibility. "It's frightening, actually, that people living now don't know much about the old things, and the people who *do* know and who do remember are dying." To capture their knowledge, Gábor has initiated research projects to "write everything down." He said, "Then, it's in the books and not only in peoples' minds."

Gábor's relationship with Judaism has taken new form during his leadership at Teleki. "Now, when we have services, I am announcing pages," he said.

In orthodox synagogues, it is not customary to announce page numbers. Gábor said, "We are because many people inside do not know what's happening and where we are in the book, so we want to help them." He wants the community to feel empowered and to feel included.

Gábor has learned to read Hebrew. He participates in international conferences on behalf of Teleki and takes part in additional projects. "For me, Judaism is a bit wider now than just Teleki," he said. "It's basically Teleki focused, my Judaism. But also the family stuff—Hanukkah, and Seder night—we do things now that we never did. Because of us. Because of my brother and me and our team."

A few lessons emerged from Gábor's leadership at Teleki. "I learned that to do something for a community, the effort cannot be your whole life," he said. "You have to keep yourself. Your aim is very important but you have to share the responsibility. If the other community members do not feel the community is their own then you are going to keep giving, giving, giving, and then, when you are not there, the whole thing will die. That is not community."

From the beginning, Gábor has been involving others in Teleki decisions and responsibilities. "Even without me, there is room for others to lead and grow," he said. "It's very important to know that even if you could do, you shouldn't, because others should. In a sense, the community is more important than any specific goal."

In my Saturdays at Teleki, while the Mayer brothers had their own presence and set of responsibilities, there were a variety of other tasks that I knew were consistently performed by other loyal community members. For example, there was always Melinda, chopping vegetables for the Israeli salad to be served with lunch, and Robbie, hauling chairs and tables around the room to set up for the meal. Teleki had developed into a close-knit family.

Gábor's voice deepened. He interlaced his fingers on the surface of the table. His knuckles grew pink as he squeezed his hands tighter together. He worried about anti-Jewish sentiment in Budapest but simultaneously felt sure of Jewish Budapest's resilience. "When there is a shark, the little fish tend to swim together," he said. "There are people who start to do more Jewish stuff, or start to dig in to their Jewish heritage, just because there are people out shouting bad things about Jews. There are people saying that Jewish life is not getting stronger, but I'm not so sure. We have more and more Jewish stuff going on, more and more festivals, and more and more people getting involved. Jewish life is getting stronger. I just don't know if the other side is growing with the same speed."

Gábor does everything in his power to strengthen the community, grow the community, involve people in the community and put the community and the area into the minds of others. "I want Teleki to be there in one hundred years," he said.

He is spearheading different initiatives for different generations and different types of people. "If anybody can relate to Judaism, they can find something at Teleki," he said. "If enough people relate, this could be a kick that lasts."

The future of Teleki depends on the next generation. "I don't know who they are. They might not even be born yet," Gábor said. "But we need the next generation to care. Let's hope that the kids take on Teleki. And then the kids' kids."

Ducking his chin to his chest, Gábor mumbled, "If we take things with Gláser's speed, it will be another sixty years before there are others leading."

He smiled. "I hope not."

I swirled my final sip of coffee around the bottom ring of my blue ceramic mug. Gábor and I agreed that there is fulfillment in doing something not for yourself, but for someone else, or for a community. The hardest part sometimes is letting go of responsibility and allowing someone else to take the lead.

"It's better to not have any expectations," he said. "Not having expectations means that you can be satisfied with whatever you have, and be surprised at every new thing."

Suddenly, Gábor's co-worker burst into the kitchen with a company emergency. I recognized the anxiety in her frantic Hungarian. Gábor glanced in my direction and we bid goodbye. I zipped up my bag. Walking toward the door, I turned back and called, "*Szia* (goodbye) Gábor, see you on Saturday."

ÁDÁM SCHÖNBERGER

"I've always thought, 'Am I on the right track?
Did I do the thing that I wanted to do?'"

MY CAMERA SHUTTER SNAPPED OPEN and closed as Tomi slowed the car, swerving in and out around various couples and groups dressed in tie-dye, summer dresses, and bathing suits. He pulled to the side of the road into a dirt parking lot and turned off the engine.

Tomi exclaimed, "We are here!" and for just over 8,000 forints (less than forty U.S. dollars), I signed on to two days at Bánkitó.

I can only describe the Bánkitó Festival as the family vacation everyone in hopeful, liberal Budapest went on together. Intimate campsites of colorful tents and hand-painted bungalows for no more than 2,000 attendees lit up the landscape. The campsites hugged one lovely lake, spotted with romance, friends, and families. Days full of swimming, sunbathing, and political philosophizing were followed by nights full of *fröccs* (wine and seltzer), beer, *pálinka* (Hungarian schnapps) and live music.

I tossed my bag into my friends' tent and headed straight for the lake lined with hot dog stands and bars. Scents of fried *lángos* (deep fried Hungarian flat bread), butter, sour cream, and Trappista cheese quickened my step. A broad stage – later the host of a series of live bands – was covered in clusters of friends tanning and chatting. Waiting in line for lemonade, I caught up with friends as various medium-sized mutts panted past us, playfully enjoying their vacation from the city. Sprawled across pillows and multi-colored towels in the shade, I met friends of friends volunteering to spread word about their community organizations taking part in Bánkitó.

The sun was setting as I made my way to the Kabbalat Shabbat service offered by *Dor Hadas*, a Jewish community from Budapest whose mission is to breathe life back into Hungarian Jewish tradition. Suddenly, the familiar faces I'd seen throughout the day were gathered in one place.

One by one, individuals and groups began to settle under the canopy, surrounding a young man perched in a red plastic chair in the center, holding a guitar and wearing a hand-woven *kippah*, or a small, circular head cover. He gracefully rose to welcome his guests.

Before he began the service, he explained Shabbat through both its literal and spiritual meanings. With soft eyes and a patient, peaceful smile, he sat back down and prepared to play a familiar sequence of songs and prayers on his guitar. A young woman with tight brown curls and lips stained red from the cherry Italian ices served that afternoon entered the circle and passed around electric blue binders that contained the Shabbat prayers in English, Hungarian and Hebrew. She announced softly that we would begin on page one.

The wind rustled the trees around us as the prayers concluded. Jews and non-Jews alike had the chance to bond and reflect over wine and *challah*, braided bread traditionally eaten on Shabbat. If there were any doubt in me about whether I could survive a primarily Hungarian-speaking festival for two days, my participation in this service confirmed that one need not speak any particular language or be from any particular background to belong.

Six weeks after the Bánkitó Festival, I met Ádám, one of the principal organizers of Bánkitó, at the entrance of Csiga (chee-gah, or "snail"), our favorite coffee shop in the Eighth District. We climbed the loft's wide spiraling staircase lined with snail shells along its handrail and sat in the far right corner booth. As we considered the beverage menu, a waitress with straight black hair and stoic dark eyes marched up the staircase, carrying with her strong scents of French fries and goulash soup from the kitchen. Ádám ordered a Club

Mate, a beer-colored beloved beverage in Budapest that combines my understandings of Iced Tea and Red Bull. I opted for a latte.

Ádám's right foot tapped against the floor under the table. He looked down and brushed his hands against his knees as construction dust from Auróra's work site clouded away from his legs. He had recently launched Auróra, a politically active Jewish pub, café and community center. He and a group of his colleagues were building out the space from scratch.

Over the past ten years, Ádám has led a number of initiatives in Budapest. In addition to the Bánkitó Festival, Ádám also is one of the leaders of Dor Hadas and MAROM Budapest, an organization of young, open, diverse Jewish adults committed to recreating Jewish culture and tradition. His name and face are widely recognized throughout the liberal, Jewish, activist world in Budapest, through which I regularly attended events, discussions and celebrations he had sparked.

Despite the two couples surrounding us, cupping cappuccinos over omelettes and sandwiches, Csiga still felt under the radar, like our own private hub. Ádám described for me a Hungarian short story by Frigyes Karinthy, one of Hungary's most famous writers, called "Meeting with a Young Person." The story illustrates a conversation between a middle-aged man and his younger self about whether he has done all he could to reach his dreams.

Ádám said, "Somehow, I always think about that story. Really, since I read it when I was twelve or thirteen, it's always been on my mind. I've always thought, 'Am I on the right track? Did I do the thing that I wanted to do? Is this the thing that I want to do?' This is one of my main life guides."

Though it is easy to cast a halo over the heads of those we admire, we sometimes forget that what keeps us up at night also often plagues our neighbors and our heroes.

Ádám was born in Budapest in 1980. When he was three, his parents divorced. His father moved to the Hungarian countryside and Ádám grew up with his mother and her parents.

With the regime change in 1989, Ádám's grandfather began going to synagogue. Ádám remembered, "It was a very strange thing because my mother's family wasn't so enthusiastic about Jewish things. They hardly spoke about it. They even had a Christmas tree at home."

Though Ádám's maternal side of the family was relatively unreligious, Ádám's father was a rabbi. Ádám spent almost all of the Jewish holidays with his father. He felt awkward about celebrating holidays with people that he did not know or did not have the chance to know. His father's town was quite small, so the Jewish individuals and families living there all knew each other. Everyone but Ádám.

He said, "It was as if I had to leave my family to go to a strange place. One thing I hated was that I wasn't able to eat hotdogs." Ádám grinned. "I like hotdogs. My mother tried to explain to me that, 'You are not able to eat these things because they are not *kosher*. At least, don't eat these things around your father.'"

During his childhood, Ádám did not necessarily have a problem with Judaism, or with the countryside. He struggled with change, with feeling like an outsider, and with challenging his version of a social norm.

At the table, Ádám picked at the Club Mate label stuck on the glass bottle until it began to fray along the edges. He explained that he was always drawn to activism. He didn't like things that felt unjust. He didn't like when classmates were bullied. As a result, he caused a lot of school scandals.

Ádám admitted that he didn't know when this attitude started or why it started, but he speculated that it might've been because he was Jewish and his primary school wasn't. He said, "I didn't really know who I was. There was my father, who is doing strange things sometimes, so okay, I am Jewish, but you know, I didn't really understand."

To Ádám, Jewish meant that he could not eat hotdogs, or it meant praying in a different language, or sitting in a particular place. He didn't understand why it was a problem for so many people. He said, "It was a problem for me only because it was boring and I couldn't eat certain things. What's the big problem with that?"

Around Christmas time in Hungary, even during communism, primary schools had a custom to perform a holiday play about the story of baby Jesus. Ádám said, "I was assigned to be one of the shepherds. I had to stand with a stick, and that was it."

The same year, the Hungarian government called for a questionnaire. Students had to answer questions about their parents' occupations and backgrounds. Before then, stud-

135

ents and schools did not discuss these things. When Ádám asked his parents for the answers, his parents told him to write that his father was a priest.

After submitting the questionnaire, students began discussing their parents' occupations amongst themselves. People asked what kind of priest Ádám's father was. His only reply was, "Uh… he is a priest and they are not eating hotdogs."

Ádám's peers and teachers put together that Ádám's father was not a priest but that he was a rabbi and Ádám was Jewish.

Promptly, Ádám's role in the play changed. He became the king and was told he had to paint his face black. "It was kind of interesting for me because I gained one line that I didn't have when I was the shepherd. I thought it was good. Still, it was so strange. I didn't understand why they did it. Maybe I will go back to that school and ask it."

Ádám chuckled, his chin bowing to his chest. He said that when the class realized he was Jewish, all of a sudden, everyone wanted to be Jewish. He remembered others in the class would say, "I am Jewish, too!" because they felt it was special. "I was a trend setter!" Ádám said.

They were twenty-five students in a class, and only six of them were actually Jewish. When it became clear that Ádám was Jewish, though, almost twenty people thought they were Jewish, too. Only four or five Christian students didn't say they were Jewish because it was important for them to be Christian. "They had their identity; the others didn't have anything."

When Ádám was nine years old, he felt his life had a normal structure. He said that it wasn't so bad then to be Jewish. A classmate of his got in trouble because he began drawing swastikas in his exercise book. Ádám smirked, "It was like everybody was Jewish, or at least, everybody wanted to protect those who were Jewish."

Then came democracy. Ádám left the school for a newly re-opened Jewish school. He said, "I wasn't able to get my pioneer tie! It's one of my greatest traumas of my life. I really wanted to have that red tie."

Children in communist countries went through two phases in school to become part of society: the little drummer and the pioneer. At age ten, children graduated from little drummer to pioneer and their uniforms changed from including a blue tie to including a red tie. "I really liked my school. I didn't want to change. When it came to my Jewish identity, I always had the feeling that I *had* to do things and I was not able to do various other things."

Despite his hesitant feelings, when Ádám's grandfather began attending synagogue again, Ádám went with him. At that point, Ádám already knew many of the prayers and practices from going to synagogue with his father.

With time, Ádám got used to his new school. "Everybody gets used to new situations," he said. "Eventually, even, I started to like it, not because it was Jewish, but because it was the new thing."

Almost every Friday and Saturday, Ádám went to synagogue. He began learning Hebrew. He had his *bar mitzvah*, the Jewish coming-of-age tradition. When Ádám turned eighteen, at his grandfather's suggestion, he went to Israel for one year. He said, "I finally felt like Judaism was something that was okay."

After his year in Israel, Ádám returned to Budapest. At the age of twenty-two, he started working with MAROM.

"That was thirteen years ago," he said. "I became active. I saw that to be Jewish is cool and interesting."

When Ádám started, there were no Jewish programs for young adults in Budapest. He said, "I felt, maybe because of my experiences, that to organize a program only for Jews is not a good way to attract Jewish people. Most Jewish people at the time didn't really feel uniquely Jewish. So we started to organize a much more open set of programs for young adults." MAROM Budapest is devoted to reinventing and re-creating Jewish culture in Hungary and across Europe. "It became very successful. People came."

MAROM's first program was a relatively small-scale Hannukah party. Today, MAROM organizes seven different large-scale projects in addition to hosting parties, discussions and informal learning events in various locations across the city.

Ádám described, "We feel great that we are Jewish. We want to think more about what comes next. If you are already working with an organization, if you are already active in society, if you already have an experience that tells you that being Jewish is more than being part of a minority of society, then what? We have to deal with what it means to be *different*."

The notion of being different led MAROM to initiate programs in cooperation with other oppressed or marginalized groups in Budapest. For the past seven years, MAROM has worked with the Roma organizations in Budapest to organize programs that spark conversations relevant to both groups and to minorities in general.

Ádám explained that the history of Jewish Hungary creates a unique Jewish experience for Hungarian Jewish communities. "Jewish life here is totally incomparable to any other thing," he said. "There is no other Jewish community with as large a number of people who have roots dating back to before the Holocaust. In other cities, Jewish communities either no longer exist or they have immigrated from somewhere else. Budapest is the only city with a lot of historical experience that still applies to the people living here. This makes us very, very special."

The couple neighboring Ádám and me stood up, causing the floor boards beneath us to tremble as they pulled out their chairs. Ádám's empty glass bottle of Club Mate swiveled in place like a *dreidel*, circling on its bottom edge, threatening to tip and break into a million pieces before stumbling back into its original place.

Ádám said, "This community is indigenous, which creates an interesting problem for the Jews here. It is difficult to relate to society because we are living in a society where peoples' grandfathers actually really killed our grandfathers. Or it could be. It's not only me that has to struggle, but also people from the other side. How they perceive this information about the past is key to how we shape the future.

What *is* the Holocaust and what does it mean for present-day generations?"

Ádám's eyes widened. He said, "This also makes us very sensitive to our political problems and issues with democracy. Of course, most Hungarian Jews didn't really learn they were Jewish or didn't really know about anything more than the fact that their relatives were Jewish. In this sense, maybe they don't feel so 'Jewish.' I think the biggest common denominator is that Hungarian Jews are open about social problems, care about other people, and feel some sort of responsibility towards other people. I think the Holocaust plays a large role in that. I think it can characterize a sort of Hungarian Jewish way of seeing things."

In a low, steady voice, Ádám said, "We will stabilize and energize the Hungarian Jewish community for the future. Maybe we could be interesting insight for the global Jewish world. We want to bring students here because we think that we have a very interesting and very special type of Judaism that can benefit others. We have learned how to relate to 'normal' life and how to be Jewish at the same time. I think it's an important thing to create dialogue around these questions and to share solutions with other people in the world."

Ádám put his right hand to his cheek and gently scratched the stubble of his beard. He said, "Over the years, especially since working with MAROM, my Jewish identity always became more and more complex, and more clear."

Ádám said he originally resisted his Jewish identity. Then he went to Israel and confronted both the beautiful aspects of having a Jewish state as well as the challenging aspects of how that state treats minorities like the Palestinians. Ádám loves Israel, but channels his frustration with injustices within the Israeli system into his drive to reform the Hungarian system and community. He is now part of a community where he is working to re-establish and create a new type of Judaism in Hungary. He said, "We have many injustices here. It's very hard for me to live with that. So, I try to change it."

Ádám is now working to figure out what it means to be running a Jewish-based, socially open, inclusive, pluralistic organization. He asks, "What is this identity and how can we formulate it?" He has figured out that the type of Judaism he relates to is his community, his friends and the people he works with to come up with creative answers to difficult questions.

"I think the main thing that has changed me is from society itself, or the people that I am around," he said. "The reason why people work with others and befriend others is that they think these people might be able to change things about themselves that they don't like. There are certain people who know the answers to the problems you are struggling with. You work with them to change your ways and change your mind. This is the effect of a community like this."

Ádám said, "You have to work in small communities to understand how the bigger communities work, how the bigger communities change you, and how you are able to change the bigger communities. The best way to understand these things is to be an active part of the community."

Ádám explained that the MAROM method to involve people in the community is to provide opportunities to volunteer. "If you come today to volunteer," he said, "next year you can be a project manager."

Ádám's smile wrinkled the skin on either side of his mouth. He said, "I really like to feel when a lot of people are coming and working together. All the people working together feel the work is important. You don't really think about yourself, but somehow, you become part of the community, which is more than yourself. You feel somehow part of the other people, you know? That's one of the things that makes me happy. I really like to be a part of a community where people are not obliged to do something but they *choose* to do something. I really like that."

Ádám turned to look me in the eye. He said, "Sometimes I feel that I really *love* the people that I am working with. It's good. Already, if you love somebody, it makes you very happy."

He placed his hands in his lap and sat up straight. "This is why I am doing the things I am doing in Jewish Budapest. I am in love and it is so good."

RÁCHEL RAJ

"Steam from the matzah ball soup makes the windows foggy. That really says everything about my mama and how I was growing up."

DECADENT SCENTS OF GRAVY AND CHEESE radiated from her kitchen. "What would you like to drink? *Pálinka*? Wine? Champagne cocktail?"

Ráchel stood in front of me as excited as a cheerleader on game day. On the wall behind her, a sea of framed newspaper articles praised Ráchel's cooking in Hungarian and English text next to romantic images of Ráchel and her family in Paris, Rome, and Israel. On the floor stood a life-sized cardboard cutout of Ráchel and her husband in superhero costumes.

I stumbled over myself as I replied, "Champagne cocktail sounds wonderful. *Köszönöm szépen,*" I added, which means "Thank you very much" in Hungarian.

With her long, dark hair in immaculate banana curls, her thick fluttering eyelashes and a fitted black dress, Ráchel did not look like she had been cooking for the past eight hours. Rather, she resembled a Hungarian Audrey Hepburn. Her round, full cheeks grew a deeper shade of pink with each guest she welcomed.

After an hour of chatting with the other dinner guests, nearly twenty of us settled around Ráchel's long dinner table graced with a hand-woven tablecloth and placemats from France.

Ráchel stood at the head of the table and cleared her throat. She announced, "The menu tonight! We will start with a fish soup. We will continue with beef tongue, pickled vegetables, spicy mushrooms and baked potatoes. I have made a special French-style stew in honor of our recent trip to Paris. We will have roasted duck and grilled chicken.

Don't forget to save room for dessert - *flódni*, of course! - and keep your glasses full!"

I looked across the table at the two Mayer brothers with an expression that begged, "Is she kidding?" They were long-time friends of Ráchel's. The boys smiled, assuring me that this was just the beginning.

Ráchel carried the dishes from the kitchen to the table, one after the other. The fish soup reawakened childhood memories of New England clam chowder, while the spicy mushrooms ignited my palate and my sinuses. Hints of sharp cheese mixed with the comfort of potatoes in the French stew.

Ráchel's hospitality was addictive; what she didn't realize was that she would have a hard time getting most of us to leave. I meandered home that evening with a full, smiling stomach and one button of my jeans undone.

Early in the morning the following week, I staggered into Ráchel's *Tortaszalon*, or Cake Salon, in the Fifth District. The salon, already steeped in smells of freshly baked cakes and pastries, was painted pink and lined wall-to-wall with images of past Ráchel Raj masterpieces and posters donning the fashion greats like Coco Chanel and Prada. An assistant chef in an apron covered in patches of flour and frosting stood at the front of the room behind a glass case of *flódni*, a traditional Jewish Hungarian dessert consisting of layered apple, walnut, poppyseed, and plum sandwiched between layers of flaky pastry.

Ráchel burst through the door behind me, dropped off her bag at a table at the far side of the room and skipped into the kitchen. She re-emerged smiling brightly holding a ball of marzipan and a cake shaped like *Süsü Sárkány*, a famous Hungarian cartoon of an adorable green dinosaur. She sat on a wide black-cushioned stool at the empty bar and placed the cake on top of a small swiveling plate. As she rolled out a ball of yellow marzipan that would eventually become Süsü's hair, she prepared to let me in on a few secrets.

Two years ago, *The Jewish Daily* described Ráchel as the queen of Budapest Jewish cooking. The daughter of a noted rabbi – the same rabbi who practiced at Teleki illegally during communism – Ráchel authored a food column for a local Hungarian Jewish magazine. She made guest appearances on TV talk shows, and a few years ago, anchored a ten-part series on Jewish cuisine on a leading Hungarian food channel.

Today, Ráchel continues to make a name for herself and her pastries in Budapest and around the world. Her cakes, most notably her infamous flódni, have received countless awards and international recognition. Ráchel also teaches about Jewish cooking and culinary culture at local institutions. A natural fashionista, she describes herself as a modern "Yiddishe Mama." In other words, she values her mother's emphasis on food and cooking, but likes to add a flash of flare and red lipstick to the mix.

Ráchel jumped from her stool at the bar to retrieve a bite-size piece of cake that she extended to me in her palm. She insisted, "You *must* try this! Do you know *zserbó*? This is Hungarian Christmas cake. Very nice."

I took the cake between my pointer finger and thumb and placed it into my mouth. I closed my eyes, swimming in flavors of vanilla sandwiching tart, fresh raspberry compote, all complimented with a dark chocolate finish.

Ráchel exclaimed, "Once, I had to do interview, answering questions about religions. Everybody was talking about what nice feelings and contact with G-d, and I was talking about eating."

She smiled cheek-to-cheek and placed a string of yellow marzipan on Süsü's head. "I was like, maybe people will think Judaism is all about food and eating. But, kind of, yes!"

She laughed as she added, "All Jewish people like food. All the festivals are about eating together. Hanukkah is about this fest of light and oil, so you have to eat just the food that is made in oil. That's why the most known cake is something like a donut. It's really, really common to eat lots of donuts. At the same time, do you know this *latke*? The fried potato pancake? Everybody calls differently this Jewish food. At home we call it *latkes*. These are example of how Jewish holidays are really for Jewish foods and eating together."

Ráchel looked up from Süsü to pinch another yellow handful of marzipan away from the ball sitting on the surface of the bar. She said that her story definitely starts with her mother. "Definitely yes, but you know, I am not doing the same as her. I always make so differently, like, make it modern."

She explained that the Jewish mother has a role to hold the family together. "Of course, with food," Ráchel said. "At the same time, she is working, having a life, looking beautiful, even after babies."

Ráchel credits her parents with helping her discover her Jewish identity. Her father empowered her by taking her seriously as a woman and an individual. Ráchel attends Teleki with her father, her mother, her husband and her children for every holiday because she went there for every holiday growing up while her father was the rabbi. She said, "For me, it means everything that my babies go there and play there just how I did, in the same place. Really, one of the most important things in my life is that he was my dad."

Ráchel appreciated most of all that her father was open-minded to and supportive of her intuitive talents and passions. "He was the one who saw me interested about fashion and told me there is a fashion school he heard about. 'Don't you want to go?' he said. I don't know too many rabbis who come to the daughter and say that. But he says, 'If you are good in something, I will be proud of you.'" She went and she excelled.

Ráchel said her mother was her culinary inspiration even though she is a very traditional cook, especially with Jewish food. She said, "I learned everything from Mama. I just make a twist. I really, really love her food but I always had this feeling like I like it but I don't like it. The gefilte fish is so... ugly. It's grey. So I made it of salmon, being pink. I like these kinds of things. I want to live more this trendy way. So, it's come like this."

As a gift, Ráchel wrote a song about her mother's cooking. "There is a verse like this," she said. "When you have the window, when it is very hot outside or cold outside, and it gets foggy. Foggy windows come from the steam of matzah ball soup. That really says everything about my Mama and how I was growing up."

Growing up, Jewish life was very important for Ráchel. Every Friday evening her family ate together for Shabbat. She explained that this set a pattern for her in many ways. "I love to live like this," she said. Her father taught her that Judaism was about respect and nice things, "but not in a saint way," she said. "To need to be a saint is not useful for me. I am not a saint! I don't want to be. This Judaism was really nicely created with this."

In Ráchel's family, it was also a highly respected Jewish value to be intelligent. "Just to be independent and clever. I am really proud of that," she said. This contributed heavily to Ráchel's success in her career.

Ráchel spun Süsü around and began adding yellow marzipan spots to his back. She remembered that as a child, she was a very poor eater. She said, "I was failed at kindergarten because I didn't eat! I didn't like that! I think the food then was wrong. I didn't like this food. When I started to get older, I started to cook and I was really excited to learn more about Jewish cooking."

When Ráchel bought her first flat, she was so excited that she could host friends and family to eat. She said, "I had a flat like twenty-three square meter." She held her hands a few inches apart from each other. "You can imagine, smaller than that! I was cooking for *eight* people. Everybody was so happy. I loved it."

Ráchel rolled a small piece of marzipan into a ball. She said that if someone helps her with something, she insists on hosting them for a good meal. She shows her emotions through food. "I think it's something my Mama did, too," she said.

Ráchel swiveled *Süsü* back around to add yellow marzipan detail to his feet. She remembered that when she went to fashion school, she loved the creative elements of the work. School helped her develop her personal style and creativity. Though she excelled in fashion school, she did not love the technical aspects like sewing and measuring.

While she was in school, Ráchel's family opened a bakery. "It became clear to me that this is what I was going to do," she said. "I can be in this shop, and I can make a name for myself. I will do that. I find the solution to take all of my love for fashion and to put that into cakes."

Ráchel spun *Süsü* around to face me. The small dinosaur smiled at me with two bright white buckteeth sticking out of his forest green face.

Ráchel explained that she is very excited to see people in Budapest becoming more interested in gastronomy. She recognized that the knowledge about Jewish food that she grew up with was not accessible for everyone, but has noticed that many young adults are just starting to regain their interest. "Somehow, this Jewish food, people like it! They don't have this kind of bad feelings like we want to go *so* far from religion. They just find their roots and say, 'I feel something in myself... something different than my Christian friends...' They find it and they want to live it."

As a result, Ráchel began teaching about Jewish food. She teaches her students the difference between traditional Jewish food, Israeli food, kosher food, and everything in between. "They all really mean the same thing for them," she said.

Ráchel raised her right hand with delicately painted red fingernails and divided the air into three columns. She explained that kosher food is food that is made in accordance with Jewish dietary law. "Butter bread can be kosher if its kosher butter and kosher bread," she said. "Israel food is Mediterranean-style with many spices. Traditional Jewish food has its roots in Europe. Israeli food is not a European thing at all." Traditional European Jewish food, like Hungarian food, has its influences in Europe, specifically Eastern Europe. Ráchel explained, "Hungary with the red pepper, Poland with the sweetness... it's all included."

Ráchel's family eats "how we call... kosher-style." She and her family prioritize observing religious holidays and their accompanying dietary traditions. For example, they keep Passover strictly, which means that they refrain from eating anything that contains barley, wheat, rye, oats or spelt. As for day-to-day eating, however, Ráchel said, "I could keep Orthodox rules for one week, but I couldn't live like this, definitely not." She is too invested in the beauty and diversity of food to adhere daily to kosher restrictions.

Despite not feeling passionately about Jewish dietary law, Ráchel does feel passionately about Judaism and her

Jewish identity. "I am very happy to be Jewish," she said. "I think this is a religion that really fit me. It's me, you know? How I feel like, 'Yes, I am.' I am not born in the wrong place, because I can live like this."

Ráchel enjoys being traditional in certain ways because it gives her life structure. She cannot think of a better way to spend her Friday evenings than with food and family. She enjoys the values imbedded in the tradition. When Ráchel looked for her first home with her husband, she was shopping more for the perfect kitchen for Friday night dinners than for the perfect bedroom or architecture.

"I cannot think of another religion that has this that strongly," she said. "I think it's so much for people to make life better." She said, "It's nice to feel that I am a good person in a way that is me. I don't have to be anyone else. I don't have to be perfect. It's very nice. I love it."

Though Budapest presents a comfortable life for Ráchel, she is not sure she will live in Budapest forever. "For all time, I cannot say," she said. "I don't know what I am doing for my lifetime. For now, yes. Budapest could be, or should be, or *would* be, a nice place. A really, really nice place. I think this is the time that we hope Budapest is not becoming like someplace to run away from."

Ráchel is working on a homemade cookbook she hopes will become an official Jewish Hungarian Ráchel Raj cookbook. Every time she creates a new recipe, she adds it to the book. On Fridays for Shabbat, she always adds a new recipe to the menu. She writes down everything.

These days, Ráchel and her mother feed a healthy competition amongst themselves. Her mother tells her, "Yeah, your cook style is much more conservative, not too much innovation," to which she replies, *"Really?"* Ráchel's eyes pulsed threateningly. She is grateful for this dynamic as it fuels her constant motivation to try new things. "I have to prove that what she said is definitely not true. Prove that I am very innovative actually."

Ráchel's assistant emerged from the kitchen with her eyes glued to the triple-layer dark chocolate cake covered in whipped vanilla bean frosting balancing between her left forearm and her right palm. She took small steps and delicately laid the cake on a second swiveling plate on the surface of the bar. Ráchel magnetically turned toward the cake. Her eyes swept from the sides to the surface as she turned the cake full circle. Her red lips curved into a subtle smile.

She pulled her shoulders up to her ears and whispered, "Ugh! It's my *favorite!*"

"I think it's especially important that despite the Holocaust, and despite all the losses, Jewish Budapest is alive."

IN EARLY NOVEMBER, THE SUN warmed my face filling me with confidence as the mild breeze kept me cool and present. I chose a seat by the window at Jelen, overlooking the street and sidewalk. A blonde woman wearing leopard leggings and turquoise sneakers strolled by the restaurant. I ducked underneath the table to pull my miniature recorder out of my backpack. When I surfaced, I was startled to find Dávid sitting opposite me. As he introduced himself, his professional air surprised me. His glasses reflected rays of light that blinded me on and off.

Dávid emitted a mature, intelligent foundation effortlessly. I was immediately self-conscious of my comparatively young age and thrown-together baggy sweater, tattered scarf and wrinkled jeans. A slim woman with a septum nose ring and short, hot-pink hair took our drink orders: an espresso shot for Dávid and a latte for me.

Dávid, a native Hungarian in his thirties, leads Jewish-themed tours around Budapest. This was all I knew. I said, "Pretend I know nothing. Start from the very beginning." Dávid grinned and took a deep breath.

Most of Dávid's family moved to Budapest nearly one hundred years ago after the Trianon Treaty of 1920, the peace agreement that officially ended World War I between most of the Allies and the Kingdom of Hungary. The Treaty defined the independent Hungarian state and its borders. Many Hungarians felt traumatized by the treaty as it left Hungary only twenty-eight percent of what constituted pre-war Hungary. Other countries absorbed five of the pre-war kingdom's ten largest cities. Its population was only one-third the size.

Prior to the treaty, Dávid's family lived all around the Austro-Hungarian monarchy. According to current borders, they came from Czech Republic, Austria, Slovakia, Poland, Ukraine, Romania, Serbia and today's Hungary. Following the treaty, like many other Hungarians, Dávid's family moved to Budapest.

It wasn't until recently that Dávid realized that there is a big tradition of culture and commerce in his family. His grandfather was in charge of the dissemination of Hungarian films all around the world. His grandmother worked for an international trade company. His mother is in advertising and his father is an architect. "It seemed natural to me that there are people who check your books, give you your balances, and that's how the world works," Dávid said. "I never realized that no, that's how *my family* works. All of us are looking for all the possibilities and all the new ideas."

Dávid's family members were all also secular people. Like many other Hungarian Jewish families, after the Holocaust, they said, "We are not Jews, we are people. That's it. There should be no difference between people."

Dávid started elementary school in the very first class of the Lauder school, Budapest's Jewish school that opened after the fall of communism. He can read Hebrew and can speak elementary Hebrew words. He has also traveled to Israel various times to visit family. He felt familiar with Judaism and the experience of what it meant to be a Jew.

"It was never a question if I am a Jew or not," he said. "Judaism for me is about culture and having fun. I never question anyone else if he or she is religious because that isn't what's important."

Dávid admitted that his Jewish identity is always changing. There are elements in his identity that he always identifies with, but he is always learning and growing. "I mean, identity is not a stable thing," he said. "I have learned a lot and I am very happy that I have a way to express this identity without oppressing anyone."

Dávid studied international development in England. He spent two years conducting research on how it might be possible to utilize international development methods with the Roma community in Hungary before realizing that he had to let the idea go.

"You know, every pilot carries the option that you fail," he said. "And I did. I understood why and I had to move forward. I always thought that pilots should be open ended. If a pilot fails, that's not a failure, really. It's another kind of success. If you fail, then you know what not to do."

Dávid shot back his espresso and clanked the small ceramic mug on the table. He laughed, "Then, I had a degree that was valuable all around the world, except Hungary."

Many people with Hungarian degrees leave for western countries, even if they work in restaurants to wash dishes or perform jobs completely irrelevant to their degrees. Dávid's friends and all the people around him thought he was insane to return to Hungary. "Nobody understood why," he said. "I wanted to express what I love in Budapest. Why it's a great city. I want to show it to people."

When he returned, Hungary was not investing a penny into international development. His wife and many of their friends had also recently received degrees from western countries and also wanted to return to Hungary. He started to think about how he could use his university training.

"Qualitative methods," he said. "That's how the idea came. These are the roots of our enterprise."

Dávid is trained as a social researcher. In his mind, one of society's largest problems now is the gap between academia and everyday people. "It's worthwhile to translate all the academic language into everyday language," he said, "and people have the right to know about the outcomes of research."

He explained that his tours are grounded in academic research. "We decided not to write articles into a journal, for which you have to wait two or three years to publish only to find one hundred or two hundred people reading it without any effect on society. Instead, what we are doing is translating the research and entertaining people with science in an urban environment."

Dávid operates three Jewish tours in Budapest, all based on a different time period. The first begins in the 18th century and ends in the middle of the 19th century. It is located in Óbuda, the northern part of the city on the Buda side, the traditional home of the Jewish community in Budapest. The second tour is called *Hidden Synagogues*, about the Golden Age of Hungarian Jewry in Budapest that started in the middle of the 19th century and ended at the First World War. The third tour is called _Kosher Budapest_ and its main focus revolves around the period between the two world wars.

One of the most important aspects of Dávid's company is that it is a for-profit cultural enterprise. They can only spend what they earn because there are no donations, no contributions and no support. "That is the idea," he said. "We want to prove that it is possible, even now in Hungary, to develop a cultural enterprise. After one and a half years, it is sustainable. It's not profitable yet, but it is sustainable."

One thing they do not offer is a tour related to the Holocaust. Dávid refuses the idea of defining the Hungarian Jewish community as a victim of the Holocaust.

"There is so much more to remember," he said. "The Jews should not be considered as a kind of target of something, as passive people who stay somewhere, waiting for things to happen. I think Hungarian Jewish life is based on being active. Doing what someone wants. I think it's especially important that despite the Holocaust, and despite all the losses, Jewish Budapest is alive."

Dávid believes Budapest is a very unique city. "There is a Jewish renaissance in Budapest," he said. While most European Jewish communities started to decline in the 20th century, Budapest was where Jewish communities grew. "It's up from the bottom, against all the official institutions, even state institutions and Jewish institutions. It's not based on religion, but something else—a Jewish spiritual culture."

He wondered why this was possible, why Budapest is so unique. He started his research and discovered various reasons why Budapest was historically so uniquely set up for growth. First, because of its traditions. Budapest was one of the homes of Jewish modernity. Theodore Herzl, known to be the father of modern Zionism, was born in and heavily influenced by the culture of Budapest.

"It's not by accident," Dávid said. "The tradition of Hungarian Jewry, and especially Budapest Jewish life, is about reforming Jewish traditions and combining Jewish and Hungarian traditions, which is really inspiring. Jewish Budapest contributes not only to Hungarian life, but to global Jewish life as well."

Secondly, the Holocaust did not affect Budapest in the same way as it did the surrounding countries. The Budapest Jewish community survived, mostly because until the very end of the war, Hungary was an ally to Germany and the Jews in Budapest were protected. When this alliance broke, there simply was not enough time to deport all of the Jewish people to Auschwitz and other concentration camps. The exact number is difficult to pinpoint, but between 80,000 and 150,000 Jews still live in Budapest, which is five to ten percent of the city.

The third factor then is the size of the community. One hundred years ago, every fourth citizen in Budapest was a Jew. The community made up a larger share of Budapest than the Jewish community in New York City.

Finally, the transition from communism to democracy. After the Hungarian border opened in 1988, it became possible for people to travel, and specifically to travel to Israel. Many Hungarian Jews had some relatives abroad, mainly in the U.S. and Israel, and a vast number of them, especially young Jews, began to travel. They went to university abroad, often to Israel because it was the cheapest option. Hundreds of thousands of Jewish young adults visited Israel and many of them lived there. When they returned to Budapest, they brought home a new spirit that embraced the possibility of being Jewish without being religious.

"The point was," Dávid said, "You could be a Jew and didn't have to follow all these copious rules. You can still be proud. You shouldn't feel ashamed of not being religious. That was, I think, the brand new thing."

Dávid explained that today, he sees both religious and Jewish cultural groups strengthening and innovating. "Budapest was always kind of a poster child for modern Jewish culture," he said. "Definitely not orthodox. One hundred and fifty years ago, only five percent of the Budapest Jewish community was orthodox. Chabad is now using their professional community building to become the second largest congregation in Budapest. If it was possible for Chabad, then I think it would be possible for any other congregation."

Dávid remembered a specific example of what he loved so much about the character of Jewish Budapest. The Hungarian football team *Magyar Testgyakorlók Köre*, or MTK, is traditionally a Jewish team. They still refuse to play on Yom Kippur, which is the holiest Jewish holiday of the year. There were once many MTK teams in Europe, but the only team to survive the Holocaust was the Hungarian team.

"MTK is still in the first league in Hungary, even though it has very little support," Dávid said. "Old Jewish people support that team. This team was always marked with geese, as the team was a team of goose-mongers—people selling geese—like my great grandmother did. A few years ago, the supporters of the team realized that they should not deny it, but they should be proud of it. Make a joke from those who are laughing. So now there is officially a mascot."

According to Dávid, the international picture of Budapest Jewry is false. He said, "When I was visiting the United States or Israel, there was talk that Israel is the home of the strong and modern Jews, America is the home of the rich Jews, and Europe is a cemetery or a museum. But if I should describe Jewish Budapest, it is a living community. It is progressive. It is not a museum and not a cemetery. It is alive and it is full of energy. Not just energy, but spirit. It is completely unique."

Hungary is often described in international media as a country that is full of anti-Semitism and racism, but Dávid said he doesn't feel it. "I know what is happening. I know there are signs. There are hatred movements, of course, and I don't want to deny it. But it's not that simple. I personally do not suffer from anti-Semitism in Hungary. Any experiences I have with anti-Semitism are from university in England, not from Budapest."

I held what remained of my latte close to my face. Smells of cinnamon and sweet milk lingered on my tongue as I set my empty mug on the surface of the table. Dávid placed his right palm over the rim of the mug and looked me in the eye.

"I would suggest to try not to listen to the prejudices," he said. "Especially when the prejudice is that all Hungarian Jews are suffering. We are not a cemetery. We are a living community."

It is very important to Dávid that his Judaism and Jewish history became his profession. "It was as natural as water, or air." he said. "I feel lucky to have a profession where I can work and live from the money I earn."

He laughed, "Well, almost."

ANDREA SZONYI

"I am a teacher. Although I don't teach in the classroom now...
you never stop being a teacher."

IF YOU ASK JEWS LIVING IN BUDAPEST TODAY about their Jewish memories and identities, they will agree on one thing: the importance of education.

At ten in the morning, in the middle of September, I walked past chalked café signs advertising pumpkin lattes and falling brown, red and orange leaves on my way to meet Andrea. I hopped onto the long yellow four/six tram that ran from one side of Pest, where my apartment was located, to the other, where I would find Andrea's office. Pulled along by electric currents surging through the wires conn-ecting the tram to the sky, the tram twisted and turned through the streets of Budapest before coming to a stop two blocks away from my destination.

Andrea greeted me at the door of her office building. We walked through the building's courtyard and up one flight of stairs to enter Andrea's office, where we were welcomed on our left by a pair of caged birds tweeting what seemed like the national anthem of autumn. I followed Andrea through the office and entered a small room in the back right. The walls were lined with books of all colors and sizes like a small personal library. Andrea offered me coffee and water as I settled into a soft, orange suede armchair next to a long brown leather couch.

Andrea tucked a wild curl that was fraying away from her face behind her ear. She said, "I am a teacher. Although I don't teach in the classroom now... you never stop being a teacher."

From 1992 to 2007, Andrea taught English as a Second Language and was the head of the English department at the

Lauder school, one of only three Jewish day schools and pivotal in the formation of the Jewish identities of countless youth in Budapest. She first became involved in Holocaust education and Judaic studies at Lauder, where she was one of three mentors for the Judaic Studies student research group.

While she was teaching English at Lauder, a friend's father asked her to translate a family member's memoir. This family member lived in the States but wrote his memoir in Hungarian.

"He wanted the family to know about his past," Andrea said. "So I translated it. I really like translating. It's like experiencing the story in a different way. You become part of it, in a way."

This family member's story was a very simple story, but it had a significant impact on Andrea. "Although I had heard several stories in my own family, somehow, it was different," she said. "I thought, 'Okay, so if it impacts me, then it probably will impact my students.'"

Andrea worked with a group of students to translate a memoir of a Holocaust survivor and edited that memoir into a book. "I started with a whole student project and it worked out well," she said. "That's how I started this whole process."

In 2007, Andrea started the Zachor Foundation, which is an educational NGO that focuses on the personal importance of remembrance and memory. She is now the director. Zachor collects written memoirs and records testimonies of survivors of the Holocaust to develop informal educational materials and programs that infuse classic approaches of teaching history with personality and a human touch.

In 2008, very little work was done in Hungary in terms of Jewish and Holocaust education. Steven Spielberg launched The Shoah Foundation after the making of Schindler's List. He wanted to record as many testimonies of survivors and witnesses of the Holocaust as possible, which resulted in a tremendous project. At the conclusion of the project, the team had recorded nearly 52,000 testimonies in fifty-seven countries all over the world in over thirty languages.

Among these testimonies were 1,320 Hungarian language testimonies. When Andrea joined the Shoah Foundation in 2009, her job was to figure out what to do with this large collection. "We had the collection, and then what?" she said. The testimonies were not online and they were sensitive in nature. At that point, there were only a few testimony access points all over the world and only one in Europe, which was in Berlin. Andrea started a program to develop educational materials using these testimonies and to make these materials accessible.

In 2009, Budapest became the second European access point at Central European University (CEU). Today, Europe has many access points, two of which are in Budapest.

Andrea and her team reached the question: *How can you use these stories in education?* She said, "These are full life stories—two and a half hour stories." Her mission was to launch a program that would create a culture of using testimony in education. "This is not only a Jewish topic and not only a Holocaust topic, but these are life stories that inspire people," she said. "It's not about the past only; it's about learning from the past for the present and future."

In 2012, Andrea became the Senior International Training Consultant for the Shoah Foundation. "In other words," she said, "I am part of the education team and I oversee education in Europe and in America."

Today Andrea works both at Shoah and Zachor, among a series of other projects. "What I do...is like my two hats," Andrea said. "What I do under my Zachor hat sometimes overlaps with what I do under my Shoah Foundation hat."

At the Shoah Foundaton, Andrea focuses on the testimonies and how they can be used in education. She runs low-touch programs where she develops educational materials and introduces the materials to teachers. She also runs deep-touch programs where the teachers participate in a week-long training, pick the testimonies they want to use, and develop their own materials. One year later, the teachers return to evaluate their lessons and receive professional feedback. 2014 marked the third year of both of these programs. Andrea has trained over fifty teachers, most of whom have returned to the program as regional ambassadors. She has also set up a system of partner schools, which have become local, regional centers for her work.

At Zachor, Andrea has begun editing printed personal testimonies. As an English teacher, she realized that a foreign language class would be a perfect place to teach these personal stories. Zachor published a series called *I Remember: Personal Memoirs*. Zachor now has eight publications which are all bilingual, in addition to a website where parts of the testimonies are published and paired online with educational materials and recommendations for how teachers may use them.

Andrea explained that for this kind of methodology, most of the teachers and participants in these programs are not Jewish. "I think this is very important," she said, "because as a minority living in a majority society, we have to spread the word. Anti-Semitism has roots in lack of knowledge and fear, so we have to reach out and educate. We have to educate the Jewish community, for obvious reasons, but we do have to reach out to the non-Jews as well."

In 2008, Andrea launched a peer guiding program called *Historic Walks in the Jewish District*. "This is not a touristic program," she said. She organizes educational walks specifically for schools in the Jewish District and in the ghetto area. A group of volunteers go through an eight-session training about Jewish tradition, history, religion, history of the Holocaust, sociology, urban history, and more. They then take an exam. Finally, they guide small groups. The guides often speak many languages so foreign groups can be guided as well.

Andrea said, "About half of these peer guides are Jewish and half of them are not Jewish. We found that participants of these walks, Jews and non-Jews alike, know so little. Non-Jews knew nothing about Jews, but have the prejudices. We decided that we would need something more. We got some funding for a publication called *Jewnior Guide Book*."

Andrea abruptly stood and left the room. Within moments, she returned holding a four-by-six one-inch-thick paperback book covered in seemingly hand-drawn graphics. Red and navy blue bubble letters floated away from the cover. She explained that the *Jewnior Guide Book* is an educational guidebook with short text and a lot of photos. It contains a Jewish dictionary at the end with Jewish basics for both Jews and non-Jews and important information about the neighborhood.

"This was compiled and edited by our volunteers," Andrea said. "The photos they took themselves, they edited the text, and they did the research. Even the designer is a young artist. Also, the translator is young man who translated the Hungarian text into English. This is what we published last year. It is very popular; we are almost out of the first 2,000 copies."

Andrea and I leafed through *Jewnior Guide Book* together, laughing at funny faces of students in select photographs and reminiscing over other pictures of familiar restaurants and museums.

Once we set the book aside, Andrea said she has been thinking about how her two organizations can work together. "I realized that it would be great to integrate Shoah testimonies into the Zachor peer-guided tours," she said.

To do so, Andrea developed a program called *I Walk*. The program contains selected clips of testimonies that are relevant to the area. For example, for the Jewish District, people speak about the ghetto or about Neolog and what assimilation is. This sheds some light on the importance of

170

remembrance. The testimony clips are on tablets and at certain points in the tour, the group watches clips and discusses, putting an educational context around the testimony and the tour.

One route is the Jewish District. Another route visits the Shoes Memorial, a series of variously sized and shaped metal shoes lining the Danube River. This monument honors the thousands of Jews who stood where the shoes now stand moments before they met their execution. "The memorial is a very important and a symbolic place," Andrea said. "We have testimonies of survivors who were actually shot into the Danube and survived. We also have Hungarian testimony strips that speak about how they were taken to the Danube but ran out into the woods and how this affected their whole life. This experience. It's very, very deep, and there is a good spot for a lot of thought and discussion."

The *I Walk* tours connect the location, the knowledge, the history and the personal, emotional element of the story. "I think it brings students a lot closer to the subject," Andrea said. "It's not just the cognitive knowledge, but also there is an emotional tie. We try to bring in the social responsibility question of, 'Okay, this was a story from the past, but what do I have to do with it? What is my role in society?' These are the programs that we run."

Seven years ago, a group of young Hungarian Jews, all third-generation Holocaust survivors over twenty-five years old and Birthright graduates, founded the *Intergenerational Program*. The young group paired up with a group of Holocaust survivors born before 1940 or 41 who had never been to Israel to discuss various topics. Because of the work she does, the founding youngsters asked Andrea to lead this program. She accepted.

The group met eight times, generally once a month. "They met and they were open, as much as they could be, to speak about their experiences," Andrea said.

After the eight meetings, the group went to Israel together. "This is a very unique program, really," Andrea said. "Things come up in this program that we have never dreamt of. Some of the stories that survivors come and tell reveal that first, they never told their grandchildren they are Jewish. Then, the grandchildren join the extreme right movement. Next, the grandfather comes to this program for months and tells his grandchildren he is going to Greece, or Rome, or something, but definitely not Israel. Finally, by the end of the program, he tells the grandchildren about Judaism."

Andrea said that the young participants also come to this program for unique and interesting reasons. "Stories come up, for example, one twenty-something-year-old, partly Jewish youngster told us that she was not told she was Jewish. She was raised Catholic. At age sixteen, something started to be suspicious, so she asked the grandfather, 'What happened to our family during the war?' Then the grandfather, very interesting phrasing, says, 'Well, we were in trouble because we couldn't prove we were not Jewish.' That's how she realized that she was Jewish! Then she got upset because there was something about her that everybody knew except for her. This is not a one-standing story."

The first year, when it started, there was no educational context involved. Andrea set up a methodology and a curriculum. "I have been doing this for seven years now," she said. "I counted the other day—over one hundred elderly have gone through this program. I mean, just, amazing."

These intergenerational bonds don't cease when the program ends. "It turns out that many elderly were very lonely," Andrea said. "They become attached to the program. They are upset when it's over."

Andrea has submitted an application for a grant for a program that is for the young and elderly graduates of the program to reunite somewhat regularly, partly for educational reasons but partly for social reasons. "You know, sometimes, projects lead to further projects," she said.

Andrea has always known she was Jewish. It was very important for her when she was growing up, though she had very limited knowledge about it. Her parents were not religious. "There was something in their lives that prevented them," she said. Andrea's father was born in 1932 and her mother in 1940; accordingly, Andrea felt "they could not live real Jewish lives."

Andrea chose to live more connected to her Jewish roots. "It was important and I always wanted to learn more about it," she said. In 1989 when Lauder was launched, she knew she would send her kids there. "They went to different schools after but it's interesting how they are in different ways attached to the community," she said. "My son does volunteer work for the synagogues and my daughter is a volunteer for Zachor. They are, in their own ways, connected."

Andrea sat upright in her chair and said, "A very important philosophy for me is that it's not enough to have a lot of good will and to be Jewish. What I do, or what we do, is a profession. It is crucial to have the professional background and commitment, knowledge and enthusiasm."

I stood for an extra moment in front of the singing birds on my way out of Andrea's office. One of the two spread its bright turquoise wings and flew from the bottom of the cage to a branch brushing against the top right corner. The other followed with its gaze but remained stationary at the foot of the cage.

I stepped away from the office and back onto the yellow whirling four/six tram, deeming it my yellow school bus for the remainder of my stay in Budapest.

LUCA ELEK

*"I think this is the thing that slowly, slowly
I manage to be… just, me."*

PLASTIC RED AND GREEN EARRINGS shaped like cherries dangled beneath her ears. Dressed in bright red stockings, a black cotton dress, and a shimmering red sweater, Luca (Loot-zah) sat smiling behind the registration table on the first day of the Me2We Conference as a volunteer. With her long, oval face and almond-shaped green eyes, Luca studied my hiking backpack and the sweat marks on my blouse.

While I thought she was sizing me up, I was surprised when she extended a warm hand and asked for my name. Crossing my name off the list and handing me my nametag and a folder containing the conference materials, Luca became my first guide to the inner workings of Jewish Budapest.

Currently, among other projects, Luca is working with Tomi on MiNYanim, a two-year international program sponsored by the Jewish Agency including one year of intensive Jewish learning and a second year of intensive project planning and community organizing. The 2014 cohort included approximately fifty young leaders from countries including Russia, Israel, Romania, Bulgaria, Bosnia, Syria, Poland, and Hungary. During the first year of this program, the cohort gathered three times. In 2014, the gatherings were in Bucharest, Budapest, and Israel. During these meetings, the group questioned and highlighted their personal Jewish identities, priorities, passions, and capabilities. During the second year of the program, the leaders are asked to turn the answers to these questions into manageable, sustainable, impactful projects that will in some way benefit their communities and the universal Jewish world.

Apart from MiNYanim, Luca, like many young adults her age, strives to reach a deeper understanding of herself and her place in the world. In order to do so, she immerses as deeply and as often as possible in the lives of others. Two days after the Me2We Conference, Luca invited me to join her and her friends at a farmers market held inside *Szimpla kert* (Simple Garden), a popular and iconic ruin-pub in the Seventh District of Budapest.

Ruin-pubs are a phenomenon unique to Budapest. Innovated out of tenement houses or factory buildings otherwise abandoned, doomed to destruction, or "ruined," and equipped with rejected furniture of old community centers, cinemas, grandmothers' flats, and cafés, these hubs radiate a retro, disheveled, enlivening aura. Ruin-pubs are not only good places to drink or party but they also function as cultural community areas with film clubs, theatre performances, concerts, exhibitions and creative workshops. Or, in Szimpla's case, farmers markets.

I walked into Szimpla, struck by how different the pub looked in the daylight. Above me, I could hardly see the sun peeking through layers of hanging bicycles, dolls, greenery, and flashing Christmas lights. To my right, the first bar was lined not with bottles of pálinka and a series of bartenders, but with fresh market cherries and vendors selling homemade jam. To my left—in the room that sells carrot sticks to drunken guests in the evenings—stood multi-colored stools topped with homemade breads and pastries. I walked through the large main room of the pub past flying wild birds and various market attendees sipping soup and peering through their canvas recycled bags to review their purchases. In the garden, fresh vegetables and fruits piled on top of a square of tables. A trapeze net hung above me, entangled with circus flags, plants, and pictures. Mirrors lined the walls of the pub, expanding the space and reflecting the sunlight. I walked the length of the square, first passing large lettuce heads, followed by carrots, cherries, more cherries and homemade soaps. In the back of the garden, surrounded by the front half of an old retro car filled with booth cushions and tall trees, two volunteers manned a soup kitchen, serving donation-based cabbage soup and a slice of homemade cornbread to all who wanted.

Upon turning the final corner, I saw Luca, sitting with her legs crossed on a bright blue stool, placing a cherry pit into an ash tray. I sat beside her and together we laughed and people-watched away the afternoon.

Nearly five months later, Luca joined me for lunch at *Kéksz* (pronounced "cakes"), what had become one of our favorite cafés in downtown Budapest. For just 900 forints, or less than four U.S. dollars, one could enjoy the lunch menu, which included the daily soup and main course. Today, that included a homemade chicken noodle soup and a chicken cutlet with potato salad. Luca ordered her usual make-your-own-salad, built with beets, chicken, onion, and topped with light vinaigrette.

As our waiter walked away with our order, Luca took a sip of *szörp* (seltzer and syrup) and widened her eyes with the straw still in her mouth, vaguely resembling a Hungarian Betty-Boop.

The waiter returned with Luca's salad and the first course of my lunch special: chicken, homemade noodles, and vegetables swimming in a golden broth.

Luca was born in Budapest on February 18, 1987 to a middle class Jewish intellectual family. Both of her parents are journalists. "I think a big part of who I am is because of them," she said, "because of the values I saw in my house. I always saw that being open to other people, to think about others and to be sensitive toward the world was a very important part of who we are."

The other thing Luca remembers is books. "All around. Lots and lots of books," she said. "I think I got this thing of love toward them from my father. I used to go to his room and read the titles when I was lonely and wished that I could read all of them."

Though both of Luca's parents were Jewish, she did not grow up in an especially Jewish home. As far as holidays went, her family always celebrated Christmas and birthdays. She remembers looking for Easter eggs in the garden without any kind of religious connotation. "Still, today, Christmas is my favorite holiday," she said, "I love the food that we cook, our tradition, that everybody is together and, of course, the presents." Luca laughed as she dug with her fork for a mouthful of salad.

Both her paternal and maternal sides of the family were heavily impacted by communism. "They had nothing," she said. "I don't really know that much about them, but for sure, I never heard anything Jewish, apart from knowing that they actually *were* Jewish."

Waving a beet captured by her fork, Luca explained that her parents enrolled her in Lauder for primary school so she could grow up and make the choice for herself whether she wanted to have any sort of relationship with Judaism. "For a very long time, being Jewish simply didn't mean anything extra to me," she said. "It was like being a girl, or having brown eyes, or living in Budapest. Not something that you have to give special attention to."

When Luca went to university and started to make friends with new people, she became more interested in her own roots. When she was seventeen, she spent one year living with a local family in Southern Spain. "Living abroad was one of the experiences that started really, really hitting who I am," she said. "Living alone and living very close to people who have different values than I do. I realized that everyone has different preferences, different activities they like or don't like, and different ways of thinking about things. I think I learned to appreciate and I learned to love people who had different values than I do. I learned to live with them."

Luca took another sip of szörp. Our waiter approached and removed my empty white ceramic bowl.

When Luca returned to Budapest, she became involved in youth work. "A friend of mine called me and asked if I wanted to go to Cyprus. 'There will be people from other cultures and you don't have to pay a lot of money,' she said. I was like, 'Why not?' That one phone call was a door to a whole new world. I felt in love. We were united by topics like urban development and human rights. When this experience ended, I wanted more."

Our waiter returned to delicately place a plate of steaming chicken and potatoes between my hands.

Luca's eyes settled on a black and white mural painted on the wall behind me. I cut a piece of chicken and held it on my fork. Luca's eyes met mine, as though coming back to reality from a dream. She said, "It's an ongoing thing, my identity."

Luca went on Taglit during her gap year between her Bachelor's and her Master's degrees. "What caught me in Israel was this mesmerizing different social structure," she said. "Just within the Jewish society, you have so many kinds of people and so many things. Israel made me want to discover more."

After Luca returned from Taglit, she began volunteering for the Israeli Cultural Institute (ICI) on a project called *Tikkun Olam* (Hebrew for "Repair the World"). "It seemed perfect to mix what I loved to do and what I wanted to learn about Judaism," she said. "The next year, I joined MiNY-anim. MiNYanim is amazing not because you make impact and a community, because we do, but we show a huge spectrum of what Judaism could be. We support values of tolerance and human rights. We go to not just religious Judaism, but cultural Judaism and all kinds of communities. You can see how many ways you can relate to others and live in a community."

Luca wanted to maintain her connection to the Jewish community, but needed to first discover what Judaism meant to her. She looked in my direction, sat up straight, and said, "Look...I don't think I have my own place. I am still figuring out how this whole being Jewish and all the rest works. All of these projects are steps, just showing me this huge whole dimension that could be mine if I want it."

Luca said that Judaism could feel very unfriendly if you didn't grow up in it. "Most of us, Hungarian youngsters, we didn't grow up in a religious environment," she said. "So, I am really thankful for people who create an opportunity to shape Judaism."

Some projects Luca participates in are related to Judaism and others are not. "I think I have become a sort of project junkie through the years," she said. She enjoys the intense moments when you have to plan a session, run a session, or participate and put yourself in it. "This is work that only makes sense if you are willing to put your whole self in," she said. "If you are ready to be vulnerable at times."

Luca fiddled with her fork before resting it neatly inside her nearly empty salad bowl.

"It's me," she said. "I am Jewish. I keep Yom Kippur, I do Shabbat in my own way, and I try to find my way. Being Jewish is a strong part of my identity. When I do all the rest, I am still me, having the Jewish part inside."

Luca plays different roles in different projects. She makes a point to really care about the work that she is doing and the people she is doing that work with. "As soon as you stop caring what are those people's names and where do they come from, then you have to take a break."

Forks and knives tapped plates around us as our neighbors continued eating.

Luca said that rather than becoming a more open and democratic state, Hungary is doing the opposite. "I love to live here, because this is my home," she said. "My family is here. My friends. I know the streets. I feel at home here speaking the language and being able to go to theatres and cinemas and museums and alternative events, and being part of the civic life. But I also see what's happening on a bigger scale in Hungary. It's not democratic. It's not respecting the human rights in the kind of way that I would want. It's becoming more and more nationalistic and conservative. It's becoming more and more excluding toward minorities. The question is: Do I want to live in a country where the main tendency and the main values are not what I believe in? Would I want to raise a kid and put my child into school here?"

She sighed. "I don't have a clear answer for that."

Luca feels that she has a responsibility toward Hungary. Not just in the Jewish community but in the city of Budapest and the country as a whole.

"Maybe for me, being Hungarian is not the same as what the Jobbik party would want," she said, "but I am Hungarian. With the tools I have, I try to influence what's happening. So far, I will stay, but it is scary from time to time. When I look around and read the news, it is usually more scary than funny, the things that they do."

Luca looked up from her bowl and said, "I would suggest everyone to visit and get to know more than that there is a castle and pretty houses and streets. I want people to not give up on us. There is so much potential. We are going through a dark period. It's getting darker. There are other people who believe in similar values that I do, and I want them to help. Yeah. Do not give up on us."

Our waiter discreetly removed our empty lunch plates. Luca tapped him on his forearm to order another latte for me and an espresso for her. She returned her hands into a tight grasp around her now empty szörp glass.

The last five years have been difficult for Luca. "There was a lot of struggling with myself," she said, "finding what I want and who I am. Learning tons of new things. It was also very exciting. I think it's a necessary learning process that happened and that's happening."

Luca interweaved her fingers and rested her chin on her hands. "I wouldn't change a thing."

Luca welcomed the small espresso cup gracefully placed in the center of our table by our waiter and prepared to pay the bill.

"I think this is the thing that slowly, slowly, I manage to be," she said. "Just...me."

Across the room, I looked at a figure painted on the wall. An abstract individual, outlined in thick black paint against the stark white wall, stood next to a skateboard and held a jagged rose toward the sky. Despite the thorns of the rose, the figure seemed to hold it with pride. Its confidence echoed, "There is so much potential. Do not give up on us."

"It used to be kind of cool and trendy to be Jewish. In certain circles, it still is. But then, the country as a whole, maybe not."

OVERCAST SKIES BARRED MY BEDROOM of sunlight while I dressed in business casual for this week's conference. During my second week in Budapest, Michael Miller, the director of the Jewish Studies Program at Central European University (CEU), hosted an academic conference called, "Narratives of Violence."

Compared to my other conference experiences—primarily designed with community organizers, non-profit professionals, teachers, social workers, and active young adults in mind—this conference catered 99.9% to PhD holders or PhD candidates presenting their most recent papers on violence. That remaining 0.01% was me. I pulled on my most professional pair of black jeans, tugging their skinny hem over my ankles and thighs, and buttoned them around a tucked-in silk royal blue button down long-sleeve shirt.

I stepped outside of my apartment and felt the humidity of the stormy morning suffocating me around my collar. My hands, clammy with nervous sweat, grasped the post-it containing my hand-written directions from Google Maps. As I meandered from my apartment to the Sixth District in Budapest where CEU is located, I noticed buildings growing substantially taller and streets growing significantly wider. As I strolled, more and more chalkboard signs advertised "Tourist Menu" and "Goulash Special" in English and the lines outside of Costa Coffee and Starbucks grew longer.

Anticipating directional defeat, I probed a waiter dressed in all black standing outside of one of the many restaurants for directions to CEU. He politely motioned with his hands that I should take one left and one right and I would reach my destination.

Despite sharing a language and an interest in violence and violence prevention, I felt more out of place among my scholarly superiors than I felt among my Hungarian peers. My mind clouded with questions of worth, purpose and intellectual capacity.

Likely noticing my heightened alienation over the course of the three-day conference, Michael helped ease me into the CEU community, as well as into his personal and professional communities beyond CEU. Originally from Boston, Massachusetts, Michael made a home in Budapest and has been living and working in Jewish Budapest for nearly fifteen years. His academic fascination and personal love of the city were beacons of hope for me in the second week of my journey.

Michael and I kept in touch as summer turned to fall. In early September, I received an email invitation to join him and his friends at his apartment to reign in Rosh Hashanah, the Jewish New Year. Sitting elbow-to-elbow around the dinner table with fellow travelers, writers, academics, and students, my self-doubt faded as my network of friends, colleagues and collaborators grew.

After an additional series of coffee-chats and another season passing, Michael and I sat down at *Stika* (sh-tee-kah), the café beneath his apartment in the Seventh District, to capture his story. I sat with my back facing the window, reading a book split open on the small, light wooden table in front of me. Michael walked into the café, announced by soft bells that swung into sound as the door opened. His brows furrowed with frustration. That morning, he had lost a handful of chapters from the history book he was actively writing about one family over the course of one hundred and fifty years. He hoped to mirror their story against the larger history of Hungarian Jewry.

Feeling a pang of vicarious heartbreak, I made eye contact with the waiter behind the bar to my left and ordered Michael a blueberry scone.

Michael first came to Hungary in 1992, three years after the fall of communism. As a recent graduate from Brown University, Michael decided to travel to Eastern Europe. He spent about six months in what was then Czechoslovakia. "I went there because I was interested in the revival of Jewish life and I wanted to take part in it," he said.

Michael wound up in the Slovak part of Czechoslovakia as a *madrich* (youth counselor) at Szarvas, the international Jewish youth camp. While he was there, he learned that one of the Jewish schools in Budapest was searching for an English teacher, so he met with the principal of the school.

"It was a very, very quick meeting," he laughed. "He basically said, 'When can you start?'"

Michael spent about five months teaching at the school and becoming more and more involved in informal Jewish life. "I was excited about coming to Hungary," he said. "I was interested in this effervescent revival of Jewish life. Everything was new. Everybody was excited about discovering their Jewishness and exploring it. There was a lot going on. Much more so then than now."

After one and half years in Israel and graduate school at Columbia University in New York City, Michael returned to Eastern Europe in 1999 to do research in the Czech Republic. He took part in a three-week summer school seminar at Central European University (CEU) in Budapest. "I decided I would stay for a couple of weeks in addition to that," he said, "and then...after a couple of weeks, I thought to myself, why do I need to go back to New York? I set up in Budapest for one year to finish my dissertation."

During that first year, Michael began to learn the Hungarian language and became more involved in Jewish happenings in Budapest. He said, "That one year became two years, and then three years, and then ten years, and then...I guess fifteen years."

When Michael finished his dissertation, he became involved in setting up the Jewish Studies Program at CEU. The idea for the program started in 1991 before Michael had ever been to Budapest. It was only around 2000 that they made progress on setting it up. "It just seemed like a good place to be," he said. "I was at the right place at the right time. There was always interest among the students in these kinds of courses, but it wasn't a specialization the way it is now."

One of the reasons Michael chose to stay in Budapest in particular was because he wanted to experience Jewish life in Hungary. In Slovakia, the Jewish community did not feel the same. "There was interesting stuff going on," he said, "but you probably had around one thousand Jews living in Bratislava compared to one hundred thousand in Budapest.

Budapest is also a beautiful city, and it was different then. It was kind of a liberal, optimistic place in the 90s. Now...not so liberal, and not so optimistic."

Michael explained that in the early 90s, everyone was curious. A whole new world had just opened up before them with the shift from communism to democracy. Not just post-communism, but also being able to explore Jewishness freely and to have so many options. Various youth groups and schools were first opening. People could travel to Israel, London or America. They could start their own organizations or import organizations that existed elsewhere but not yet in Hungary. Michael had friends who moved to Israel in the early 90s and then came back to Hungary in the mid-to-late 90s because they thought things were better in Hungary than in Israel. "I mean, in general, there was this feeling of optimism," he said. "People came back because they felt like Hungary was not only their home, but was where their future was. I think that feeling lasted until the end of the 90s."

Our waiter dropped a glass ashtray that shattered against the porcelain floor. He fled the scene to search for a broom.

Michael explained that conditions in Hungary are becoming increasingly ominous. Though he cannot predict the exact number of people who are leaving, Michael regrets to admit that he knows very few people who haven't recently at least discussed it. "There's this general sense of malaise," he said. "Economically, this country is not doing well. Politically, the country is...pretty horrible. I think the whole political discourse has changed. It used to be kind of cool and trendy to be Jewish. In certain circles, it still is. But the country as a whole, maybe not."

The political climate has not heavily impacted the Jewish Studies program at CEU. Michael imagined that one reason might be because many of the students involved in this program are not Hungarian. He said, "This year, my students are Lithuanian, Serbian, Croatian, Hungarian, Romanian, Ukrainian, Japanese and Italian. There are people who don't have large Jewish communities at home. They don't have Jewish Studies programs either. This is really the only program of its kind in the region. So, students come."

Michael has found that even if Judaism is not a customary topic of conversation, people are interested in learning more about it. "I don't know necessarily *why* people are interested," he said. "In some cases, they feel like in order to understand their own country's history, they need to understand Jewish history. For example, how can you understand Romanian history without understanding the role of the Jews? Or Hungarian history? Or Ukrainian history?"

Some students are interested in learning more in order to better understand their own personal familial history. Michael recently discovered that his Croatian student has a Jewish mother. Some years, he has many Jewish students, and other years, he doesn't have many at all.

Upon graduation, regardless of their personal Jewish roots or lack thereof, many of Michael's students go on to contribute to the European Jewish world. One student worked for the OSC in the division that fights anti-Semitism and xenophobia. That student is now the head of the

Warsaw Jewish community. Another student is at Harvard furthering his studies in the Jewish field. Others go on for a PhD at CEU. One student teaches Jewish history in the Czech Republic and another teaches Jewish history in Bucharest. "We have a little network," Michael said as he mimed figurative piles all over our coffee table.

Over the course of the past fifteen years, Michael has encountered many students who have unique stories about discovering their Jewish roots. "The student who is now at Oxford," he said, "her grandmother made one of those deathbed confessions fifteen years ago. She was about to pass away when she confessed her Judaism to her family. She embraced it."

Michael laughed, "I had a student named Christian once. A nice Hungarian Jew named Christian."

Through his students and his research, Michael has anecdotally discovered immense knowledge about Hungarian Jewish life. "It's always interesting when I have a random student who I assume is not Jewish, and they make some sort of comment that reveals that their grandmother was Jewish," he said. "I think this experience has given me some insights into the complexity of Jewish identity in this region."

Michael stood to retrieve a straw from across the room. He delicately placed his straw at the bottom of his sparkling juice and it bounced to the surface, tinkering on the edge of falling out of his glass.

"Not everybody has the same definition of what it means to be Jewish," he said. People embrace their Jewishness in different ways. Some are Jewish by law, others have one Jewish grandparent. Sometimes the person with one Jewish grandfather feels more Jewish than the person with two Jewish parents. When international students come to study in Budapest, their perspective on Judaism in their home country changes upon their return.

Michael has spent most of his adult life living away from America. "Living here has changed me," he said. "In some ways, living here has made me feel more American, which is not necessarily a central part of my identity when I am living in the States. When I am here, being American is something that people identify me as and there are a lot of things that I appreciate about America that I appreciate from afar and didn't necessarily appreciate before. It's also just, you know, a sense of home. I have lived here for fifteen years, and I am very much at home here, but this is not home. Home is the States. That's an interesting realization."

Hungary has changed a lot during Michael's time there, as well. "I don't know if Hungary could have at some point felt like home," he said. "I think what I like about living in Hungary is that it can't be my real home."

A glare of sunlight pierced through the window and rested upon Michael's right hand. "This is a beautiful city," he said. "This is a wonderful neighborhood. The university I teach at...I'll never have this kind of job again. CEU is a remarkable place. The diversity of the student body, the diversity of the faculty, the pretty light teaching load, the flexibility in terms of travel and research, the relative lack of bureaucracy. It's unique. It's very easy to be here. Now, it's time to challenge myself a little."

Michael does not see Judaism growing in Budapest in a religious sense. He explained, "I get a sense that there is a finite number of people who sometimes move from one place to another but the number is not growing. My sense is that there are eight thousand or so Jews in Hungary that at least once a year step inside a synagogue or do something Jewish, and it's those eight thousand. The other, let's say, ninety thousand, are out there, but they're out there as statistics, not necessarily as involved people. I don't know how much that is going to change."

Michael predicts that eventually, many of the synagogues are going to close down. "There are going to be a lot of Jewish individuals here," he said, "but I don't know what the Jewish community is going to look like. This isn't a religious community right now, so much, and I don't think that's going to be different in ten or fifteen years. So the question is: what kind of institutions *are* going to be in place that are going to give Jews in Hungary meaning?"

Already, synagogues are not necessarily what give the average Hungarian Jew meaning. "People go there for the communal, historical, cultural, traditional experience," Michael said. "Jewish life is already being redefined."

When outsiders come to Hungary, they look for the synagogues, but the question that has been occupying Michael for the last ten to fifteen years is: what is the content of this non-synagogue-centered Jewish life in Hungary? "There are only so many people who are going to find meaning in community centers," he said. "These places are important institutions but I don't think they attract a following. Occasionally, there is an interesting lecture or event, and people go, but that's it."

Michael sees Jewish excitement in some of his students but is not convinced that the big wave of excitement from the early 90s still exists. "This may be a result of the political climate," he said. "People are less willing to out themselves as Jews or talk about their Jewishness publically. We are also one generation further removed from the Holocaust. People that grew up in the 80s, their grandparents were Holocaust survivors. Their parents probably knew a little something. People that are coming of age right now, they didn't know their great-grandparents, and their grandparents were born under communism. The tradition has been severed. The people that are involved in Jewish organizations now are by and large the people that were starting them ten years ago. There's not a new generation that's taken their place."

Michael peered out the window. "What I have learned is that I still don't know the answer," he said. "What's next for me is...eventually back to the States."

He pinched a crumb of blueberry scone off the ceramic white place and placed it back down.

"I will always keep a piece of Hungary with me. I've been here fifteen years, and I'll probably keep coming back. But fifteen years is a long time. I have connections to this city that I am not going to cut off. But, this place will probably no longer be my home."

Though many of my Hungarian acquaintances maintained a strongly optimistic, determined and altruistic perspective about Budapest and its future, Michael's blunt doubt left a gnawing void in my chest.

Michael lifted his watch on his left wrist and realized he was late for a meeting. We stood and kissed once on each cheek before the bells announced his rushed departure.

I observed the waiter, fumbling with the buttons of his tuxedo vest behind the bar. I imagined that he would gain confidence and skill as he gained practice balancing glasses and treats on large, round trays. I glanced around the room at the otherwise unoccupied café. I slipped my miniature recorder into my messenger bag and walked away from Stika, the sound of bells ringing in my ear as I passed.

KATA NÁDAS

Photograph by Merlin Fox

"We need to believe that certain things happen for a reason. They might not be good at the time, but in five or six days, or weeks, or months, or years, you will understand why."

IN EARLY AUGUST, I TRAVELED TO STOCKHOLM, Sweden for a ten-day Project Incubator at Paideia—The European Institute for Jewish Studies. Paideia hosts a one-year Jewish Studies curriculum as well as a ten-day Project Incubator, a brief gathering that yearly trains twenty social innovators and entrepreneurs in how to successfully launch and execute an initiative that plans to create a positive impact in the European Jewish world. After one hour of meandering the streets of Stockholm in search of Paideia, I stared at my phone's unforgiving screen. Lost.

"Not again!" I breathed heavily and continued to walk up and down the street. The number I was looking for suddenly caught a flicker of light. A narrow door nestled between a coffee shop and a clothing store, the entrance looked more like an abandoned apartment than an institute. I squeezed past the various coffee patrons splayed across tables perched outside the entrance to reach the door.

I walked up two flights of narrow stairs to meet Erik, the program director of Paideia's ten-day Project Incubator. As he gave me directions to the hostel where I would be staying with the other program participants, he informed me that I would be sharing a room with Kata, who must have been a friend of mine. I stared him blankly in the face.

"Kata Nádas? You're both from Budapest! You went to a conference together in June. Of course, you know each other?"

I tried my best to smile, admitted that I am no good with names, and fibbed that I was excited to reunite with Kata.

Hours later, while I was unpacking my hiking backpack in the comfort of our small hostel room that fit no more than two bare twin beds resting directly next to each other, Kata arrived. I definitely did not know her, but to my relief, she did not know me either. When she learned the Erik story she released an outrageous laugh that warmed my heart and instantaneously relieved my anxiety.

"Well, hi. I am Kata. Nice to meet you."

Each morning of the Incubator, one participant had the opportunity to share their Jewish journey with the rest of the group. On our final morning, Kata unfolded a large board covered in multi-colored pieces of construction paper and pulled two dice and various plastic pieces out of her purse. To illustrate her journey, Kata created a board game. For one hour, the group of twenty participants huddled together over a long, plastic table, drawing cards that told stories of Kata's youth and begged questions of Jewish identity and purpose. Walking away from the plastic table to our first lecture, the group whispered to one another their remaining questions and thoughts that lingered from the brief interaction with Kata's game.

A few weeks after the Incubator, Kata and I settled into the multi-colored chairs of Jelen, the funky, alternative restaurant-pub around the corner from my apartment. Kata nervously fiddled with the strap of her purse as she insisted that her story was not the most exciting. Her thick ginger-brown hair bounced as we walked to our table. We collected ourselves and ordered a round of drinks: a szörp for Kata and a latte for me.

Kata was born in 1983 in Hungary into a Jewish family. "Everyone was Jewish, but still, it wasn't a topic to talk about," she said. All four of Kata's grandparents were Holocaust survivors. "So, I always knew everything about the Holocaust, unfortunately, but I never really knew what Judaism was."

Kata distinctly remembered one Jewish celebration from her childhood. She guessed it was a Seder night. "It was one of the most *boring* times of my life," she laughed. "I was very small and I had no idea what was going on. It was great."

Kata does not remember exactly when her parents told her she was Jewish. "I remember that in primary school, I really wanted to go to Catholic learning classes," she said. "Four or five of my classmates went twice a week. It was something really interesting. They came back with these beautiful golden Mary and Jesus pictures and I always wanted them! So, I told my mom that I want to go. She said no. That was probably when they told me." Kata pressed her lips together refraining from laughter. "She said that I was running up and down the house yelling, 'I don't want to be Jewish!' She really understood but she couldn't do anything about that."

Due to the impact of communism, Kata's parents were not very familiar with Jewish customs. Her grandmother, however, took her father to synagogue fairly regularly. "He even had a bar mitzvah," she said, "but, for him, it didn't really mean too much. It was just too much for him."

Since age eleven or twelve, Kata spent her summers in England and in the States. In the States, she went to a

Christian camp. "Maybe two of us were Jews there" she said. "Actually, this strengthened my Jewish identity. Everyone knew that I was Jewish. To be there, as a thirteen-year-old, and to realize that you can survive, and not just survive, but *enjoy* a seven-week camp, was really something."

Kata's favorite aspect of camp was that the staff was positive. "That was the first time in my life when every day, someone is praising you. To say, 'Well done. You are great.' I went there three times and it really added to my strength. I bring my strength from home, as well, but I think being abroad, and being quite stubborn, it all adds up."

Kata pulled a menu to her face. Our waiter—a stout, dark-skinned man with tattoos lining both arms and the left side of his face—approached to take our order. Kata and I each ordered the lunch special: vegetable ratatouille, spinach quiche, and a chocolate mousse for dessert.

Growing up, Kata did not receive a very expansive Jewish education. When she was about fifteen, a friend of hers took her to one of the Chabad centers. "I really liked it," she said. "I met a few friends and I got captured." Kata erupted into a bold laugh, causing our waiter to turn around on his way back to the kitchen.

Chabad became a large part of Kata's life. She participated in the community for about ten years. "I never thought I would be religious," she said, "but it really interested me. I wanted to learn the customs and everything. I was there almost every Friday night."

The first time Kata felt at home at Chabad was when she started helping. She said, "When you realize that it's dinner and you can get up from your ass and collect the dishes, I think that's when you really feel at home."

Our waiter returned to place our first course on our table. Layers of steaming zucchini, tomato, squash, and mushroom swam in a thick marinara sauce.

Kata's family was originally disturbed by her choice to become involved in Chabad. They feared they would lose Kata to the Jewish community. "At the same time, I didn't see any alternative," she said. At that time, Kata wasn't familiar with any other Jewish programs. Eventually, her family understood that Judaism was important for her and made her happy. They grew more comfortable when they realized that her becoming more involved in Judaism would not make her less involved with her family.

After high school, Kata spent one year in Switzerland and New Zealand. "It's interesting that my identity got stronger when I lived abroad, alone, and I didn't have a Jewish community," she said. "That's when I really started to feel something inside."

While Kata was away, her mother started to go to synagogue. Kata remembered, "She said that I am not here, so she needs to represent me. So, her relationship to Judaism changed, too."

The following year, Kata went on Taglit. "I already had my Jewish identity, I never thought I needed to do anything with Israel," she said. "I thought they were two different things. Honestly, if it wasn't for free, I probably would have never gone."

While Kata was in Israel, she learned that you can truly be Jewish even if you are not religious. "You can be Jewish in a cultural way," she said. That became her focus. She tried to become an ambassador of this realization and is now helping others find their identity in any form that fits.

"Maybe there was always something inside me looking for a Jewish community," Kata thought. "Honestly, I think when you are sixteen, you just look for a community. I really don't know what I was looking for. Of course, now, I see Judaism's unique beauty."

Kata feels at home within almost all of the Jewish organizations in Budapest. She knows many of the leaders and participants of projects. Every six months, Kata finds a new project or organization to become involved in as Jewish Budapest grows. On a Friday night, there are at least fifteen places where she could celebrate Shabbat, religious or non-religious.

Kata delicately stacked one of each vegetable onto her fork and dunked the forkful into a pool of sauce on the side of her plate. She said you can only get to this place with patience. "A lot of people ask me how they can learn the holidays and the traditions, and it's not like you buy a book and you will learn it," she said. "It's just with practice. For at least one year, or two, go and listen to all the traditions. Go to more and different places, not just to one place, because if you only go to one place then you think that's the only choice. Just be patient and build it up for yourself. Maybe there are fifteen communities and you will have a sixteenth view of life in Judaism. That's okay."

Kata scraped a forkful of marinara sauce onto her fork and pushed the ceramic plate away from her. She said, "I hope Jewish life here can reach more and more people and not just the same people over and over again. I love Budapest. I think the culture here is amazing. The vibe is amazing. With the festivals and cultural events, especially in the summer, but also during the winter. I think there are a lot of possibilities for the Jewish communities."

Our waiter removed our plates and replaced them with circular bowls holding fluffy spinach quiche burnt slightly brown along the edges.

Kata admitted that there is anti-Semitism in Budapest, and it is a problem, but it doesn't take away from the amazing Jewish life she experiences. "We need to be careful" she said, "but I don't think it's an anti-Semitism problem. I think it's a political problem that I am more afraid of. I just hope we are not going backwards into what we used to have. At the moment, the future is not very bright."

Kata poked her quiche with her fork, popping an air bubble that rested on the surface. She said, "There is a problem and it should be stopped, but there are amazing things happening here. We are okay, thank you."

After working more than five years in the professional Jewish community, Kata is now thinking about broadening her professional experience. While her heart, community, and weekends revolve around Jewish Budapest, professionally, she plans to take a step away. "I am happy to open my eyes a little bit and see what is in the outside world," she said.

Two small silver cups holding chocolate mousse replaced our empty quiche bowls. Kata tasted the swirl of whipped cream on top with her finger and said, "People really appreciate my creativity. People will follow me, they told me. That is the best recommendation letter. People know me in the community, I know the community, and the personal feedback I get keeps me alive in the hard periods."

Kata dug her spoon to stand straight up in her mousse. "I think life, it's amazing," she said. She paused, resting her glance on the floorboards beneath us.

The air between us stood still.

"It's very difficult. Life is very hard. We need to believe that certain things happen for a reason. They might not be good at the time, but in five or six days, or weeks, or months, or years, you will understand why."

Kata sat up straight and lifted her gaze. She shook her head from side to side as though shaking away cobwebs.

She added, "I really want to say that I am fantastic and I am looking for a man around thirty-five, tall, handsome, rich... My number is..." she started laughing.

I laughed with her and warned, "Be careful what you wish for," hoping that somehow I could grant Kata her man in exchange for the spirit and heart she so gracefully shared with me.

ANDRÁS MOLNAR

"It is the responsibility of those who are not Jews to stand up and say this is not acceptable."

ON APRIL 26, 2014, ONE WEEK AFTER my Kickstarter campaign and one month before my departure for Budapest, a man named Dávid Barkóczi sent a message to my Kickstarter inbox to express his excitement about the project's mission and initiation. He began by saying, "Dear Alyssa, I am so happy because this project backed successful. I live in Budapest, and would be great if you drop a line when you arrive here or any update."

After a few back-and-forth messages with Dávid, he signed a heartfelt message with a note that read, "P.S: Lot of enthusiastic people organize an interesting program on June 21, call Yellow-Star Houses," accompanied by a link through which I could find out more information (http://www.yellowstarhouses.org).

Yellow Star Houses, organized by András Lénárt, Gabriella Rothman, and Miklós Tamási, was an all-day commemorative event held in Budapest on the 70th anniversary of "the day Hungarian political leaders forcibly expelled Budapest Jews from their homes." In the words of the organizers, "220,000 targeted individuals were obliged to move... subjected to a series of 'Jewish laws,' and forced to wear a yellow Star of David on their clothing. They had to leave their own apartments by midnight on June 21, 1944 and move into one of the 1,944 designated apartment buildings also marked with a yellow star, the 'yellow-star' houses."

I drew a bold star in my planner around the date June 21 and outlined it with a yellow highlighter. Two months later, I found myself on my way to the event.

I walked the then familiar forty-five-minute route from my apartment into the more bustling heart of Budapest, assigning shapes and names to the elusive clouds whispering through the sky. The commemorative event began at the American Embassy, located in what I had come to call politics square (its real name being Szabadság tér, or Liberty Square) – a park boasting politically charged monuments surrounded by the international headquarters of countless nations. Each stroke of street art and the toothless grin from an elderly woman mumbling pleasantly in Hungarian reinvigorated my drive.

As I turned the corner to enter the Embassy, a woman in a suit opened the door to the security check-in, stepped away and motioned for me to enter. She entered behind me, swiftly removed her black pin-stripe suit jacket as I removed my white cotton cardigan, both of us preparing to place our phones, keys, and jackets into the security machine. Together, we collected our belongings on the other side and entered the event.

I quickly realized that I had arrived slightly late. Specks of blue, green, red, grey, white, and black colored the immaculately gardened lawn of the American Embassy. I estimated nearly three hundred people were in attendance. André Goodfriend, Deputy Chief of Mission, was speaking about the importance of memory and solidarity in Hungary. Dressed in a grey suit paired with a white button-down and a red and blue striped satin tie, standing in contrast to the white, looming American Embassy building towering behind him, Goodfriend wondered rhetorically about what he would have done in 1944. Despite his record of responsible and humanitarian-focused decisions, he questioned: *How was it that so many people stood by and watched as their neighbors were deported and killed?*

An eerie silence fell over the crowd. Goodfriend's messages struck a nerve. *What would I have done?* Would I have offered myself in place of my neighbor? Would I have felt confident and courageous enough to make a difference? Would the fear of death and the Nazi party's immense influence have triumphed over my ideals?

Following Goodfriend's introduction, one by one, the crowd dissipated to follow their own self-chosen path for the day. The Yellow Star Houses event offered various choices of houses to visit, people to listen to, and cultural events and historical recounts to immerse in. I used language as a guide and chose to attend every event that would be held in English.

First, I listened to an anonymous woman recite the well-known statement from Martin Niemöller, a prominent Protestant pastor who emerged as an outspoken foe of Adolf Hitler and spent the last seven years of Nazi rule in concentration camps:

First they came for the Socialists, and I did not speak out—
Because I was not a Socialist.
Then they came for the Trade Unionists, and I did not speak out—
Because I was not a Trade Unionist.
Then they came for the Jews, and I did not speak out—
Because I was not a Jew.

Then they came for me—and there was no one left to speak for me.

The woman, with her long, curly brown graying hair tightly pulled back into a bun behind her head, read the quote in Hungarian, followed by English. As she read, she kept her eyes glued to the piece of paper in her hand, which shook ever so slightly. Light grey hairs sporadically frayed away from her face like they were rebelling against the structure of the bun.

Upon finishing, she looked up. She made intense eye contact with the crowd, deepening a feeling of emptiness and responsibility. I walked away from her feeling as though one dark cloud were hovering over my head despite the bright blue sky and warm sun suggesting otherwise.

On my way to listen to a speech by the Israeli ambassador, a massive crowd surrounding one of the Yellow Star Houses lured me off track. The event was being held in Hungarian but a number of video cameras the size of motorcycles and microphones as tall as the surrounding buildings kept me intrigued. I whispered to the person standing next to me, on his tiptoes hoping to see and hear over the tall woman standing in front of him. He informed me that George Soros, an eighty-four year-old Hungarian-born American business powerhouse, investor, and philanthropist, was seated at the center of attention.

Finally, as the sun set and a cool breeze replaced the heat of the day, I walked toward what once was Tom Lantos' apartment to hear a speech given by the Tom Lantos Institute's director, Anna-Mária Bíró, and Tom Lantos' daughter,

Katrina Swett, along with the recital of memories of Tom Lantos by four young Hungarians. Lantos, a Hungarian-American born in 1928, was the only Holocaust survivor to have served in the United States Congress. Speaking before the House of Representatives after his death in 2008, House Speaker Nancy Pelosi stated that Lantos "devoted his public life to shining a bright light on the dark corners of oppression... He used his powerful voice to stir the consciousness of world leaders and the public alike."

I arrived early. In contrast to the crowd mobbing George Soros as though he were a member of the Beatles, I stood alone at Tom Lantos' apartment, nervous that I had come to the wrong address. I gazed at the strikingly ordinary building above me displaying light grey stacks of cement and windows guarded with white vertical bars. To the right of the doorway, a silver plaque stated that Tom Lantos once lived in this apartment.

A young man in a navy-blue suit approached me. Though he was nearly twice my height and pulled off a distractingly strong jaw-line, I took ease in my estimation that he was no older than nineteen. His dark eyes met mine and the corners of his mouth curved into a smile, unveiling dimples that were almost as charming as his lavender tie. He began speaking to me in Hungarian to no avail. He continued to look straight through me, raising his eyebrows as his smile crinkled into an unnerving frown. In his next effort, he said, "Hi, I am András, I am with the Tom Lantos Institute. May I get you anything?" He thought I was with the press. Thank you, Canon T1i DSLR camera.

I replied, stuttering through a burning desire to learn Hungarian, "I- I am not with the press, but it seems we have some time. I think I will grab a coffee. Would you like to join me?"

His frown reversed as his English had solved the mystery behind why the first attendee of his event was ignoring him. He looked around, scanning the scene, noticing four fellow colleagues of his setting up a large projector and another two greeting guests and handing out colored pamphlets with more information about the Tom Lantos Institute. His extra hands would be put to no use. His gaze returned to meet mine as he replied, "I'd like that."

We crossed the street and walked through the Thirteenth District along the deep teal River Danube. As we strolled past Szent István Park, sounds of children laughing and scents of unattended dog feces swept over my senses.

Approaching the café glamorously designed with an outdoor patio overlooking the river, András and I discussed his current educational experiences at Durham University, his role at the Tom Lantos Institute, and his perspective regarding the Yellow Star Houses initiative. This evolved into discussing his views on diversity, on minority rights, on being Hungarian, and on the world.

András is a twenty-two-year-old white, Hungarian, non-Jewish, non-Roma, male. Though not himself a minority, when talking about minority rights, his voice hardens like an army general's. As I handed my credit card to the cashier to pay for my latte, András banged a fist against the marble counter to emphasize that minorities and disadvantaged communities deserve the same rights as everyone else. We walked back to the event at Tom Lantos' apartment, by then hugged by a small crowd of attendees in suits and flowery summer dresses, and secured a time to finish our discussion.

One week later, I stepped onto the train platform to meet András for dinner. The bright red-orange sun splashed the sky with stripes of violet and magenta. I pulled my thin cardigan close around me, mildly underdressed for the chill of the evening. I met András at the end of the platform and we walked together toward an oversized mall perched in the distance, reflecting the purples and pinks of the evening in its multiple stories of windows.

Before long, András and I settled into a small table in a crêpe restaurant on the second floor of the mall. Smells of deliciously thin and buttery crêpe batter made it difficult to focus on András, despite his dapper baby-blue-checkered button down and loosened navy blue tie. András closed the menu quickly, sharply contrasting my incessant indecision about whether to order a savory crêpe with Swiss or Muenster cheese. A knot in my stomach tightened, heightening the fear that I would simultaneously order the wrong crêpe while butchering an interview with mountains of potential. I felt like a rookie baseball player recruited to the major league before my time with the weight of the game on my shoulders.

András and I placed our orders with our waitress, a short, full-bodied woman who patiently humored my indecision. Smiling as though he could see through my shaky exterior, András said that he was unaccustomed to formal interviews. He, too, was nervous. He picked up where we left off.

András placed his right hand on his chest and his left hand cleanly on the table as though he had meditated such precise motions in debate class. He explained that seventy years ago, very few people stood up and said, "You are taking away my neighbor? Stop it, you can't do that." He said, "Now, as a person who is coming from a non-Jewish family, I believe it is much more my responsibility to stand up and do something in a time when anti-Semitism is evolving again. It is the responsibility of those who are not Jews to stand up and say this is not acceptable."

András was born in Budapest in 1994. His family originally lived in various cities around Hungary, mostly in the countryside. His grandparents all moved to Budapest. András' father is a first generation intellectual and his mother is a second. He said, "It is really good to know how my family could build up their own future."

András' family was very much affected by World War II and other Hungarian historical events. András' great-grandfather was an illegal communist. He established the communist party locally in the village where he lived. "He actually believed in equality and believed communism would bring equality," András said. "He hoped that finally, classes would be destroyed. He was very rich and gave up his land to help other people." András' great grandfather didn't agree with the measures that were taken by communists after they came to power. "He died because of that," he said. "He was harassed by communists. He didn't get proper medical treatment and he died in the hospital."

Consequently, András' grandfather was very poor. "He was picked up by the communists," András said. "He gained his education and his future because of the communists. This is a very stereotypical Hungarian story: there are those who lost everything because of communism, and there are some who gained everything because of communism. In my family, there are both."

András attended an average primary school. He said, "In primary school, no one read books and no one was interested in what we were studying." Due to his grades and determination, he was offered the opportunity to go to an excellent high school. András received an impeccable education and widened his perspective on world issues and disciplines. "It was shocking for me that people were actually interested in what we were studying. It was a very good feeling," he said. "We were discussing not just in class, but outside of class, and not just books but what was happening in our country, and politics."

András remembered his history class placing a strong emphasis on human rights. Students had discussions, debates, and led presentations about topics they were interested in. In this way, András felt eternally grateful for his education. "On the other hand," he said, "I felt some topics, like the Holocaust, were ignored compared to how much we dealt with issues such as city state." András felt there was an injustice in the prioritization of certain topics over others and took his personal time to research topics that seemed glossed over.

After high school, András enrolled at Durham University in North East England to study history and politics. He began working at the Tom Lantos Institute (TLI) as a research fellow to fulfill a summer internship. András values that TLI addresses human rights violations not just in Hungary but also all over the world. He said, "Society often thinks about human rights as something that is off topic. Oh, so idealistic. But it's not. Human rights are women's rights, or human rights are Jewish rights, or human rights are gay rights. Those things are important. Until those are respected, we cannot rest. I value that."

As a Hungarian, András feels that it is his responsibility to keep Hungarian tradition alive. "People leave Hungary and make Hungarian Jewish populations elsewhere, like in the U.S., but they cannot really compare to the communities that existed in Hungary before the war," he said. "We owe it to the people to respect their legacy in a way that we ask others, 'Why is that synagogue a shoe shop now, or a florist, or a mall? Well, because those people were killed.' There is no one else who can keep that legacy alive and they have an amazing legacy."

In a levelheaded tone, András said, "It is not without reason that I was born in Hungary. There is a purpose. I am responsible for all the people who live here." Many young adults András' age leave Hungary for professional or educational reasons and never return. He explained, "I feel that if I do something good in the UK, it hasn't got as much value comparing to the fact that I can do something good here, in a country which is less developed, less open, and I can bring back a culture, an idealistic view as you can see, and a lot of experience."

András explained that in Hungary, the culture of loyalty and improvement regarding human rights is not implemented in politics or everyday culture. He said the people who are outside of the country now have a responsibility to stay involved in Hungarian life and human rights whether they realize it or not. "They don't have to necessarily come back," he said, "but at least from outside, help somehow."

This is one of many reasons why András highly respects George Soros. Though he does not live in Hungary, he established institutions like the Open Society Institute, now the Open Society Foundation, a grant-making network aimed to shape public policy to promote democratic governance, human rights, and economic, legal and social reform. He founded Central European University (CEU), an international postgraduate institution located in Budapest and focused on the humanities and social sciences. He also initiated the Roma Access Program (RAP) within CEU, which aims to help promising Roma students from Europe realize their full academic and professional potential. András said, "These are very important initiatives, which, without his presence, are still working and doing very good things."

In light of his own path, András said he would like to live in Budapest after finishing his degree and obtaining a few years of professional experience. "Start from the bottom and eventually do something at the top," he said.

András envisions a future in which Hungary better understands human rights and the importance of open discussions. More than tolerance, András hopes for integration. He said, "Tolerance is, 'Yeah, I accept you, but I am keeping a distance.' With assimilation, with acceptance, and with being in other peoples' shoes, you can do something. You can change attitudes and prevent terrible events such as the killing of Roma people or the killings of Jews in the 1940s. Those things shouldn't happen again."

András believes that in Hungary, racism and discrimination exist culturally, but the government is formally hostile against discrimination and anti-Jewish sentiment. On the other hand, he is weary of the rising racism, discrimination, and anti-"other". "We have to convince each other that this is unacceptable," he said. "Everyone can be targeted by a party that is searching for an enemy."

Though András does not identify as a Jewish individual, he empathizes with the Jewish perspective. He defines his religion as his values of equality and a society in which people can live alongside each other. As a non-Jew, he feels even more mobilized to defend Jewish rights. "That's how you stand up when neighbors are taken away," he said. "You say no, you cannot do that, he is my neighbor, and he is my friend." He sees Jewish Hungarians as especially targeted and vulnerable, despite having contributed heavily to Hungarian culture, politics, and society.

András remembered that two months ago, his best friend tried to prove that Jews are selfish and as such, not worth protecting. He said, "I have experiences with Jews, and they are never gonna protect you," to which András replied, "Well, have you ever protected them?"

Prior to meeting András, I believed that the most vivid fighters for justice channeled a personal feeling of isolation or experience of wrongdoing into the achievement of equality and justice for others. However, András challenged that theory. He seemed to have generated the need for protecting others simply because he was human and they were human, too.

András said that two weeks ago, he went to a "worse than average" school. He screened a video about whether a movement called "Give Gas" should be permitted during the March of the Living. March of the Living is an international educational program that brings Jewish people from all over the world to Poland to learn about the Holocaust and present-day Jewish life in Poland. The "Give Gas" movement revolted against the March of the Living's mission with picket signs, demonstrations and aggressive acts.

In the school that András visited, the majority of the students agreed that such a movement would be unacceptable. András remembered, "Students age fourteen and fifteen were standing up saying, 'I don't know much about this issue because we never covered it in history, but it is hurting others and it is showing that we want the terrible events to happen again." He said, "Without any knowledge, the students were standing up for those who were attacked."

András used this story as an example to illustrate his belief that the majority of Hungarians, especially the younger generation if they receive a strong education, still believe in justice and want the best for their neighbors. He said, "A strong country can be built on the fact that we work together, not against each other."

During his summer internship, András organized a debate series at TLI that involved two groups: students from an elite school and students from disadvantaged backgrounds. He mixed the two groups and initiated debates about human rights topics. In the beginning, he imagined the elite students would be patronizing and the disadvantaged students would be shy. Then, he hoped for the disadvantaged students to recognize that they deserved as much of a voice as any other student. "That will be amazing," he said. "Then, they will see that they are not stupid. They have the same abilities. We can work together."

Though he knew this would be challenging for both sides, András hoped that this project would create a path for the two sides to realize the potential of "the other" and to apply that lesson to broader circumstances in Hungary.

András placed his fork in the center of his empty plate and folded his unused white napkin on top. "Don't give up hope on Europe," he said. "There are many people who are trying to do what I am trying to do."

We stood and hugged, unsure whether we would ever see each other again.

I retrieved a narrow rectangular subway ticket from my purse and awaited the train beneath a street lamp. The light flickered on and off, periodically illuminating the faces of those who waited alongside me and abandoning me in the dark of the night.

"You cannot teach how to believe in G-d."

ON A WARM DAY IN EARLY AUGUST, I made my way toward Dessewffy Synagogue, where there would be a Torah-scroll-dedication ceremony. My eyes strained to adjust to the sunlight as I exited the dimly lit Massolit and stepped onto the hot concrete.

My dress covered my shoulders but did not cover my knees, as would be customary among an orthodox community. I did not have enough time to go home and change if I wanted to make it to the ceremony on time. Tugging at the skirt's flowing edges, I hoped that maybe in the fifteen-minute walk my dress would stretch. I did not have a shawl or a scarf and my hair was probably four times wider than my face due to the humidity.

I closely followed my directions and made it to the some-what hidden synagogue. If not for the two security guards standing in all black with crossed arms in front of the tall wooden double-door, I might have missed the entrance. The guards looked at me inquisitively and said something in Hungarian.

"I am sorry, I don't- Oh! My friends!"

Before I could plead with the guards to let me in, despite not speaking Hungarian, I spotted two people I knew inside the synagogue's courtyard. They waved and summoned me in. The guards looked at each other and stepped aside.

Before the ceremony began, people of the congregation and other interested members of the surrounding Jewish community gathered in a small open-air courtyard between the gated street entrance and the formal entrance of the synagogue. One by one, the crowd proceeded upstairs. On any other day, the upstairs section of the synagogue would be reserved for the women of the congregation; however, both genders climbed upstairs today to witness the final letters being painted onto the Torah scroll.

A dozen chairs in rows of two lined the right side of the bright room, the size of a small elementary school classroom but with bare walls and stone floors. The crowd filled the sturdy metal chairs in seconds. The rest of the visitors—about fifty of us—were left to stand. Though four windows resting above the chairs were cracked open, the faint breeze provided little relief from the heat of the day. With limited space to move or breathe, I could feel my back dampen. A bullet of sweat rolled down my spine.

As the ceremony proceeded in Hungarian, Viktor, who I recognized from the Me2We Conference in June, walked across the front of the room to greet the community. He stood somber and angular behind the light wooden podium. Thin, dark hair swept across his face, striking a strong resemblance to a younger version of *Harry Potter's* Professor Snape. With precise words, Viktor introduced the rabbi who would finish the Torah scroll and floated back to his seat.

The crowd's attention swerved to the man sitting to Viktor's left behind a long table holding an open Torah scroll. With a slender face, a long, crazed beard and a black kippot atop his head, the rabbi delicately painted the final Hebrew letter onto the scroll.

A celebratory madness immediately ensued. Flashes from cell phones and cameras filled the room, the Torah scroll was lifted and kissed, and men danced around the newly finished scroll while the women gossiped about who was who, who has been where, and what they were wearing. The scene reminded me of my older brother's bar mitzvah. My eyes were glued to Viktor, who complemented his stoic stance and stormy presence with the faintest hint of a smile.

Viktor prioritizes a religiously observant mentality and lifestyle, and yet, to the naked eye, dresses and behaves like an ordinary secular millennial. Viktor stood in the corner of the room and leaned against the wall in black pants and a white t-shirt, unlike his fellow orthodox peers in suits and ties. For Viktor, Jewish identity is a lot of things, but most of all, Viktor's identity is his faith and his community.

A few weeks after the dedication of the new Torah scroll, I met with Viktor for a drink at Csiga to discuss his story in more depth. I placed my microphone atop the surface of a wooden table wedged just to the right of the bar, reserving a small nook to ourselves. A cool breeze blew my hair into my face and clouded my vision. Viktor walked into the bar and sat opposite me, the two of us sandwiched around our long, graffitied table that wobbled slightly if you put too much pressure on either side.

Viktor was born in Budapest on December 22, 1989. "I was raised in one of those rare Hungarian families where Judaism was kept, where it had a deeper meaning than the title of a book on a shelf," he said. Viktor's father's family was Hasidic, meaning they followed the Hasidic branch of Orthodox Judaism. His mother's family kept Jewish traditions and holidays, "nothing more, nothing less."

As the two sides of his family followed Jewish law to different degrees, they rarely got together. Viktor said, "My maternal grandmother had three husbands and many, many lovers. We never had family dinners or celebrations with the entire family because the orthodox side of my family would never sit at the same table with my mother's mom. We organized everything separately."

Every year, Viktor celebrated the first Seder Nacht—the first night of the Passover Seder—with his father's parents, which usually took at least six hours. His grandfather read the entire Haggadah, or Jewish text that sets forth the order of the Passover Seder, explaining each intricate detail, usually in Yiddish. "My mother and us kids did not really understand it," Viktor remembered. He spent the second night of the Passover Seder with his maternal side of the family, which lasted for no more than two hours and most of the time was spent eating.

The person who influenced Viktor's Jewish identity the most was his paternal grandfather, Pinches. Pinches and his family came from what is now Czech Republic, but at that time was also a part of the Habsburg Empire, just like Hungary. His father was a kosher butcher. They settled in a town not far from Budapest. They formed an orthodox *kehila* (community) with families like them, all coming from different areas. Eventually, they separated from the locals because the Jewish community was not religious enough for them. They bought a house, which still stands today. When Viktor travels there with friends, he is moved that even after so many years, he can still sense the Jewish presence. "This is a piece of my history," he said.

This grandfather married Viktor's grandmother, Bathsheba. She was from a very small village, which in Yiddish is called *Ratzfert*. This village is in the eastern part of Hungary in Satmar Country. Together, they managed to survive the Holocaust, unlike most of their siblings.

After the war, Pinches and Bathsheba moved to Budapest. They kept Jewish traditions. They did not escape from Hungary during the Revolution of 1956 as most other orthodox Jews did. Instead, they began to build their lives, again, from nothing.

They were separated from most of society. They lived in an outer district of Budapest perhaps as the only Jewish family in that neighborhood. They built their own small ghetto. They had separated a kitchen for Pesach (Passover), a dark prayer room with many important books, and everything one would need for a Jewish life. They built *Sukkah* every year, a temporary hut constructed to eat, sleep, and relax in during the week-long Jewish holiday of Sukkot, which Viktor especially enjoyed. "I learned the traditions from them," he said.

Viktor struggles to understand his parents' faith. Growing up, his father had a strong faith. He adhered to orthodox practices and his first marriage was arranged for him when he was eighteen years old. He and his wife had a boy, Viktor's half-brother. They divorced after two years, which greatly challenged his faith. "When my grandparents learned of the divorce, my grandfather considered my father dead to the family," Viktor said. Ten years later, Viktor's father met Viktor's mother. By that time, he was no longer religious.

There is a tradition in Judaism that says that if a father theoretically loses his son, or the son leaves the religion, the father can make a Tikkun in the grandson, or the grandson can provide redemption.

"That would be me," Viktor said. When Viktor was born, Viktor's grandparents began speaking to his father again.

Since before primary school, Viktor attended Talmud Torah, elementary classes in Hebrew, Scriptures, and Talmud for young boys. "I am pretty sure that if it would be something that I could not accept, I would reject it," he said. "I cannot say since I was born I had faith, but I can say that for as long as I can remember, I have had a strong connection with G-d."

Throughout Viktor's childhood, he spent much of his time with his grandparents on both sides. "I got used to respecting Shabbos when I was with my father's side and it was totally natural that I was able to do whatever I wanted to do when I was with my maternal grandparents," he said. "Generally, growing up, I did not realize that Jewish is meaning something different from the others. In that time, I didn't have any idea that there were others. I thought that everybody was Jewish."

Viktor attended a secular primary school. During the school days, the students celebrated many holidays, including Christmas, Easter, and the national holidays. Viktor was the only Jew in his class. The first time he saw a Christmas tree was in primary school. At that time, he started to realize that *he* was "the other," not "them."

"I was a bit confused," he said, "but I accepted that there was the school world and then there was my world because at that time I still thought that my world was much bigger than the school's. Later, when I started university, I understood that I was wrong."

Viktor went to a non-Jewish but very liberal high school. In his class there were ten or twelve other Jews and more than eighty percent of the teachers were Jewish.

"I felt like I wasn't the 'other' anymore," he said. At this school, students celebrated Christmas, but they also celebrated Hanukkah. "We spent a whole day remembering the Holocaust through various activities," Viktor said, "which is very rare." Most other Hungarian schools had Holocaust Memorial Day every year, but they commemorated for one hour or less, or just mentioned that now it is Holocaust day, and that is all.

When Viktor went to a Hungarian technical university in 2008, he received a big shock. "Basically, nobody was Jewish," he said. "The bigger problem was that they came from totally different backgrounds than what I experienced until that point. Most of them came from the countryside. I've always loved to read, to go to theatres, and all kinds of intellectual stuff. I realized that nobody was loving the same as me."

Before Viktor could continue, a bartender leaned over the bar and tapped him on the shoulder. He asked in Hungarian what we would like to drink. Viktor ordered us two draft beers. He looked back in my direction and said, "It was a real culture shock. Until that point, even though I studied in non-Jewish schools, I was in a bubble. And this bubble just...*pfft.*"

Viktor doesn't have many friends from university. In truth, he has just one. "We met in line on the first day," he said, "waiting for our student cards. She was in front of me in line and was using hand cream with Hebrew letters on it. I approached her and said, 'How come you have this Hebrew hand cream?' The question sounded silly but she answered naturally and said, 'It's from Israel.' I said, 'Okay, what's your name?' and that's how our friendship started."

When he first started university, Viktor was very depressed. "Not because of my classmates, but because my results were very, very bad. During high school, I was one of the first in the school, and then I was one of the last. Also at that time, my grandfather Pinches passed away."

Viktor coped with this transition by becoming more involved in the Hungarian Jewish world. He went to the first Bánkitó Festival, Budapest's progressive Jewish music festival. It was a brand new festival that he knew nothing about, but his friend from university was going, so he went, too. "From the moment my bubble burst," he said, "I was desperately trying to make a new bubble."

At Bánkitó, Viktor met a girl who was looking for someone who could help her in a Jewish youth organization. He joined the organization and later became the Vice President. In that time, he also began organizing the Synagogue Tours program, which brings Jewish young people together who don't feel comfortable entering a synagogue alone. Many of them have stayed as active members in synagogues they were introduced to by the Synagogue Tours. Later, Viktor became a guide for the Hungarian Jewish Heritage Foundation and started conversations between Jews and non-Jews.

"During that time, I found what I needed," he said. "Something new and something Jewish, but something wider than what I knew before."

The bartender—a short, full-bellied man with a grey sweatshirt tied around his waist and French fry oil splashed across his punk-rock t-shirt—stepped around the bar to drop two dark red beers in pint glasses at our table. The foamy liquid swayed along the surface of the glass until it found solid ground.

Viktor was born into a fairly observant family. Originally, he did not choose his own community but rather frequented the synagogue closest to his family's flat. In high school, he felt he needed some space, so he stopped attending synagogue all together. When he turned sixteen, he started going to Chabad. At university, he began finding his new way, and finally, in 2010, he visited Budapest's main orthodox synagogue for Hanukkah. He has been an active member of that synagogue ever since.

"I have to tell you," he said, "most of the community members are not just orthodox but they are Hasidic. At first, the place didn't feel like home and the people were a bit suspicious like, 'Who are you? You are not from us.' Later, they totally accepted me."

In 2013, Viktor became an official member of the Hungarian Autonomous Orthodox Jewish Community. "I think I find myself there," he said. "I love the fact that I can improve my knowledge. Being part of this community is challenging me. If I would be a member of the reform community, I would not grow as much. I would miss having the choice of what traditions I keep and what I don't."

Though he is a member of the Hasidic community, during the weekdays, Viktor does not dress in suit or *kaftan*, the robe traditionally worn by Hasidic Jews. He wears *tzitzit*—specially knotted ritual fringes or tassels that serve as constant reminders of the Jewish obligations to G-d and fellow Jewish people—under his shirt and tucks his *payot*—side locks or side curls worn by men and boys in the orthodox tradition based on the interpretation of the Biblical injunction against shaving the corners of the head—behind his ears. "I don't break the laws," he said, "and of course, during Shabbos and holidays, I dress up properly and I put on my big hat that I got for my wedding."

Viktor took a long sip of beer. "There are many, many different ways to connect to Judaism or Jewishness," he said. Many Jews from Viktor's generation don't feel enough motivation or energy to start becoming involved in a community. Most of them find some Jewish documents while cleaning their grandmother's flat and go to Taglit because it is a free vacation. When they return to Hungary, they have enjoyed their holiday, but that's it. "It was a holiday with palm trees, seaside, some weird Jewish content and friends," Viktor said. "That's how much young Hungarian Jews are connecting to their Jewishness."

Many of these people grew up in non-observant families without strong Jewish backgrounds or knowledge. "During communism, it wasn't popular to talk about Jewish roots at all," Viktor said, "so the children don't have Jewish identities. Communism has been over for more than twenty-five years now. If our generation doesn't start to become involved somehow in a Jewish community, then our children won't be able to build strong Jewish community in Hungary either."

Viktor acknowledged that the individual must choose whether or not to engage. "In the Jewish world," he said, "it is very hard to divide the religion and the other stuff like culture and people. It's a very big step to light candles during Hanukkah, even if it's in a Jewish pub. If you are celebrating also Christmas, that's okay, too, it's a big step that at least you are doing both. The hardest task is reaching out to people and helping them to take those first steps."

Viktor's faith is the strongest aspect of his Jewish identity. "Faith is not about practice," he said. "You can practice Judaism but you cannot practice a Jewish life. Those are different. I think that if you don't have faith then you don't have a real motivation to keep the traditions and the *mitzvot* (good deeds or commandments)."

Viktor realized that his path wasn't necessarily the easiest but there was something within him that begged him to press on. "I ask myself, 'Why am I doing it?'" he said. "It would be much more easier if I don't want to be part of the orthodox community. But if I would leave the orthodox community, I would miss it so much. I am enjoying it, to be with them. That's the first community that is recognizing me, perhaps because they really need me. They are counting on me. And I am counting on them. I think that's a very good thing."

Viktor's newlywed wife entered the bar and sat alongside him. Her narrow profile turned toward Viktor as she tapped her fingers on the surface of the table. He returned her gaze and kissed her hello.

As she rose to order a glass of rosé, Viktor gazed out the window and said, "You cannot teach how to believe in G-d. You can tell people that there is a G-d, and all the stories from the Torah, but everybody has to decide for him or herself if they want to believe in HaShem (G-d) or not. Though sometimes I considered myself to be religious and other times not, my question or doubt was never whether or not I believe in G-d. Mostly, I was too young to accept all of the religious rules."

Viktor feels grateful that everyone in his family is Jewish. "I have some friends who were born into mixed families," he said. "If they had Jewish roots from their father's side but not their mother's, communities didn't accept them as full members. Some of them decided to convert to Judaism. I helped some of them during the process. I was amazed by their strong faith; all they needed was to study the laws. This is great example of how G-d can clearly exist without practicing Judaism."

Viktor also feels gratitude toward his teacher, a Hasid man who was raised in a Neolog environment. "Maybe that's why he can perfectly understand me," Viktor said. "He experienced that 'not so religious' Jewish life. He knows very well what are the challenges. He is not blind."

Viktor tipped his beer glass along the edges of its bottom rim. He narrowed his eyes and said, "I think even if you are or became religious, you have to keep the balance. I guess that if both sides of my family were orthodox when I was born, most probably I would never sit with you here and tell you about my Jewish identity." His glass stood upright on the table as he placed his hands in his lap. "You don't have to go to extremes," he said.

Viktor's thin face widened with a grin as his wife return-ed to our table with her glass of wine – the first full ear-to-ear smile I'd seen on his face since we met. The night was becoming late and our time was nearly finished. Viktor nod-ded his head to the music playing over the loudspeaker and said, "Just speak to people, with people. So many, many things in Budapest."

The three of us ordered one more round of drinks. On my walk home later, Viktor's words, "You cannot teach how to believe in G-d," bounced around the walls of my mind.

Prior to talking with Viktor, when surrounded by people who seemed to believe with the entirety of their being, I would question what disabled me from believing. Maybe I was too skeptical, or too rational, or too eager. I realized, though, that there was no right or wrong way to believe. My belief was different than Viktor's, but equal in value. Viktor confirmed in me the belief in belief, in all its diversity, colors, and forms.

"People need to realize that diversity is a value and not something to be afraid of."

IN A CLIMATE OF PESSIMISM AND DOUBT, Haver's mission and optimism encourage a spark of hope. According to its website, the Haver Foundation is a Hungarian non-profit organization that has worked for twelve years to combat prejudice and discrimination in order to promote social cohesion through dialogue, training, education, and advocacy. Haver aims to start an open and honest dialogue between Jews and non-Jews that leads to tolerance and common understanding. The staff at Haver believes it is essential to give special attention to the colorful modern Jewish life of 21st century Budapest.

I arranged to meet with the staff of Haver in their office on Károly körút, an avenue in the Seventh District. The office, located above a series of restaurants serving street-style gyros and sit-down Hungarian goulash and potatoes, is perched just a few shops away from the Dohány Street Synagogue, the largest functioning synagogue in Europe. Nearly lured away by smells of fried falafel and grilled onion, I rang the bell to the Haver apartment office. A jolting buzz signaled the release of the lock. I walked up four flights of narrow, scuffed cement stairs to reach Haver.

Bence (Bent-say), a large, stoic man, met me at the door and extended his hand. His broad shoulders and unyielding expression walked with me around the office. I discussed Haver with a stout woman preparing coffee in the kitchen and a tall, lanky man blowing cigarette smoke out of the kitchen's window. Together, Bence and I settled into swiveling chairs alongside a cluttered office table supporting stacks of papers, post-its, capped and uncapped pens and an old desktop computer.

Originally, I was sure that I was a splinter in Bence's thumb. As he escorted me toward the exit after our meeting, I mentioned I was searching for a bicycle. Bence said he had an old bike in storage that he wasn't using. He offered that I could borrow it if I wanted to.

The next week, I met Bence in the Thirteenth District to see how much it would cost to touch up his bike. His ability to negotiate with shopkeeers in Hungarian paired well with my excitement and sanguinity. Unfortunately, the shop-owner, an elderly man wearing a grease-ridden t-shirt with a slight hunch in his stance, took one look at the bike and shook his head. The bike would cost more to touch up than a used bike would cost to purchase. We left empty-handed. Technically, we left strolling with an old bike that neither one of us would use.

Rather than returning home, having offered a generous proposal that did not happen to work out, Bence made it his mission to find me a bike at an affordable price. We visited five used bike shops that afternoon. Some were closed, some were displaying bikes that were too expensive, while still others were pushing bikes that weren't worth the cost. Somewhere between the sidewalks, shops, and tires, Bence and I had a chance to talk about life beyond Haver.

Bence's hard exterior softened as we shopped. I learned that, like many of us, Bence hadn't entirely planned his life out in concrete steps, but was now trying to navigate his vocation. Bence pulled the bike to the nearest bike stand

and locked it. He nodded toward a small confectionary to our left and suggested we take a break. In Hungarian, Bence ordered two teas.

I wrapped my right hand around the body of my ceramic mug and caressed the string of the tea bag with my thumb. Bence pulled his tea bag out of his mug and laid it on a napkin, avoiding my eye contact.

Bence was born in Budapest and raised in a secular Jewish family. Three out of four of his grandparents were Jews who did not particularly identify as Jewish. All three survived the Holocaust: one in Hungary and two in concentration camps outside of Hungary. "They lost their Jewish identity," said Bence, "or they never really had one."

Following the Holocaust, they spent a significant portion of their lives in Socialist Hungary. "I imagine that was quite depressing and quite grey," Bence said. "Even though I was born in the year of the democratic change, black and white pictures and images come to my mind when I think of what it must have been like for them."

Jewishly, Bence's grandparents preferred not to differentiate themselves from any other Hungarians. They felt this way even before World War II, but after the war, they felt they had no choice but to surrender their Jewish identities. "Even my grandmother from my mother's side, who was brought up in a religious orthodox family, who used to talk Yiddish with her grandparents. Her Jewish identity did not survive the war, not after the Holocaust."

This was the environment in which Bence's parents grew up. "My parents had no connection to Judaism," he said.

"They didn't even know they were Jews until their teenage years." Years later, they realized that not only were they Jewish but many of their friends were Jewish, too.

The first generation that started to deal with the Jewish question a little bit more in depth was Bence's generation. Bence's older brother was the first person in his family to face questions of identity and spirituality more seriously. He brought tradition and knowledge about Judaism into Bence's home.

Bence kept his eyes focused on the table as he blew on the surface of his tea, preparing to take a sip. He said, "For me, I always knew I was Jewish, but for a long time, I couldn't do anything about it. I knew, 'Okay, this is something different,' but I wasn't really connected to it or its content."

At twelve years old, Bence explored the religious side of Judaism. "At first, you know, I thought Judaism is a religion, so if you want to be Jewish, you have to practice religion," he said. So, he went to shul every week on Friday night to study a different text. "I found text study to be much more interesting than doing prayers," he said. "I went to synagogue and davened but realized soon that it wasn't for me. Religion wasn't my path."

Bence set his mug on the table as a woman walked into the shop with her puli, a medium-sized Hungarian dog that presents as a sea of dark grey dreadlocks. The dog's long, corded coat spread into a circle around Bence's feet as it settled on the floor. Reaching down to pet the dog, Bence reflected that he didn't feel very comfortable at the synagogue. "I started to feel *uncomfortable,* actually," he said. "It wasn't a good feeling, but it was good that I realized it. Enough people don't realize it and they are still part of a community or an environment which they are feeling uncomfortable in."

When Bence realized that the religious aspects of Judaism weren't for him, he also realized that there were a lot of other elements to Judaism that he could discover. "Judaism is not only going to shul," he said. "There is a lot to learn, a lot to read, a lot to study."

Bence started to take part in various Jewish communities. He attended Szarvas year after year. "On a cultural level, my identity became stronger," he said. "My Jewish cultural identity is still, until today, very strong."

Bence leaned forward, his chest grazing the edge of our table. He said in a clear, meditated tone, "I realized recently that I need more."

For the last couple of years, Bence's main connection to the Jewish community has been through his work at Haver. His career with Haver is rooted in his interest in education. For a long time, Bence yearned to become a teacher. To test the waters of education, in 2009, he became a volunteer at Haver. Since 2011, he has worked full-time at Haver as an employee. "The work I do at Haver stimulates me to cultivate myself and my knowledge about Judaism," he said. "It makes me act on it."

Bence has found a place of belonging at Haver. "Diversity is the very concept," he said. "Different people who affiliate differently with Judaism somehow work together and think together."

"I think this is very important work today," Bence said. "You experience a lot of issues in Hungarian society related to anti-Semitism. There is a huge lack of solidarity and tolerance among people. You have to work very hard if you want to live in a society which is open and tolerant, where anyone with any religion, belief or culture can be free."

Haver is one tool working toward that society, but alone, it is not enough. "People need to realize that diversity is a value and not something to be afraid of," Bence said. "For that, you need to educate people."

Outside of Haver, Bence works on a variety of projects to generate meaning in his life. "I want to do something that benefits the wider community or wider society," he said.

Right now, he sees those projects based in Budapest. If Bence were to ever move away from Hungary, it would not be because of his Jewish identity.

"I will not move because I am a Jew and I feel threatened," he said. "I may feel uncomfortable being a liberal, a free, independent thinker, or a critic of the system, but that's different."

For Bence, to be a free, independent thinker is like being an outsider anywhere, anytime. "It's connected to Judaism but it's bigger than that," he said. "On a psychological level, from very early ages, I felt this thing like being an outsider. It's good, I mean… once you realize it, you become more aware of things and you can become a more conscious person.

"Feeling like an outsider, though, is intimidating. It's a positive thing only if you convert it to a positive thing. Asking questions or facing a dilemma and not having answers all the time can be scary."

Bence bent to pet the puli's head but the dog lifted its chin to lick his fingers instead.

"For me, I am okay with being alone," he said. "I am okay with standing up for rights, or to say stuff out loud when I feel that it must be said out loud. It wasn't always that way and I understand that it can be very hard. Just know that it gets better."

Bence sat up and took a deep breath. "I try to live my life making as little harm as possible, to nature and to people," he said. "That is what makes me the most happy."

Gazing at the dog between our feet, I realized that my first impression of Bence was flawed. What seemed stoic or uninterested was confidence and stability that did not need to be externally affirmed.

Bence stood to pay the bill and I walked outside to unlock the bike. Together, we walked away from the café toward our respective homes, wheels wobbling between us.

VERA FÉNIÁSZ

"After a while, you have to realize that you have the power, too.
Our work is to put the power in everyone."

I SAT IN JELEN AT A LOW-TOP wooden table for two, lightly decorated with Sharpie tags of those who sat there before me. I picked at a slab of lavendar paint chipping away from the surface. A beautiful teenage woman approached me. She introduced herself as Vera (Veer-ah), tossed her shoulder-length blonde hair out of her face and sat down at the other side of the table.

Vera is nineteen years old. She is co-running Hanoar Hatzioni Hungary, a youth organization utilizing informal education to teach children to shape their own opinions, think for themselves and make decisions based on core human values. Like Szarvas, Hanoar provides an avenue for young Jews to find themselves and to find community. As the co-director, Vera is a role model by trade.

A mutual friend introduced me to Vera while I was selling clothes at a vintage clothes market in mid-autumn. Within a few days, Vera and I set a time to meet to discuss our mutual perspectives further. Her hair reflected the red and blue lights of the café and her voice was smooth and clear over the live music playing behind us.

Vera tapped her foot on the floor at a quicker tempo than the music. In her charming Hungarian accent, she told me a short story.

"This is one of my favorite one," she said. "It says that the king Herodes in Christ's time ask the people, 'Who should I kill?' You know the story, right? Everyone alone said the killer's name. But together, the whole nation, sounds like 'Jesus.' So this is why Jesus died. This is my life's philosophy. Everyone is good...but when it's a society, when it's a group...it's harder."

Vera's grandparents on her father's side were Jewish. From her mother's side, she is half Gypsy and half Christian. "So, I am a good one!" she laughed, shaking her shoulders but maintaining a steady, upright posture.

A young waiter approached our table and admiringly smiled at Vera. She ordered a soda and I ordered my usual latte. She explained that actually, her father did not know that he was Jewish until he was about eighteen. "It was war, it was communism," she said. "It was a lot of problems." People hid not just that they were Jewish, but that they were any kind of religious.

"They could have faith only in the government at that time," Vera said. "But me? And all of my brothers and my sister? I wouldn't say they treat us as Jewish. They told us, 'Your mom is Christian and your father is Jewish. You can choose whether you want to go to synagogue or church, if you want to pray or not, if you believe in G-d or not.'"

Vera first connected with Judaism as a child when she spent weekends with her father's parents. Her grandfather went to synagogue alone every Friday night while she spent time with her grandmother. In the morning, when Shabbat was still in, Vera went to synagogue with her grandfather. "I remember that, just the grandpa and me," she said. "I got my best dress on, I was the most beautiful little girl, and we went to synagogue."

This experience inspired a real passion in Vera. "I remember everything," she said. "The Kiddush, the prayers. I was almost the only girl, so I had to be separately, but it was so good for me. I was really interested and I loved it."

When Vera was seven, she spent the summer at Szarvas for the first time. "It's two weeks and it was the best two weeks of my life," she said. "Opening for me, totally. I saw that there are some other kids who know about Judaism and some who don't. Actually, it wasn't about Judaism or not, it was friends, and good people, and teenagers looking after us, no parents or old people. It was only the youth. We were together and we had fun. The biggest thing was that during the dinner, or the lunch, we could stand on the chairs to cheer song. It was unbelievable for a kid." This past summer was Vera's thirteenth year at Szarvas.

A few years ago, one of the Szarvas staff members asked Vera to be a counselor at Szarvas, which would require two years of training. Vera remembered, "I think I was already in the training, because I knew that you born, you be a *chanich* (camper), you be a *madricha* (counselor), and then you die. This is the rule of life." At that moment, however, she did not have the time to commit.

"It's not true," she said. "It's not about time. I was sixteen and my dream was boys and parties. I love kids, but I was like, 'No, not now.'"

Vera hinted a sarcastic smile but kept a serious face. Our waiter dropped off our drinks and lingered to listen to pieces of Vera's story. She said the same staff member asked her a second time to become a counselor. She remembered he said, "Vera, we have to sit down me-and-me, not in Facebook, but me-and-me." She met with him and he told her,

"Okay, I won't say any lies, we want you." She immediately responded, "Okay, I want it." She was ready.

So, she began the training. "Best two years of my life," she said. "Just knowledge, knowledge, knowledge. I changed a lot in that two years. I learned how to work in groups. We were such a community. I was always a one-work person. But now I know: I need to learn more."

Then, the group leader, who was twenty-one years old, announced his departure from the program. "He felt he has to move on, that he was robbing someone else's place," Vera said. "I cried for an hour. He was the one! He could not do this!"

Vera ducked her chin to her chest and looked at the bubbles of paint on the surface of the table. "I cried a lot, like, really, a lot," she said. "I felt I lost my place in the world. I was confused. Then, the big change happened in me."

Vera traveled to Turkey for an international meeting of the youth counselors. She saw that physically her community was massive. "A lot of people really believe in the same thing," she said. "They treat kids in the same way."

She went to the group leader and said, "I want more." He responded, "I know."

Vera's eyes widened. "It was all planned!" she exclaimed. "Everything was a big play because they knew that I have something which will make me the leader." Vera's sass shined through her teeth-bearing grin. "It was a big scene," she said. "I was so terrified."

I envied how instinctively Vera admitted fear. In the face of a new chapter and a momentous leadership opportunity, of course she was terrified. However, it is not every day you hear someone say it.

Today, Vera is leading the Hungarian team with her partner. They manage ten active counselors and host programs every Saturday. "I love it," she said. Last year, she and her partner hosted around one hundred and forty campers, the youngest of whom was only five years old. Vera said, "I think it's a really big thing that there are parents that say, 'I believe you and I think my child will be safe with you.'"

Vera teaches not only about Shabbat and the technicalities of Jewish holidays but also teaches about values and human ethics. "You teach them that everyone is equal," she said. "They will always remember that. It's really hard work, but this is why we do it, actually. If it wouldn't be hard, they wouldn't need me."

Vera's favorite aspect of her community is that every person has their own goal. "This is how you find your motivation," she said. "I cannot tell you that this will be your goal so reach it. Everyone has to find: *Why are you doing it? Why?*"

Regarding her own goal, Vera said, "I really want to change the world. I know it's stupid, but I'm nineteen. I have to think like this." Vera's primary focus is the school system. "It's really bad in Hungary," she said. "It's always one step forward and two steps back. I just want the kids to *think* and to ask questions because if you ask questions, you have something in your head with the answer, too. And if you have answers, you can build a better place."

Our waiter cleared our empty glasses and hesitated, as though he were eager to leave his number on a napkin.

Vera said she hoped that one day, there would be many more movements like Hanoar in Hungary. "It can be without Judaism," she said. "It's not about Judaism. It's about having something, every week, where we can *speak*. People are not speaking anymore. This is the main goal, to sit down and say, 'What is your opinion?' I don't care about what. But open your mind. Communicate. Everyone thinks, 'Okay, if you are online, I communicate with you.' It's not communication. This is my main goal. It's a big one, I know, but you have to dream big to reach something."

Vera uncrossed her legs and placed her hands in her lap. She sighed, "I hate that I don't want to be here. I *want* to be here. This is my dream to live in Budapest. This is my country, my language. I love this place. I hate that there are some really, really bad opinions. It's taught me to be happy. I mean, really happy. My parents have money, I have a good boyfriend, I have friends, I have clothes, I have a good school. I am happy. I know I am clever enough to go to a really good university. But what about my kids? What if I don't have work? The problem is not with my life. My life is really good. But actually, I am living in a bubble. What happens outside of it?"

For Vera, her life is Budapest. "People should come to Budapest," she said. "I love this city, I love these people. But Hungary is everything outside of Budapest, actually," she said. Much fewer people live in Budapest than in the countryside. Few movements work to make things better outside of Budapest. "I am not patient," she said. "I want big steps. We have to change a whole nation's thinking."

Vera is not exactly sure what her next steps will be but she looks to fields of pedagogy, psychology, and social work for inspiration. She has found courses on drama pedagogy in university catalogs. "It's pedagogy, but with games," she said. "For example, if there are some kids who are really behaving a bad way, or it's really hard to catch them to concentrate, I could build a group from these kids, and play once a week. I have to learn those games that are helpful. But actually, I already know a lot of games like this because we are teaching informally at Hanoar. I like it."

Vera credits her family with her strength. "Somehow, I know that if I want something in my life, I will reach it. I am that kind," she said. "Everyone is like this in my family. And actually, we do it. We are really hard workers. I believe in work. I know it's not the same for everyone, but for me, the shape of what I saw is that my mom worked, my father worked, my brother worked, and they achieved; so this is what I believe in. I believe in work and people. I really believe that everyone is good. You just have to find in what. Maybe someone is not the kindest person, but maybe he is really good at math. I hate math, but it's good that he's good at math. I believe in everybody."

Vera lifted her gaze. "People always think that someone else has the power," she said. "They don't know that the power is in *us*. They are thinking like someone else has to fix the problem. I was the same. Remember? I was really afraid when our leader told me he was going to leave. After a while, you have to realize that you have the power, too. Our work is to put the power in everyone."

Despite the political or economic hardships felt in Budapest, I found that individuals native to Budapest were more passionate about their city than I was about any of the cities I had ever lived in. Before parting from Vera, we planned excursions around the city that we would embark on together. We paid the bill and migrated toward the band playing at the far end of the bar.

I nodded my head in rhythm with the drums and tucked my hands into my jacket pockets. Vera wrapped her arm around my shoulder and swayed.

MARCELL KENESEI

"The uniqueness of our stories is that they are about Jewish life and not Jewish extermination."

I WALKED THROUGH THE MAIN ENTRANCE of Köleves, a Jewish-and-Hungarian-themed, locally-sourced, home-style restaurant. I expected to see a gathering of familiar faces for Mircea's farewell party. Mircea, the director of the Haver Foundation, was stepping down from his position.

Amidst a slew of pieces of hand-drawn wall art by local Jewish artists, tables full of diners, and smells of roast goose leg and sweet red cabbage, I saw no one I recognized. I walked outside and turned the corner to enter Köleves' adjacent outdoor garden bar and dining area. Past multi-colored hammocks, wooden painted tables and bright red, green, and blue chairs, still, I saw no one I recognized.

Suddenly, I remembered there was a formal event space upstairs and returned to the restaurant. I climbed the stairs, out of breath, and saw Bence at the top. Bence was responsible for coordinating Mircea's farewell party and had scored me my invite. Pacing from one side of the corridor to the other, practicing his speech, he did not notice my arrival. I chose not to disturb him and proceeded through the crowd in the hope of finding other friends and acquaintances.

The space was more expansive than I remembered. One entire room was devoted to drinks and appetizers; plates of hummus, falafel, and chopped tomato and cucumber Israeli salad floated around the room. Glasses of white, red, and rosé wine stood atop a table along the wall, patiently waiting their turn to be held and enjoyed. I walked into the next room to find a dozen tables decorated with romantically lit candles and blue and silver metallic balloons. I scanned the room and noticed quite a few friends who were all volunteers for Haver. I took the time to prepare a plate of Mediterranean appetizers and relieved a glass of white wine before sitting alongside my friends at a table in the back of the room. Within moments, Bence clinked his glass with his fork to initiate the event.

The entire celebration took place in Hungarian. I simultaneously felt out of place and grateful to have been invited. I sat quietly with curious eyes, examining body language and overanalyzing emotions. Bence seemingly thanked everyone for coming and introduced the first speaker. Then the second. Then the third. The series of individuals spoke, I imagined, about how Haver has changed their lives and how Mircea was an irreplaceable leader. My mind examined eyes welling with tears, hands wafting the air mid-speech, and laughs erupting from the crowd after a joke or a story. I longed to understand their words but felt moved by the rare opportunity to ponder their emotions as they were: raw and out of context.

Next in line was a man with slender brown eyes, bushy black eyebrows and an arched, prominent nose. He stood tall, lean and confident. When he laughed, I found myself laughing, too. I asked my neighbor for more information about this man. She whispered to me, "His name is Marcell (Mar-tzell) Kenesei (Ken-eh-she). He used to volunteer with Haver and has since nurtured a strong relationship with Mircea. Now, he is the director of Centropa."

Marcell's dark skin tone and defined bone structure set him apart from the average Hungarian physique. In place of note cards, he spoke with a charisma that warmed the room.

His hands flowered around him. As he spoke, I realized that I had actually quoted him in my original Kickstarter campaign video. As a young, influential activist, his name and picture appeared in many of the news articles I was reading about Budapest. As fate would have it, I had scheduled an interview with Marcell via email for two days after the farewell party.

After Marcell finished his speech, I timidly introduced myself and congratulated him on a speech-well-delivered. I parted from the event eager to learn more about Marcell and his perspective.

I met Marcell near his office at a restaurant-pub that close friends of his owned and operated called Konyha, or "kitchen" in Hungarian. I explained my project briefly to Marcell, though he assured me he was already familiar with it. Our waiter approached our table and we each ordered the lunch special: cabbage soup and a fried zucchini patty with potatoes.

Marcell was born in Budapest in 1983. He grew up in a secular, liberal, non-religious home. He is the younger brother to one brother and one sister. He comes from a mixed marriage; his father is Jewish and his mother is not.

Marcell, widely known as a Jewish and human rights activist, is not Jewish by law. Judaism is a matrilineal religion, which means that only individuals with Jewish mothers are legally Jewish. "I never thought of this as a problem," he said. "My Jewish identity is very strong in me, and some people who are Jewish by law have less of an identity than I do."

It is not uncommon for members of strong Jewish communities to view mixed marriage and intermarriage as a threat to Judaism. "I think it's bullshit," Marcell said. "I understand the concerns, but in Europe, I think the biggest threat to Judaism is not to allow mixed marriages and not to allow people to be Jewish because they have a non-Jewish husband or wife and to think in Jewish absolutes."

After all, Marcell questioned, "You know, what is Judaism? Is it the people? Is it a nation? Is it a religion? Is it a cultural heritage or a shared faith? The answer is always: name it. It is whatever you want it to be. It's all of it, or a combination of them. Judaism will survive if more and more people who are Jewish find their Judaism in some way or another. If people don't realize this, then that will be the end of Judaism."

Marcell explained that he didn't gain his Jewish knowledge from his father's side or his mother's side. Judaism wasn't really talked about when he was growing up. Judaism was a taboo particularly for Marcell's father, who grew up in a communistic environment. He was born in 1944, making him a Holocaust survivor. He did not know he was Jewish until he turned twelve or thirteen when his brother came home and started to say anti-Semitic things. At that point, Marcell's grandmother decided, "We don't want you to be Jewish, but you have to know that you have some Jewish ancestry, so be careful what you say."

Marcell never met his grandparents. He said, "They belonged to a generation that wanted to protect their children from what happened to them during the Second World War.

They were hiding, you know. Most of my family was unfortunately exterminated. Those who survived, it was their survival strategy not to identify with Judaism."

Marcell's grandparents welcomed communism and socialism as an opportunity for religious differences to be nullified. He said, "Just imagine a person who lost his whole family comes back and is hated by everyone. There was no feeling that 'Oh, you survived, it's so good you came back.' No. Jews who came back, others were shouting at them that, 'Oh no, more of you came back than there were.' Judaism was a burden for these individuals because it almost killed them. Communism provided something that eliminated all of the religious differences. It didn't, but they didn't know that. With time, they got to know. My father said that it was part of his health getting worse that he saw the system failing. You never know."

It wasn't until Marcell was researching different high schools that he was first presented with Jewish education. His mother asked him what he would think about going to Lauder. Lauder is a Jewish school that opened in 1989 when Hungary transitioned from communism to democracy. Marcell said, "I knew that it was a Jewish school, and I knew that it was a new school, but I didn't consider it as a Jew school. I thought my mother wanted to send me there because of this liberal, alternative school, which gives a different kind of education. It's not a regular state school. I thought she wanted to provide her youngest son with something different."

Marcell thought attending Lauder was a good idea. He said, "It was a fabulous building with a lot of happy people. The classes were small and very focused on the individual. I never thought it was because I was Jewish." He enrolled with his cousin for the next year.

At Lauder, Marcell learned about Jewish philosophy, Jewish holidays and Jewish summer camp. He started to ask questions. During this process, he realized, "Oh, we are Jewish!"

Marcell smirked, teasing himself for not realizing this sooner. Eventually, Marcell and his cousin convinced their parents to begin celebrating the Passover Seder. Seder is a religious dinner celebrated during the first and second nights of Passover, an eight-night holiday commemorating the Jews' emancipation from slavery in Egypt.

Prior to these dinners, Marcell's family only celebrated the Christian holidays, especially Christmas and Easter. Marcell said, "All of a sudden, the Christian and Jewish holidays started to compete with each other. Seder night and Pesach (Passover) became enormously popular because of the glasses of wine you had to drink and the whole family getting together. At first, my cousin was the rabbi, and then I was the rabbi. It was a huge laughter. Everybody had a great time. Over the years, it became the main holiday. It even beat Easter!"

Marcell's excitement about Judaism spread to other family members, including Marcell's brother, sister and other cousins. "They also developed some kind of Jewish identity," he said, "or, if not a Jewish identity, then some kind of connection to this Jewish *thing*."

At this time, Marcell confronted the word *identity*. "Before that, I had no idea where I belonged or what I should do," he said. "My family's Jewish roots became a thing I was very interested in. What happened to us? What would this family have if the Second World War never happened? What is this whole genocide? What do the Jewish people know that they wanted to exterminate them so badly? What is the big secret?" Marcell furiously sought the answers to these questions.

Marcell sat back in his chair as the waiter placed a steaming bowl of soup in front of each of us. He said in the end, he discovered that being Jewish meant being surrounded by Jewish friends and family. "And then...it stuck," he said. "I had all my friends from these Jewish schools and these Jewish summer camps, I attended Jewish events. It became slowly, slowly important to me to do something."

After high school, Marcell earned a university degree in political science. "When I finished," he said," I didn't know what to do with myself. I certainly didn't want to practice my profession. I was looking for a way out."

Then came Paideia, the European Institute for Jewish Studies in Stockholm, Sweden. Marcell said, "I finished university studies in June or July 2007 and I went to Sweden in August for one year." The one-year Paideia program is designed to immerse young Jewish adults in Jewish education, text, culture and politics. While studying at Paideia, Marcell decided he wanted to do something Jewish professionally. "It was very inspiring," he said," not only intell-ectually, but mostly because of the connections I made and different communities I saw."

When Marcell returned from Paideia in 2008, he had already been volunteering for the Haver Foundation since its foundation in 2002. His mentor, Mircea, and his colleagues hired Marcell as one of the first employees of the Israeli Cultural Institute (ICI). Marcell was responsible for reso-urce development and fundraising. "I don't know if it was a good idea for the state of the institution," he said, "because I had no experience in fundraising. Then again, not so many people actually did in this country. Mircea and the people who hired me thought, you know, I am an investment."

Once Marcell began working at ICI, he wanted to remain in the Jewish professional circle. In 2011, the Director pos-ition opened at the Hungarian branch of Centropa. He jum-ped at the opportunity. He has been acting as director of Centropa ever since.

Centropa is the Central European Center for Research and Documentation. Marcell is primarily responsible for all of the public school programs Centropa has in Hungary. He has also created a network called the Centropa Jewish Net-work, which is an association for teachers who teach in Eur-opean Jewish Schools.

Centropa has conducted 1,300 audiotaped oral intervi-ews with Holocaust survivors in Central and Eastern Eur-ope. These interviews focus more on how Jews lived before and after the Holocaust than how they perished during the Holocaust. Centropa gives the interviewee the freedom to discuss any topic they wish. If the interviewee chooses to go into more detail about the Holocaust, they may. However, Centropa staff asks more questions about the person's life, for example, how the person was raised, how they fell in love, and how they had come to live. The interviewees tended to not want to speak as much about the Holocaust because they had already been interviewed so many times about that topic.

Marcell said, "The uniqueness of our stories is that they are about Jewish life and not Jewish extermination." The other uniqueness is that Centropa digitized 22,000 family photographs after conducting these interviews. The photographs come from both pre-WWII and post-WWII. "The photos help us understand what it looked like to be Jewish in Hungary," Marcell said. "There are different stories. There are religious people from the countryside, there are urban people who are more secular, and they all tell their stories. They tell stories about how they were fired from their job, how they went to school and how they went on vacation. What kind of bathing suit they were wearing. Everything."

These stories help teachers approach Holocaust education in a different way. "A lot of teachers have a great problem with the Holocaust because they don't know how to make students interested in the topic," Marcell said. "Students will not be interested if you show them the extermination and the horror. That's how to make a distance between the topic and the student. If you start from the beginning, if you start from the story of this little girl, who grew up here, and went to this school, then they themselves will ask the question: What happened with her during the war? If you arrive at this point, then something will stick."

Centropa creates short multi-media films from their best interviews. They animate the family photos and tell the family story in ten to fifteen minutes. These stories engage students in something different. "If you give a lecture and they have to write a test at the end," Marcell said, "they might remember the historical facts and the statistics for the test. One week after, they will forget everything. However, if they participate in something, if they do a video project of their Jewish history, if they become student tour guides for our traveling exhibition, or if they watch one of our films, there will be a much better chance that they will actually remember what they have learned during the process."

Centropa utilizes training programs and seminars to share its methodology with public school teachers. "You don't want to teach history, you want the students to explore history," Marcell said. "We develop a partnership with teachers rather than giving them lectures and sending them home with a box. We don't have a box curriculum. We don't even have a box. What we do is we show them how our website works, our interactive online everything, reachable for everyone, how they can look for photos, for stories, and for films, and then we ask them to work. We have them sit together in small groups and write lesson plans. Then, the lesson plans are uploaded to our website under educational materials and teachers use them."

Centropa not only involves the teachers in the development of programs and lessons but also tries as often as possible to involve the students themselves. All of Centropa's interviews, media, and lesson plans can be found on its searchable, key-worded online database called *Jewish Witness to a European Century*. Its complex online education platform is currently used in more than five hundred schools in sixteen countries.

Our waiter reappeared at our table, removed our empty bowls and replaced them with large plates of long, golden patties filled with soft, flaky slices of zucchini and spotted, grilled red potatoes on the side.

Jewish Hungarians believe that Hungary has the biggest potential for reviving European Judaism because Budapest has 100,000 Jewish people living within its walls.

"That might be true if 100,000 Jewish people living here had some kind of Jewish connection," Marcell said, "but only ten percent of these people have a Jewish identity. More than two-thirds of these people do not even consider themselves to be Jewish. Some of them do not even know they are Jewish."

Marcell proposed that the way to approach these individuals is not the same way you would approach a group of Jews. "This is the main mistake people make," he said. "They want to strengthen Jewish identity. The biggest challenge is not strengthening identity in those that already have it but forming identity in those who don't to make the circle bigger."

One struggle Marcell identified in Jewish Budapest is a lack of transparency. Jewish events, people, and communities are well and strong but the formal institutions like government and synagogues are not transparent. The arguments between the institutions threaten potential community members into keeping their distance.

Another obstacle is that many people who would otherwise be interested in Judaism and verbally identify as Jewish culturally are uneducated about Judaism and its various applications. Marcell explained, "They would never think of celebrating a Jewish holiday because they are secular people. They don't give a shit. They don't think it's worth it. How I see it, it's worth it to do it even if you are not religious. It's a lot of fun. It gives a special taste to our kids. It's identity."

Marcell would like to see more initiatives that encourage an open dialogue about spirituality and community. "We have Jewish communities where people can find themselves," he said. "They have a very different approach, I would say the 'hippie-cool' approach, and I think that is a very good direction. I don't say it's *the* direction. I say it's a very good direction to reach out to more and more people."

Marcell sees Judaism as more than a religion. "People have to understand and see through thinking of Judaism as a religion or Jewish people as those people who support Israel. Yes, there are some Jewish people who support Israel and there are some Jewish people who are religious but it actually does not cover even half of the people who we should consider becoming members of the community."

Despite challenges, Marcell maintains that Jewish Budapest is headed in the right direction. "Hungarians have the tendency to complain about a lot of things," he said. "They have a tendency to complain about the number of Jews because 'it's not growing' or 'we are not reaching out.' Just look at the number fifteen years ago. It's not something that will happen in a year or two. It happens over decades and I think we are on the right track."

The next needed step is for Jewish Budapest to become financially self-sustainable. Marcell predicts that the money the official Federation of Jewish communities receives from the Hungarian government does not actually reach at least twenty percent of Hungarian Jews.

Additionally, Marcell worries that the Hungarian synagogue members tasked with representing Jewish Hungary in government fail to represent the wide variety of individuals in Hungary who actually identify as Jewish. "I don't see that the formal synagogue members represent me," he said, "and most people I know don't see them as a representation, either. Yet, the same synagogue members continue to sit in parliament."

Marcell fears that the current representation does not do enough to grow the circle of Hungarian Jews because they are so attached to their particular interpretation of Judaism. "The circle can only get bigger if it gets more colorful," he said. He looks forward to Heisler, the new president of the Federation of Jewish Communities, opening the door to new communities. "He has this vision to open the gate in front of civil non-profit Jewish organizations and reform movement and all this kind of stuff. It's not just a good idea, it's a complete necessity. What the hell are you waiting for?"

While Marcell supports the new government's idea to reform the Jewish system, involve more perspectives in the discussion and distribute money to more institutions, he does not trust the government not to create double standards or to say one thing and to do another, especially against those who disagree.

Marcell's values have evolved with his relationship to his Jewish identity. "I am definitely more secure in myself and what I believe in," he said. "I think one of the core values of Judaism is to pass it on. All the Jewish parents are investing everything they have in children and in education. I think the Jewish value of debate as a constructive way of getting to know our own ideas is very inspiring. These are things that originate in a religious tradition but can be saved in a secular background. When we talk about Jewish continuity, how Jewish people can survive, and what Judaism will consist of, if it will not be religion, then it will be the values that we embrace and it will be the things that we prioritize."

For Marcell, being Jewish carries with it a sensitivity to minorities and minority rights. "I am so glad I have this sensitivity in me," he said. "Whenever I am in a situation, I always try to look at myself from the outside and see the perspective. Always, there is the example of what happened to Jews and my family. Without Judaism, I don't think I would have that perspective. I am sure I wouldn't."

Marcell is fairly sure that his grandparents would be upset with what he is doing and where he is heading. His father's mother, who died before Marcell was born, was very much against anything Jewish. "Even mentioning Jewish things upset her," Marcell said. He imagines that if his grandparents saw the way the Hungarian government is behaving, they would feel a resemblance to pre-WWII Hungary. He said, "I am not among those people who think that it's the same. I certainly don't think we are on a corner of the next Holocaust."

Marcell credits his confidence and fortuitous circumstances partially to luck but mostly to his parents. Marcell's parents have always been very supportive of his decisions. He admires his father for his grace and acceptance of Marcell's decision to pursue a Jewish life. "My father always made jokes about me, that he is the only halachically Jewish person in the family and I am telling him what Judaism is," he said. "He was making fun of me all the time but in a way that is proud."

The waiter gracefully placed the bill on the table. Marcell admitted he needed to run to a meeting at the Centropa office. He stood and placed his portion of the bill on the table. He shared one final story.

Marcell remembered finding a picture in an old family album from when he had first celebrated Hanukkah with his family. He was lighting the candles with a kepot on his head. As he flipped through the album, he noticed that his father subtitled each picture with an anecdote. The subtitle he gave to this picture was, "Only if my mother saw this..."

Marcell smiled and stood to bid me farewell with a kiss on each cheek.

I sat at our table for a few moments after Marcell's departure. The waiter carried away our paid bill with our empty plates. He returned with a moist towel and wiped the surface of the table clean.

A couple entered through the front door of the café with a scurrying black dog only to find that all of the tables were occupied. They asked whether they could share my table with me. The dog, whose eyes hid behind its frizzy curly hair, settled between my feet and began licking my toes. I knelt to pet my new friend and offered the table to its owners.

As I prepared to leave, Marcell's friends waved goodbye from behind the counter. I smiled, waved and turned toward the door.

TAMÁS VERÖ

"Strength is a blessing. It's family and community.
Just like that."

THE FOUR/SIX YELLOW TRAM crosses the city of Budapest east to west and takes me anywhere I want or need to go. I am able to take the tram to *Margitsziget* (Margaret Island), which has a 5.35 kilometer circumference lined with track perfectly designed for runners, or to Jászai Mari Tér, where youthful Jews with artistic tendencies and young families live, eat and drink. The tram also runs beyond Pest into Buda, the half of Budapest on the other side of the Danube River.

This morning, I rode the tram from my apartment in the Eighth District of Pest across *Margit Híd* (Margaret Bridge) to *Frankel Leó utca* (Frankel Leó street) in Buda. Stepping off the tram, I walked the length of the tram platform, covered in bright yellow cautionary paint warning against stepping onto the tram tracks, and turned right. I walked another ten minutes, up and down small hills of pavement, past various homes, stores, and neighbors, until I reached the *Frankel Leó Zsinagóga*, or Frankel Leó Synagogue.

I was relieved to find the synagogue, well hidden inside the courtyard of a beige and white six-story apartment building. My relief was shaken when I realized the cold, thick black gate guarding the synagogue was locked. Scratched, silver metal bars peeked through layers of deteriorating black paint. Peering through the bars, I realized that this synagogue took over almost the entire courtyard. Rows of red brick surrounded two white pillars that hugged great wooden doors engraved with two large Stars of David. The roof of the synagogue, resting just one story lower than the roof of the apartment building boxing it in, boasted white ceramic tiles ascending like stairs climbing to heaven. I lifted my gaze to the buzzer box. There was no button for Frankel Leó Zsinagóga. I agreed to meet Rabbi Tomi in seven minutes. The crisp air raised goose bumps on my forearms as I waited.

Two minutes passed. I continued to wait, tempted to ring every buzzer until the synagogue answered.

A stranger approached the gate from the inside, preparing to exit. He released the lock and let me inside.

I walked two meters through what remained of the courtyard and pushed firmly on the door of the synagogue. It budged open. I slipped inside and closed the door.

Upon entering the prayer hall, children whizzed past me, yelling and laughing. Papers flew off of benches. One woman standing by the door observed the chaos.

At the opposite corner of the prayer hall, I noticed a man whose large, round eyes, plump build, and booming laugh were unmistakable. This man was Rabbi Tomi. He drew closer, whispered, "One minute," and motioned toward a seat.

"Still or sparkling?" he offered. He handed me a bottle of still water and I sat peacefully, swishing the water around in my mouth before swallowing each gulp. The children left in pairs and the synagogue grew increasingly quiet.

As I waited for Rabbi Tomi, I took in the beauty of the synagogue. The prayer hall simultaneously embraced history's traditional decor and innovated a modern presence. The *bimah*—the raised platform in a synagogue from which the Torah is read—stood strong in the front center of the room, illuminated by natural light. The rows of wooden benches facing the bimah looked maintained yet lived in.

Rabbi Tomi politely interrupted my gaze. "Hi, nice to meet you. Ready to begin?"

Talking with Rabbi Tomi reminded me of what it might feel like to talk with a close grandfather. Scents of fresh wood and distant cigarettes filled the air as Rabbi Tomi, dressed in a light blue button down, a sweater vest, and jeans, sat next to me. His protruding stomach and deeply broken English were effortlessly charming. Tomi was average height and balding beneath his oversized black kippah. He emphasized an open-door policy and insisted that I come visit the synagogue more often.

Both sides of Tomi's family were made up of Holocaust survivors. His grandmother on one side was an Auschwitz survivor, while his grandmother on the other side survived by hiding in the home of a generous and courageous non-Jewish family. Judaism was important to his family, he said.

Tomi's parents' wedding was the first Jewish wedding in Hungary where both the bride and the groom were born after the Second World War. "Their wedding was here in this synagogue," Tomi said. "I grew up here, too, in this synagogue. My Talmud Torah—the school where young boys learn elementary Hebrew, Scripture, and Talmud—was here. My bar mitzvah was here."

Tomi's eyes welled. "Now *I* am doing here the weddings and the bar mitzvah!" he said. Not only did he wind up where he started, but he was also able to give back to other children, young adults, and adults a piece of what this place had given him.

During the Communist Era, it was forbidden for people to pray in groups. "If people practiced," Tomi said, "the next day, you would always be asked, 'What was happening yesterday night in your house?' People knew everything you were doing and it was dangerous. The communists wanted to show that everybody can do whatever, but really, it was like...you can go, *if you want*."

Still, Tomi's parents wanted to show him and his siblings what Judaism meant to them. They didn't keep kosher or the Jewish holidays very strictly, but they did go to synagogue with their children.

In the context of a discouraging external political and social environment, Tomi took pride in the reality that his parents continued to prioritize Judaism. He peered over his shoulder and gazed at the prayer hall behind him. He turned back to me and extended his arms like a tour guide. "Frankel Leó," he said. "We are calling every synagogue in Hungary the same name like the street. On Frankel Leó utca, we are Frankel Leó Zsinagóga. We are a Neolog synagogue."

The Neolog sect of Judaism in Hungary began one hundred and fifty years ago. One group of orthodox Jews disagreed with another group of orthodox Jews over Judaism's best practices. One of the two groups founded the Neolog sect. There are four main differences between Neolog and orthodox: first, Neolog allows the organ to be used on Shabbat and on other Jewish holidays; second, Neolog allows the sermon be given in the Hungarian language;

third, Neolog allows male congregants to sit on the same level as female congregants; and fourth, Neolog allows for less formal dress.

"Neologs want to bring the Jewish people back to the Judaism," Tomi said. "It is about starting a new Judaism but still keeping what it was before. New but old." Neolog practitioners follow traditions but adjust regulations in a way that hopes to be more inviting to more people.

Tomi explained that though Neolog was originally intended to be far more observant than reform but less legalistic than orthodox, the practice of Neolog has changed in recent years. Congregants tend to cling to the title of Neolog and hold tightly onto particular rules while still limiting their education and knowledge in many ways. He said, "I think that most of my congregants, like, ninety out of one hundred person, they are Neolog and they know less about Judaism than the reform, they keep less rituals and traditions than the reform, but they won't accept anytime a woman rabbi, they won't accept mixed sitting in the synagogue, or they won't accept if we try to call the woman to the Torah to read. They don't know so much but they do want to hold on to some aspects of the past."

Tomi has made his own adjustments to the practice of Neolog Judaism in his synagogue. "Here I kicked out the organ," he said, "because the people were just sitting here. When I came with the organ, they would just listen, they didn't pray. Now, without the organ, we are praying together and singing together. Good feeling."

I appreciated that Tomi was able to embrace the importance of tradition while still acknowledging the value of adaptation. He grew up Neolog but does not feel attached to the Neolog tradition. "I'm a little more modern orthodox," he said. "I try to teach, but the first step is always to get people here. Then, when they are here, we can teach."

Various Jewish communities in Budapest support a mindset that encourages practice, Jewish values, and Jewish tradition, but embraces community above all else. Tomi recognizes that not everyone was raised in an observant home; thus, he tries to meet people where they are.

The Frankel Leó Synagogue community is growing. "We have more young people and many, many who had the children in the families," Tomi said. In Hungary, and specifically in Budapest, many young adults attend the synagogue that their parents went to, if their parents went to synagogue. "It doesn't matter that they don't live in that area," Tomi said. "So, in this synagogue, people come from everywhere Budapest. It's very diverse."

Tomi did not decide as a child that he wanted to be a rabbi. "The rabbi seminar was the only place where I could study Judaism and also work with people," he said. "It's not because I want to become a rabbi, but then slowly, the people accept me like a rabbi, so I accept myself like a rabbi."

Tomi's shoulders slouched and he exhaled slowly. He tilted his head side to side, searching for the words.

He said there are two sides to the story of Judaism in Hungary. "One side," he said, "it's very dangerous here and we have guards, security in the synagogue, and guarding me at home also. But the other side, it's true that more and more people are trying to find the roots and that's why they are coming to the synagogue. Many, many people are finding Judaism as the place where they can relax, find the *sholom* (peace). With my wife, we are making a Seder night for two hundred families, so I can say that now, it's like *Canaan* (Promised Land)."

Szarvas is not only Tomi's favorite thing about Jewish Hungary, but is also Tomi's favorite thing about Hungary as a country. He was at the camp in 1989 when it first opened and has gone every summer since. "So, if you ask Hungary, that's Szarvas," he said. "Every summer I spend there. Every year, we have American students coming. It is strange because in U.S.A. they have everything, and yet, they are saying that they are coming here and *then* they understand!"

Tomi marveled at how the camp was able to educate the future generation. "We are saying that now, it's not the parents teaching the children, but the children are teaching the parents," he said. "They are going home from Szarvas and they are asking to light candles for Shabbat like they do at camp. Slowly, the parents are doing this together with the kids. Fantastic."

Over the last several years, Tomi's life, his Judaism, and his mind have changed. "I feel connected to everything here," he said. "The places, the language, the history. But now, with the political situation, when I hear the Hungarian nationalistic hymn and when people are putting up the national flag, I don't know. Every year before, I also put it, but now, I feel like many, many Hungarians are not feeling as loyal."

Tomi said that Budapest now is beginning to feel like it was before the Second World War. "Hungarians think that I stole the jobs and I am Israeli spy and something like that," he said. "They are really scared because they have a bad situation. That's why they have to find something, and the thing they found is again the Jews."

Every four years, Tomi watches the Olympics with his wife's father. He remembered, "We are always saying, 'Let's the Hungarians win the cup!' and everything." Whenever the Israeli team competed with the Hungarian team, they would root for the Hungarians. "Now, if it happens and they are playing," Tomi said, "he is still with the Hungarians but I am with the Israelis. So that's the change."

Despite his changing opinions, Tomi chooses year after year to stay in Budapest. He sat upright and explained in an even tone, "My home is in Israel and my home is in Hungary, too." Tomi's Jewish life is a Hungarian Jewish life. "The people, the atmosphere, the way they react, everything," he said. "There is no question that everything in me is Hungarian."

When Tomi thinks about himself, he knows he has to stay in Hungary. When he thinks about his daughters, however, he thinks they have to leave. "One is eleven and one is seven," he said. "But where to go? To Israel? I don't know. Now, Israel also is not such a safe place. But they would be better someplace else because of better education elsewhere. My wife and I want something open for them."

Despite his worries about Hungary, Tomi feels confident that Jewish Budapest will prevail.

He paused for a moment, his hands woven together and resting on his stomach. "Strength is a blessing," he said. "It's family and community—just like that."

I stood to bid Tomi goodbye, promising I would return to the Frankel Leó Zsinagóga that Friday evening for Shabbat.

I paced back and forth on the tram platform. With each step, my feet brushed along the bright yellow cautionary paint. I squinted my eyes at the sun unceasingly working to shine through a thick sky of impenetrable grey clouds.

I wanted to hug the individuals and families who had chosen to stay in Budapest. I believed that their investment in their city and their country would make a difference.

EPILOGUE

"Would you tell me, please, which way
I ought to go from here?"
"That depends a good deal on where you want to get to."
-- Lewis Carroll, Alice in Wonderland

Below is a brief timeline of my personal journey to create this book. You may read more about my path on my personal blog that showcases short pieces I wrote during the project period: resilienceinbudapest.tumblr.com.

Day one. I was not entirely sure where I wanted to go. All I knew was I felt a guttural lure to immerse myself in a certain identity crisis in Budapest. I stepped out of the car and onto the concrete. My heart raced. One long, deep breath. I was sweating even before mounting the probably one-hundred-pound pack on my back. The blazing heat reminded me that summer *does* exist in Chicago and an adventure was ahead. I squeezed my brother as hard and as close as I could. This was the beginning of my journey to write an anthology style nonfiction book about resilience. Years before, I might have thought that emotions ought to make sense. That day, though, I embraced uncertainty from all angles.

Day four. I completely miscommunicated with the man working at the store next door. Despite the emotional roller coaster of leaving something familiar for the unknown, I mustered a sense of certainty in Budapest, at least with regard to the inevitability of learning new elements about myself and about the world around me. I was proud to have been mistaken (twice!) for a local Hungarian.

Day ten. I had already attended three conferences about Jewish life in Europe. My mind was racing with questions like, "How have direct experiences with violence been memorialized?" "Is it not everyone's job to somehow help the larger community to which they belong?" and "What motivates people to be everyday heroes, even in the face of severe hardship?"

Day twenty-one. I conducted my twelfth interview. I was at the edge of my seat, eager to transcribe and edit narratives that were incredibly unique, heartfelt, and thought provoking.

Day twenty-eight. I learned that my grandmother's hometown, Munkacs, was not only once a part of Czechoslovakia, but also was once a part of Hungary. One month into my journey in Hungary, I learned that I was one-quarter Hungarian.

Day thirty-three. The end of my first month in Hungary posed a series of challenges - most noticeably, my allergies. Until this point, my allergies were uncomfortable but not severe enough to address. They quickly graduated to vision inhibiting. I woke up asking myself questions like, "What am I doing here?" "What is the point of all of this?" "Can I really do this?" and "Who will even *read* this?" It would have been relatively easy to surrender to the questions begging me to spend over ten percent of my remaining budget on a round trip flight to the United States, crawl into my boyfriend's arms and eat my body weight in Lay's sour cream and onion potato chips while watching a chick-flick. Instead, I reminded myself that I signed on to this. I reminded myself that this was the body's reaction to realizing it was in unfamiliar territory. I immersed even deeper.

Day forty. My eyes opened further to the warmth of the Jewish Hungarian community. I started Hungarian language lessons. I attended music festivals and strengthened friendships.

Day fifty-one. I learned that it is possible to create a sense of community even in the most unlikely of places. I experienced how powerful both individuals and communities can be. I discovered that innovation, social justice, and positive impact come in all forms.

Day sixty-three. I announced a change in book plot and structure to my funders, supporters and blog audience. The original book was proposed to be an anthology of Jewish millennials in Budapest discovering and embracing their Jewish identity in positive ways, despite growing anti-Semitism. After a ten-day intensive skill-and-project-development workshop, I decided that the plot would revolve around a foreigner's perspective - my perspective - traveling through Budapest and other European cities, discovering how the search for identity linked international Jewish individuals. I hoped the dialogue between my voice and the voices of my interviewees would encourage a sense of unity among searchers yearning to understand more about their spiritual and personal paths.

Day eighty-two. I began Torah study with the rabbi from the small apartment-style synagogue and community center I had been attending weekly. My textual Jewish study began to enhance my personal and cultural Jewish discovery.

Day ninety-nine. An American rabbi sat to my left. I turned to him and asked, "Were you always so observant? What is your background?" He recited his upbringing and current stipulations and celebrations. He turned to me and asked, "And you?" Until this point, I had been asked, "Why Hungary?" "How are you qualified?" "Where are you from?" "Why would anyone leave New York?" and "Will you learn Hungarian?" Until this point, though, I had not been asked about my Judaism or my identity. There was something magical about discovering myself in a land without ties to the person I once was or the person I was "supposed" to be. I looked the rabbi wearily in the eyes and said, "I don't know yet." As we rang in the Jewish New Year, I wrestled with introspective questions and realized that the answers would only come from within.

Day one-hundred-and-three. Autumn brought with it red and orange falling leaves, pumpkin flavors, increased layers of clothing, holding tighter onto my comforter in bed, and a slew of Jewish holidays. After the conclusion of Rosh Hashanah, Yom Kippur, and Sukkot, I reached a wider conclusion more comfortably: there are various definitions of spirituality. There are various traditions and practices within Judaism, and even further diversity within each sect of Judaism. We must let go of the idea that there is only one way to be religious, or that the more observant community is the holiest or most respected choice. As I embraced Sukkot as the "festival of insecurity," I embraced the previous four months and the uncertainty that lay ahead.

Day one-hundred-and-twenty-eight. I returned to my original book structure. Despite the various twists and turns the book had taken throughout the preceding months, my gut reaction from the beginning shined through. After Skype sessions with mentors and indecisive journal entries and conversations with myself about which direction the book *should* take, I realized, staring myself in the face while brushing my teeth, that there was a reason that I was drawn to Budapest. The Jewish individuals that I had the privilege to meet inspired me. I knew that they would also inspire others. I needed to share their stories as honestly and as transparently as possible. While my voice would still be integrated into the work, the emphasis would not be the foreigner, but the local - the community member, the mother, the brother, the sister, the co-worker, and the friend.

Day one-hundred-and-thirty-four. I asked an interviewee what it was like to grow up in Budapest. As he described his life in elementary and high school, he said, "Somehow, I felt different. I didn't know why, but I felt it." Previous interviews flooded my mind. Something in me clicked. Somehow, we *all* feel different. Somehow, this is innately linked to our search for why that is, for who we are, and for who we want to be. Somehow, I *am* different; different from who I was, different from who surrounds me, and different from who I might've expected or wanted myself to be. Somehow, that is beautiful, and somehow, I found a title to my book.

Day one-hundred-and-forty-one. I wondered about community. I pondered about what it takes for a person to be admitted to one. Beyond the particular methods and means of each community, I thought about the feeling of belonging. When does the individual feel at home? When does the group feel the individual to be a part of their home? Is there a length of time that marks this milestone, or a common experience, or a rule of thumb? The more I pressed for answers, the more I yearned to let go of asking.

Day one-hundred-and-sixty-two. I abruptly and inconveniently realized that often we fail to recognize ourselves as authoritative or reliable resources. We are quick to dismiss our instincts in order to embrace societal or more quantifiable paths. We only feel we know something if we have a formal degree in the subject or have received recognition from the *New York Times*. I did not believe that trusting too much was a problem. In fact, I believed a life without trust would be a mess. I determined that learning to trust is powerful and tuning the ear and heart to trust ourselves would be much more valuable than to receive bottomless external affirmation. I found a newfound priority.

Day one hundred and seventy. I visited my grandmother's hometown and discovered her birth registration, full name pre-immigration, and parents' names and professions. I marveled at my Hungarian roots. I rode a train to Budapest consumed by feelings of existential wonder and gratitude.

Day one-hundred-and-eighty. I conducted my final interview. I celebrated with a close friend and a local draft beer at my favorite neighborhood coffee house and pub.

Day one-hundred-and-eighty-four. Newfound Hungarian friends began to realize my time in Hungary was limited. My chest welled with bittersweet longing to stay and determination to carry the book to completion.

Day one-hundred-and-eighty-six. I crowdsourced the first round of formal edits to my manuscript from twenty-four unpaid professional and non-professional editors. These individuals – dear mentors, friends, and family to me – helped shape the direction and impact of *Somehow I Am Different*.

Day one-hundred-and-ninety-five. I organized twenty-one edited narratives, Content's Page, Author's Note, Prologue, and Acknowledgments into a manuscript to be sent to a paid professional editor. I prepared a book proposal to apply to publishing houses.

Day two-hundred-and-seventeen. I left one home for another. I boarded the flight from Budapest to New York. Similar to the guttural feeling drawing me to Budapest in June, I knew somehow that this was not goodbye.

January 2015

ACKNOWLEDGMENTS

*"If the only prayer you said in your whole life was, 'thank you,'
that would suffice." - Meister Eckhart*

I want to extend an expansive *köszönöm szépen* ("thank you very much" in Hungarian) to my entire team. This project would not have been possible without the personal and financial support of countless individuals who formed an unconditionally giving project-oriented community.

This book was a group effort from start to finish. *Somehow I Am Different* was funded through Kickstarter crowdfunding and the first round of editing was completed using crowd-sourced editors.

The following individuals, listed in alphabetical order, were financially invaluable to "kickstarting" this project:

Nate Bartlett | Hinda Bodinger | Keri Disch
Audrey Haque | Kimberly Hopes | Becky Levin
Kenneth Petersel | Lois Petersel | Karen Sheehan
Kerry Stauber | Maximilian Sternberg | Shirley Tuckey

The following individuals, listed in alphabetical order, generously contributed the first round of edits for the twenty-one personal narratives included in this book:

Natalie Bergner | Jackie Burns | Stevie Burrows
Ezra Erani | Réka Forgách | Sarah Gokhale

Acknowledgements

Michael Greenblatt | Stefanie Groner | Audrey Haque
Shaker Islam | Andrea Jacobs | Arjuna Jayawardena
Lorraine Ma | Amalia McDonald | Samantha Offsay
Joshua Petersel | Lois Petersel | Nirit Roessler
Naomi Rosen | Daniel Schlessinger | Lauren Schwartzberg
Maximilian Sternberg | Caz VanDevere | Lisa Wang

Thank you to the following donors for your thoughtful support and generosity:

Amanda Baker | Alyssa Barba | Barkóczi Dávid
Lareece Dunn | Kirby Barth | Mike Barton | Joshua Bay
Alexander Beer | Daniel Bergner | Natalie Bergner
Kristen Binda | Gail Brodkey | Stevie Burrows | Katy Cherish
Annabelle Clemente | Elizabeth Cooper | Jocelyn Cooper
Joni Cooper | Sue Cotter | Crazy Benjee Productions
Caryn Curry | Kelli Day | Jack Doppelt | Emily Marie DuBois
Carlo Francisco | Britinia Galvin | Joshua Gippin
Sarah Gokhale | Simon Goldberg | Jonathan Gordon
Elizabeth Gore | Ben Gorvine | Michael Greenblatt
Marie Gunning | Helene Haber | Adam Haiken
Samantha Haltman | Miles Harvey | Matt Haywood
Lauren Kadow | Jonathan Kretzmann | Sherry Lewinter
Matt Marcus | Elisa Mattenson | Mississippi Mike
John Mjoseth | David Nagy | Bruce Petersel | Joshua Petersel
Project 2x1 | Annette Regan | Barbara Rekant
Julie Reynolds | Emma Rosen | Naomi Rosen
Jonathan Schild | Daniel Schlessinger | Philip Schlossberg
Daniel Sher | Michael Simon | Zachary Stauber | Julie Strand
Rachael Swetin | Kerry Vanden Bos | Lisa Wang
Colleen Webster | Jake Wilkoff

Special thanks to Joshua Petersel, Kenneth Petersel, Lois Petersel, Zachary Petersel, Maximilian Sternberg, Amalia McDonald, Audrey Haque, Jody Kretzmann, Miles Harvey, Jack Doppelt and Caryn Curry for your irreplaceable professional and personal guidance.

Köszönöm to Acorn Author Services and Publishing for *Somehow I Am Different's* developmental edit and professional publishing guidance. Specifically thank you Holly Kammier, Jessica Therrien and Shelly Stinchcomb for your spirit and commitment to the success of this project.

A heartfelt thank you to my interviewees for the courage and openmindedness of sharing your perspectives and experiences with me and the other readers of *Somehow I Am Different*. You are enriching the world with your light.

Thank you to Dane at Ebooklaunch and Zsili, a reknown artist in Budapest, Hungary, for your creative genius with *Somehow I Am Different's* cover art.

Finally, I am deeply grateful to the friends and family who have nurtured me throughout this experience and all others. You know who you are. I would not be who I am or where I am without you.

Köszönöm szépen.

CONTEMPORARY HUNGARIAN HISTORY, POLITICS AND ECONOMY

Written by **Ákos Keller-Alánt**

Edited by Alyssa Petersel

Hungarian History 1920-1990

World War I and World War II

At the end of World War I, under the peace Treaty of Trianon, Hungary lost two-thirds of its territory and one-third of its population. A brief but bloody Communist dictatorship followed. Admiral Miklós Horthy was the leader of the White Terror (1919-1921), a repressive and violent counter-revolution to the communist dictatorship. The anti-Semitic Horthy gained power as a regent in 1919 and remained the head of the state for twenty-five years. In his first decade in charge, Horthy had little to do with public affairs. After the Great Depression in the 1930s, Horthy assumed more and more control. He acquiesced Hungary's allegiance to Germany in World War II. Although initially he was against the deportation of the Jews, he deprived Jewish Hungarians of rights as early as 1920, forced labor services, and oversaw the first mass killings of Jewish people in 1941. Hungary fought as a German ally for most the war, but after an unsuccessful attempt to abandon the failing Germany, the Nazis occupied Hungary on March 19, 1944. A new collaborationist, the Arrow-Cross party, led by Ferenc Szálasi, came to power. Szálasi seized the property of Jewish people and killed approximately 600,000 Jews within a few months, mostly in Auschwitz-Birkenau. Jews in the Hungarian countryside were executed; only Jews gathered in the Budapest ghetto survived because there was no time to deport them. On

January 20, 1945, an interim government initiated an armistice with the Soviet Union.

Communism

In 1945, the Independent Smallholders' Party, supported by most of the right-wing anti-communist politicians and landowners, won the election. The new coalitional Soviet-supported government instituted radical land reforms and nationalized mines and heavy industries. As the informal power of the communists grew, the power of the governing coalition was undermined. By the 1947 election, the communists' political tactics had disarrayed the Smallholders' Party. Additionally, the revised electoral law resulted in the exclusion of about one tenth of the electorate. The communists created a ballot that enabled individuals to vote away from home. As a result, communist voters traveled across the country and voted fifteen to twenty times each, leading to approximately 100,000 extra votes for the Communist Party. In this way, the communists won the defrauded election of 1947. By 1949, all other parties were forced to merge with the Communist Party under the name of the Hungarian Workers' Party. A new constitution was passed and the state became the Hungarian People's Republic, following the Soviet example. Free press, religion, and travel abroad were restricted. Additionally, the Soviet economic model was adopted, which meant that all industrial firms were nationalized, the land was collectivized, and forced industrialization began.

Due to growing economic problems, in 1953, Imre Nagy replaced the former leader of the country, Mátyás Rákosi. Under Nagy, various elements of the Soviet-style economic reform were eased or undone and thousands of political inmates were released from prisons. However, the political changes could not resolve

Hungary's economic difficulties. In 1955, Hungary joined the Warsaw Pact Treaty Organization, which was a collective defense treaty among eight Communist states led by the Soviet Union.

The Revolution of 1956

The Revolution began on October 23, 1956, after security forces fired at peaceful students marching in Budapest. As the news of the shots spread, disorder grew into a massive popular uprising across the country. As a result, the government collapsed, Soviet troops started to withdraw, and Moscow promised free elections. Nagy announced Hungary's neutrality and exit from the Warsaw Pact. In early November, the Soviets changed their mind about the status of Hungary and launched a military attack on the country. During the uprising, more than one thousand people were killed and two hundred thousand Hungarians fled to the West.

János Kádár, the first secretary of the Communist Party, formed a new government with Soviet support. The reprisal was severe: tens of thousands were imprisoned and hundreds were executed, including Imre Nagy.

Easing under Kádár

In the early 1960s, Kádár introduced a relatively liberal cultural and economic course to Hungary. In 1966, the Communist Party approved the New Economic Mechanism with the aim to overcome the economic difficulties caused by central planning, to improve living standards and to ensure political stability. By the early 1980s, the New Economic Mechanism achieved some economic reforms and limited political liberalization, at the cost of growing foreign debt.

Transition to democracy

By 1987, the reformist wing within the Communist Party and various intellectuals were pressing for change. Young liberals formed several organizations that later became parties in the first democratic Parliament. Kádár was replaced in 1988 and the Parliament adopted a number of new regulations, which resulted in trade union pluralism, freedom of association and freedom of the press. The Soviet-style constitution was rewritten and a new electoral law was adopted. During the so-called Roundtable Talks in 1989, leaders of the Communist Party negotiated the details of the transition with the opposition (newly formed parties and social groups) and laid the groundwork for the new multi-party constitutional democracy. The Republic of Hungary was born. The Hungarian transition to a parliamentary democracy – complete in 1991 when Soviet troops fully withdrew from Hungary – was the smoothest among the former Soviet bloc.

Viktor Orbán's Road to Power 1988-2014

Many critics describe present-day Hungary as an authoritarian regime under the rule of Prime Minister Viktor Orbán. Orbán – the once liberal and promising politician who fought to gain democracy in Hungary – became a conservative right-wing leader facing protesters shouting "Viktator" because of dissatisfaction with his governing style. Orbán's first governance between 1998 and 2002 was already a conservative one, but when he returned into power in 2010, Hungary arrived at a tipping point.

Viktor Orbán was born in 1963 and grew up in Felcsút, a village near Székesfehérvár, 70 kilometers southwest of Budapest. He became the secretary of Communist Youth Organization (KISZ) of his school at the young age of fourteen and held the position for two years. According to Orbán's account, he was devoted to the Communist Regime at the time. His views changed during the course of his obligatory military service in 1981-1982. A year later, he moved to Budapest to pursue a law degree at Eötvös Lóránd University. After his graduation in 1988, Orbán and his like-minded peers (including János Áder, current President of Hungary and László Kövér, Speaker of the National Assembly) co-founded Fidesz – the Alliance of Young Democrats. At the time, Hungary was still governed by the Communist Regime; thus, Fidesz was the first and only independent youth organization.

During the last years of the Communist Regime, Orbán became well known for protesting against Hungary's Communist dictatorship. In the summer of 1989, Orbán delivered his famous speech at the ceremonial reburial of Imre Nagy and other victims executed by the Soviets after 1956. The twenty-six-year-old Orbán called for free elections and the departure of Soviet troops from Hungary. This was the first time such demands were made in public and the nation was electrified by the bold and radical stance of the young politician. Orbán represented Fidesz at Roundtable Talks and played a very important political role in the last years of communism as one of the prominent members of the liberal, anti-Communist Party he helped set up. Orbán entered Hungary's first democratically elected parliament in 1990; however, Fidesz received less than ten percent of the votes.

In 1993, Orbán became the leader of Fidesz. Four years after the end of communism, the public was in a state of shock from the mass layoffs and the economic uncertainty brought about by the transition from a planned to a free market economy. In 1994, the old Communist Party, rebranded as the Hungarian Socialist Party (MSZP), came back to power, and the former right wing parties collapsed. This was the time when Orbán said goodbye to his radical liberal views and Fidesz became a conservative right-wing party. Noticing the space left empty by right-wing parties, Orbán seized the opportunity to make Fidesz a major – and later the only – party on the right.

Four years later, in 1998, the thirty-five-year-old Orbán became Prime Minister of Hungary for the first time. He was able to form a government in coalition with two minor right-wing parties. By this time, Orbán and Fidesz completely re-positioned to the conservative side. Orbán reformed the structure of Fidesz, making it a hierarchical and centralized organization. Fidesz limited Parliament's power, while promoting national values and competing with the radical right for votes. In opposition, Orbán always acted as the defender of the democratic rights, but once he gained power, he put his policies through forcefully.

The period from 1998 to 2002 was one of rapid economic growth for Hungary. Hungary became a member of NATO in 1999 and Orbán was a popular leader. However, the opposition and some critics complained of his authoritarian style and questions were raised over government control of the state-owned media. For example, an OSCE election report in 2002 noted that, "state television consistently demonstrated a bias in favor of the government and Fidesz."

It was a big surprise for Hungarians when Fidesz lost the 2002 elections and MSZP won in coalition with the Liberal Party. The frustration within Fidesz was enormous. Orbán refused to give up; he asked for the re-counting of votes, claimed "electoral theft" and ordered his supporters to demonstrate on the streets. After 2002, his speeches became more and more radical. This was the time when he started using wartime rhetorics, calling his political opponents "enemies" – not only his enemies but also enemies of the Hungarian nation. By this time, Hungarian politics became extremely divided and the two major parties running for power became more and more mischievous.

Four years later, in early 2006, the coalition led by the Socialist Party was able to win the general elections again. Fidesz seemingly lost confidence in Orbán. However, in September 2006, a speech by the socialist Prime Minister Ferenc Gyurcsány leaked to the press. The speech was given in Balatonöszöd after the winning parliamentary elections to the representatives of MSZP and was supposed to be confidential. In the most controversial part of the speech, which was broadcasted by the national radio, the re-elected Gyurcsány said the following to his audience (regarding the economic situation of the country):

"There is not much choice. There is not, because we have fucked it up. Not a little but a lot. No European country has done anything as boneheaded as we have. It can be explained. We have obviously lied throughout the past two years. It was perfectly clear that what we were saying was not true."

The speech immediately ignited rioting in the streets of Budapest and anti-government mass protests around Hungary. Crowds gathered for months in front of the Parliament building, calling for early elections.

Orbán led the call with Fidesz, declaring the Socialist-Liberal Coalition "illegitimate" at a mass rally in the capital in October 2006, at the 50th anniversary of the Revolution of 1956. That event was marred by heavy-handed police suppression of riotous far-right protesters round the corner. Many Fidesz supporters were caught up in the chaos of tear gas and rubber bullets, which only served to strengthen Orbán's popularity. As a result, Fidesz has won the local elections in 2006 and has consistently come out way ahead of any other party in opinion polls.

Still, the socialists clung on to power and Gyurcsány remained Prime Minister. Prior to the financial crisis in 2008, the Hungarian economy was characterized by electoral budget cycles followed by austerity. The big systems run by the state, like education or healthcare, were malfunctioning but remained untouched. The crisis hit an already weakened country. Due to the crisis, Hungary's GDP shrank by almost seven percent. Gyurcsány finally stepped down in April 2009, acknowledging that his lack of popularity prevented the consensus needed to make structural reforms to tackle the economic crisis. There was no early election, but a technocrat government under Prime Minister Gordon Bajnai was installed. The country reached an agreement with the International Monetary Fund for a 25 billion USD bailout. The resulting austerity package was a difficult economic blow for Hungary's citizens. By this time, quite a few high-profile corruption cases came to light.

Hungarians not only left the governing Leftist Party but they also craved something totally different; Orbán gained the opportunity to offer that. Orbán triumphed in the elections in 2010. Fidesz claimed a two-thirds majority in the Parliament that eased the way to changes in the constitution and major laws.

Declining democracy 2010-2014

After the elections of 2010, Orbán started to change the whole political system in Hungary to the "System of National Co-operation" (NER). Orbán mandated that the "Statement of National Co-operation," which states that the last twenty years were the "two chaotic decades of the transition" but in 2010 "a constitutional revolution in the voting booths" occurred in the country, be hung in every government office and state-run institution (e.g. theaters, museums). The nation voted for "a new social contract of national consolidation" and for a new future of Hungary based on "work, home, family, health, and order."

According to Freedom House, the Washington D.C.-based human rights watchdog, in its latest "Nations in Transit" report, Hungary's democracy is in serious decline. The report states,

"Without counterbalancing improvements, any further deterioration in governance, electoral process, media freedom, civil society, judicial independence, or corruption under Prime Minister Viktor Orbán's recently re-elected government will expel Hungary from the category of 'consolidated democratic regimes' next year."

In the same report, Freedom House writes,

"In Hungary, abuse in public-procurement practices, to the benefit of business groups and communities that are loyal to the government, became increasingly obvious in 2013. After a scandal over reports that the nationalization of Hungary's tobacco industry had deliberately favored some local allies of the ruling party, the government made its freedom of information law more restrictive."

Many things led to this structure, including the regulation of the media, the new constitution and legislation, and the high level of corruption.

Seizing the media

The state-owned television and radio not only became a mouthpiece of the government after the elections of 2010, but also regularly falsified news. The government, through the new regulation, had more effect on independent media outlets. One of the new government's first steps was to change the media law, which created a new media board. The Media Council and the Media Authority were led only by Fidesz Party loyalists. The government was the largest advertiser in the country. The Media Council also had very strong power; it could suspend a media provider or fine it up to 200 million forints (750,000 USD). Consequently, the most common phenomena among journalists became self-censorship.

Defamation is considered a crime, which seriously hinders investigative journalism. For example, in 2014, one of the most popular Hungarian news sites, Origo.hu, reported that János Lázár (then Undersecretary, now Minister of Prime Minister's office) had spent millions of forints for some trips abroad. The journalist who reported the story was fired in response and the rest of the staff resigned in protest. Additionally, when the most watched television channel, RTL Klub, began to criticize the politics of Fidesz and report its members' involvement in corruption, the government adopted a tax on advertising revenues. The tax was clearly adopted to reduce the Hungarian RTL's revenues, but it harmed all independent media in the country, of which only a few remained, resulting in a media market dominated by media linked to the ruling party. The regulation of the media was just the beginning; Orbán's new government changed the whole legal system, including the constitution.

Writing a new constitution

In order to heighten "effective governance," Orbán systematically eliminated checks and balances on his power. Using its majority in Parliament, the government amended the constitution ten times in its first year in office. In April 2011, Parliament adopted the country's new constitution, the "Fundamental Law of Hungary." The constitution, written by very few people within Fidesz, passed without cross-party accord or a referendum. The new constitution became effective January 1, 2012.

The new constitution includes not only telling symbolic statements but also worrying policy changes. The document changed the country's official name from Republic of Hungary to Hungary, referred to the role of Christianity in "preserving the nation," and constitutionally banned gay marriage and abortion.

Moreover, the document denies Hungary's culpability for the organized murder of some 600,000 Jewish citizens in World War II. It namely states that the country lost its self-determination in 1944 when Nazi Germany occupied the country until the collapse of communism.

The Fundamental Law also mandated a process requiring the passage of several dozen "cardinal laws" on issues such as the church, the media, the restructuring of the judiciary, the elections, the level of taxes, the fiscal policy and the central bank. The majority of these laws were passed in 2011 and their future modification would require a two-thirds majority in Parliament.

There were a number of mass protests against the new "Fundamental Law." Moreover, it attracted a great deal of criticism from the Council of Europe, the European Parliament and the United States. However, the government led by Viktor Orbán seemed deaf to criticism. The government's policy remained the same: those who criticized the government were the enemy of the nation.

Elimination of checks and balances

The judiciary system suffered the most harmful hit. The Constitutional Court previously had the right and the responsibility to review whether all the laws were in line with the constitution. However, the court could no longer review any law that had an impact on the budget, such as taxation laws or austerity programs.

Only after a long process in the ordinary courts could an individual go to the Constitutional Court, which made it more difficult for the body to review whether laws were in line with the constitution. The government added four loyal-to-Fidesz judges to the body, expanding the number of judges from eleven to fifteen. Before 2010, the Constitutional Court was the major check on executive power, but this role was practically diminished by 2011.

The ordinary judiciary system was "reformed" as well. Judges in the most important positions and those with the most experience were replaced because the retirement age for judges was lowered from seventy to sixty-two. More than one hundred judges had to retire within one month of the new law coming into force. The president of the Supreme Court was replaced as well, because according to the new regulation, his seventeen years of experience as a judge on the European Court of Human Rights didn't qualify him to fulfill the position. Furthermore, the president of the newly created National Judicial Office had the power to move any judge to any other court, to name future judges and to replace retired judges. The head of the Office could move any hearing from one court to another, which meant it was in his power to decide which judge would hear a case.

Changing the whole system, the government not only filled the most important positions with people loyal to Fidesz, but also extended the terms of office for the head of the state audit office (twelve years), the public prosecutor (nine years), the head of the national judicial office (nine years), the head of the media council (nine years) and the head of the budget council (six years). All of these positions could be replaced with a two-third majority of the Parliament. Instead of the three ombudsmen positions (human rights, data protection and minority affairs), now there was only one. Under the new constitution, the central bank merged with the

Financial Supervision Authority. The minister of economics became the new president of the deemed independent central bank.

After the elimination of all of the legal checks and balances, the independent NGOs remained the only control on government power in Hungary. Hence, the government reduced the already thin budget of civil society, which is now fully dependent on foreign funds. In the summer of 2014, the ruling power initiated a legal corruption investigation into the organizers and beneficiaries of Norway Grants. The Norway Grant is a seventeen-million-dollar fund offered by Norway to support NGOs, focusing on organizations whose activities range from Roma advocacy and LGBT rights to investigative journalism. According to Fidesz, Norway was "meddling in Hungarian inner politics" and abusing promotion of organizations with "leftist political ties." The police raided the office of organizations that were assigning the funds and sequestrated documents and computers.

Education and Culture

Radical changes were occurring not only in the political field, but the government additionally impacted the educational system and cultural institutions. In the twenty years prior to 2010, the Hungarian right-wing felt excluded from the Hungarian educational and cultural spheres. They disliked the modern and progressive way of self-expression, claiming modern art "ultra liberal" and "foreign, not part of the Hungarian tradition." After 2010, state funds for culture were radically reduced and almost all of the directors of theaters and museums were replaced with conservative, loyal followers.

Schoolbooks were rewritten and all public schools were organized under one central institution. The local municipality and the parents had no influence on the nomination of principals. The teachers had no freedom to choose what and how they taught; there was one central syllabus and the government had the authority to check whether it was kept.

According to the government, there were too many youngsters with a "useless" degree. Consequently, the government decided how many students could enroll in a university and generally reduced these numbers. The prior totally free education system was replaced; now, the majority of students had to pay for their education. There was no proper scholarship; those with less wealthy families had no chance to receive higher education. The lucky students who could get one of the few free places were obligated to work in Hungary after graduation or else they would have to repay their education's cost to the state. The cuts affected not only the scholarships but the universities' budgets as well. Many professors were forced to retire.

Keep the power – a new electoral system

The radical changes adversely affected many Hungarians with still no sign of the promised economic growth. Experiencing decline in their popularity, by the end of 2011, Fidesz changed the electoral system as well. The number of representatives was reduced from 386 to 200, which opened the opportunity to gerrymander. The new electoral districts were drawn in favor of Fidesz. If the new boundaries were valid during the three previous elections, the party would have won all three despite only winning one election under the old system. Fidesz tried to keep voters at home, as well; the ruling party cut the campaign period from 90 to 50 days and banned campaign advertising on private (and most watched) TV stations. To divide the opposition, Fidesz eased the requirements of nominating candidates. Additionally, legal supervision of elections changed. Before 2014, there was the Election Commission, with politically diverse members. However, in 2014, Fidesz replaced all five members of the body with members nominated from within.

In the elections of 2014, Fidesz won two-thirds of the mandates again, but this time, their qualified majority depended on only one representative. If the old electoral system were in place, Fidesz would have won the election but would have lost its qualified majority.

"We are building an illiberal state"

Behind all these moves, Fidesz was consciously distancing Hungary from western democratic values. In his speeches, Orbán declared that the western model of rule of law and free market economy was declining, if not already dead. In his view, Hungary tried to adopt the western model. As the problems of the country were not solved in the last decades, Orbán deemed this adoption a mistake. The former leftist governments were not protecting Hungarian interests, but rather, the interests of banks and foreign powers. Hence, after the financial crisis of 2008, Orbán insisted the time had come to do something different. In an infamous speech given in July 2014 to his supporters, Orbán said, "We are parting ways with western European dogmas, making ourselves independent from them." He declared, "We have to abandon liberal methods and principles of organizing a society. The new state that we are building is an illiberal state, a non-liberal state." In an interview in December 2014, he said, "Checks and balances is a U.S. invention that for some reason of intellectual mediocrity Europe decided to adopt and use in European politics."

In practice, instead of rules equal to everyone – competition and separation of powers – the new system is highly centralized and hierarchical, where success depends on personal relations. In general, the legislation after 2010 was used as a tool to gain the government's political goals. Laws passed through Parliament without any dialogue or debate. Accordingly, the political and economic environment of Hungary became extremely unpredictable.

The Hungarian Economy after 2010

Increasing taxes

In 2010, Orbán inherited an economy plagued by economic crisis. After the elections, the government adopted an "unorthodox economic policy" led by the then Minister of Economy (now President of the Central Bank) György Matolcsy. This meant the introduction of new taxes targeting the most successful sectors: banking, energy, telecommunications, and retail. Orbán claimed the taxes adopted on multinational companies working in Hungary reclaimed the country from foreign control. Most of these "crisis taxes" should have phased out after three years, but instead, Orbán introduced new taxes in the next years. For example, the general VAT was raised up to twenty-seven percent (the highest in the world), there was a new fee on withdrawing money from ATMs, and a new tax on potato chips ensued because of their salinity. Ironically, one of the few promises of Fidesz in the campaign in 2010 was the reduction of taxes.

Despite the increase in taxes, in 2010, the government discontinued contributions to the voluntary private pillar of the pension system and imposed financial disincentives on those who chose not to return to the state system. The money of individuals gathered in the previous years was nationalized and depleted. The government used the money to reduce public debt, but debt remained high, around eighty percent of the GDP.

Increasing corruption – Land and tobacco

One of the vows that made Fidesz popular on the countryside was that local farmers and young families would have access to state lands. However, across the country, the winners of the land were friends, relatives and political supporters of Fidesz. For example, in the neighborhood of Felcsút (Orbán's hometown), almost all of the available state land around the village went to only two groups, one of which was a company linked to the Mayor of Felcsút who is a friend of the Prime Minister.

Similarly, in 2013, the Hungarian government introduced a state monopoly on the retail sale of tobacco. The concessions to open a "National Tobacco Shop" were distributed via public tender but the results were very similar to the land lease tenders: the major part of the concession was won by people linked to Fidesz, while many small shop owners lost their business. A Hungarian tobacco company, Continental, and its CEO, are linked to János Lázár, the Minister of the Prime Minister's office. Continental's sales unit won about 90 concessions, and pro-Fidesz grocery store chain, CBA, was also among the big winners.

Increasing corruption – Közgép

The most flagrant example of corruption is the case of the construction company Közgép. The owner of the company is Lajos Simicska. Simicska attended university with Orbán and participated in the formation of Fidesz. In 1993, he became the financial director of the party. During the first Orbán government, Simicska was the head of the Hungarian Tax Authority. Later, he withdrew from public service to build his own empire. Beside his right-wing media outlets and advertising companies, his biggest business is Közgép, which conducts all kinds of building and connecting activities. In 2013, Közgép won state tenders worth more than 475 million USD, generating revenue of about 223 million USD. In 2009, this figure was 144 million.

The political panacea – cuts of utility prices

Despite these scandals, Fidesz was reelected in 2014. In addition to its dominance in media, the new electoral system, and the lack of capable opposition, there was another factor that made the victory possible: the cuts of utility prices (rezsicsökkentés). In 2013, the government reduced the centrally regulated household price of utilities. The fees for electricity, gas and heating were reduced by a total of twenty percent and the fees for water, sewage and garbage collection were reduced by ten percent. The results of the rezsicsökkentés were advertised on billboards and TV during the electoral campaign. Reducing the profit margins of the providers gave the government the opportunity to purchase foreign-owned utility companies. The German E.On already sold its gas operation to the Hungarian state, but Fidesz had more ambitious plans. Orbán wanted to turn all public utility providers in Hungary into non-profit companies.

Transfers keep Hungary alive

As the Hungarian economic environment was not business frie-ndly, the country remained highly dependent on its exports and on the European Union. Hungary became a member of the European Union in 2004. As Prime Minister between 1998 and 2002, Orbán worked hard for the joining. But later, Orbán accused the EU and the European regulations of holding Hungary back and hindering the country's sovereignty. In reality, without the European funds, the Hungarian economy would probably collapse. The EU accounts for 95 percent of Hungary's public investments. Between 2007 and 2013, 36.5 billion USD went to Hungary, and in the next seven-year period, this sum will be 22 billion USD.

Unfortunately, despite its gains from the EU, even if the Hungarian government is not respecting some of the EU's core values (all member states have to preserve democratic governance and human rights and have a functioning market economy), the EU has no effective instrument to intervene.

Increase of poverty

As of 2014, the Hungarian GDP was still below the pre-crisis level. About three million people were living in poverty in the country, approximately one third of the total population. The unemployment rate remained high. The government launched a large-scale public work program, which the unemployed by necessity had to participate in. The problem was that these jobs generally involved menial work, paid less than minimum wage, and rarely lasted for more than a few months.

Growing dissatisfaction after 2014

Despite Fidesz winning three elections in 2014 (parliamentary, European Parliament, and municipal), its popularity fell sharply. The immediate cause for the discontent was a planned tax on Internet, which was withdrawn after demonstrations brought tens of thousands of protesters onto the streets. Discontent grew as some stories came up about the luxuries and expensive properties enjoyed by some government ministers and their friends. Furthermore, Fidesz ordered the obligatory closure of retailers on Sundays and turned all the main roads in the country into turnpikes. In October 2014, the United States banned at least six Hungarian officials, including the President and three other leaders of the tax authority, from entering the United States due to suspected corruption. This was a highly unusual sanction against officials of an ally. By early 2015, according to pollster Ipsos, Fidesz had lost one million voters over one quarter. According to the poll, the popularity of opposition parties had not changed at the turn of the year. The second most popular party, and only significant competition for Fidesz, remained the far-right Jobbik party, which absorbed some of the disappointed Fidesz supporters. The left and liberal parties remained divided and disorganized. Forty-one percent of the respondents, i.e. about 3.3 million people, would not vote for any of the parties.

In spite of its drawbacks on economy and democracy, Hungarians feel nostalgia for the Kádár-Regime. The decades before 1956 in Hungary were characterized by uncertainty and war, while under Kádár, security and increased standards of living became more important to society. In change, political rights and freedoms were not considered to be as vital. During communism, unemployment was an unknown phenomenon. After the collapse of communism, families were plagued with new loss of money and loss of employment. In 1991, 74 percent of Hungarians approved of the adoption of democracy; by 2009, only 56 percent still approved. Economic difficulties of the market economy caused support for capitalism to fall from 80 percent to 46 percent. This feeling explains not only the nostalgia but also contemporary Hungarian politicians' promises to extend the role of state.

Far-right politics in Hungary

Anti-Semitism and racism among Hungarians

Other than growing poverty, the most worrisome phenomenon in Hungary is the society's shift to the far right. According to public opinion research, large segments of the Hungarian population are open to far-right ideals and half of Hungarians are extremely prejudiced, mostly against the Roma people. Specifically, the lower middle-class is responsive to extremist views due to fear of heightened poverty, the economic and social crisis in the country, and general disappointment and job loss.

Anti-Semitic views reappeared in Hungary after the collapse of the Communist Regime in 1990, along with freedom of the press and freedom of expression. Between 1990 and 2009, the proportion of anti-Semitic respondents remained steady at around ten percent of the population. When the far-right party Jobbik became popular, things changed; by 2013, about one third of Hungarians gave anti-Semitic responses to pollers. The number of anti-Semitic Hungarians likely did not grow, but Hungarians' attitudes changed as Jobbik's openly racist and anti-Semitic rhetoric toppled a taboo in public speaking. People who were used to hiding their anti-Semitism views saw and heard the racist politics and started speaking openly about their views.

Moreover, the far right is becoming more and more self-confident. The right-wing extremists are paying tribute to Miklós Horthy, the anti-Semitic leader of Hungary between 1920 and 1944. Far-right leaders are erecting statues in his honor – one can be found only few steps away from a nationalistic World War II monument at Szabadság tér in Budapest. Even some members of the Fidesz party support the trend.

Far-right politics of Fidesz

As a result of this shift in society and the growing popularity of Jobbik, Fidesz adopted several policies from the nationalist right's agenda. For example, the new constitution refers to the so-called Holy Crown and to Christianity. Additionally, the justification of the newly introduced "crisis taxes" was nationalistic; according to the government, the foreign banks and multinational companies were taking out the profit from the country. Moreover, the transformation of the media, culture and education was reflecting slightly nationalistic and very conservative viewpoints, as well. In public schools, ethics and religious studies became obligatory and some anti-Semitic books from the pre-WWII period became part of the central syllabus.

Fidesz and Orbán support extreme stances. For example, György Fekete, the head of the MMA, or the Hungarian Academy of Arts, declared the Holocaust-survival writer György Konrád as not Hungarian but someone "who seems to be Hungarian," because Konrád was criticizing Orbán's politics. Additionally, the government created a new historical research institute, Veritas, "with the explicit goal of studying and reevaluating the historical research of Hungary's past one-hundred-fifty-years." Its Director, Sándor Szakály, declared that the deportation and massacre of tens of thousands of Jews in Kamianets-Podilskyi by the Nazis was a "police action against aliens." Furthermore, in the summer of 2014, Orbán selected an anti-Semite, Péter Szentmihályi Szabó, to serve as Ambassador to Italy. Furthermore, in a lawsuit against a school that segregated Roma children, the Minister of Human Capacities, Zoltán Balog (a Calvinist pastor), defended the convicted school. Not by chance, Jobbik politicians complained the government was "stealing their issues and ideas."

The second most popular party: the far-right Jobbik Party

Founded in 2003, in its first years, the far-right Jobbik (the Movement for a Better Hungary – "jobb" means both right and better) was a marginal party. In the national elections of 2006, Jobbik received 2.2 percent, but during the anti-government riots of the autumn, the party became more popular. The rising popularity was not visible in the polls, so it was shocking in 2009 when Jobbik received nearly 15 percent of the European Parliament votes. With 17 percent, Jobbik got in the national Parliament in 2010. In 2014, the party received 20 percent. The party has representatives in city councils and more than a dozen towns across the country. By the end of 2014, the far-right party was the second most popular party in Hungary. As the leftist and liberal parties remained divided, Jobbik became a serious competitor for Fidesz. They describe themselves as the EU's "most successful radical nationalist party."

Jobbik has a good relationship with all the main radical-nationalist organizations in Hungary. In 2007, Gábor Vona, the head of Jobbik, co-founded the Magyar Gárda (Hungarian Guard), a paramilitary neo-fascist group, which helped the party to gain fame and popularity across the country. The Hungarian Guard was formed to "defend a physically, spiritually and intellectually defenseless Hungary." In reality, the group's structure reflected a hierarchical, paramilitary approach; for example, they marched in formations and had their own uniform. The founding ceremony of the Guard attracted nearly 3,000 people in the heart of Budapest. The group played a major role in introducing the racist term "Gypsy crime" to public speech. The expression was based on the assumption that the Roma people were criminals. The Hungarian Guard regularly organized anti-Roma rallies and marched through villages with Roma populations to intimidate them. The Guard was dissolved by the court in 2009. On his first day in Parliament, Gábor Vona appeared in the uniform of the already dissolved Guard. Later, the Hungarian Guard was reorganized as the New Hungarian Guard.

Jobbik claims that Roma people are not part of the Hungarian nation, as they live outside of "laws, work and education," and they don't want to assimilate. Jobbik is anti-communist, nationalist, and considers itself the only true representative of Hungarian national interest against the foreign – especially American and Israeli – powers.

Anti-Semitism is a very important part of Jobbik's rhetoric. According to Jobbik, Judaism is a symbol of globalization, foreign capital and banks that are "buying up the country." In May 2013, several hundred Jobbik supporters took part in a Jobbik-organized anti-Jewish rally in Budapest on the eve of the World Jewish Congress (WJC). The WJC held its meeting in the Hungarian capital specifically because of the rising anti-Semitism in the country. Furthermore, in late 2012, one Jobbik representative called Parliament to "register all the Jews living in Hungary, particularly those in parliament and the government, [to prevent] potential danger they posed to Hungary." Another party member (a Calvinist pastor) claimed that Israeli powers use Roma people as "biological weapon" against Hungarians.

In mainstream media, Jobbik is relatively underrepresented, but the party has its own outlets. Jobbik has its own weekly paper and its very strong online presence is characterized by a very popular, openly racist and anti-Semitic website.

Anti-Semitism translates into occasional anti-Jewish incidents. Verbal aggression in the streets and on the Internet is common. From time to time, Jewish cemeteries and Holocaust memorials are desecrated. Poverty and growing tensions lead to a number of violent attacks against Roma people, as well, including a serial killing that lasted for one and a half years.

Responses from Society

Increasing emigration

One of society's most troubling and harmful responses to the economic and political crises is emigration. In 2014, everyone in Budapest had at least one friend who had recently left the country.

Hungary had been a low emigration country for many years after the collapse of communism. Until 2006, the Hungarian GDP was converging to the western European countries; economic prospects were quite good and the living standard was relatively high in Hungary. Hungary joined the European Union in 2004, opening the door to free movement to other EU countries, but the level of emigration out of Hungary accelerated only around 2007, and there was another wave of emigration after 2011.

Migration is driven by expected wage gain and better employment opportunities. In 2003, only 20,000 Hungarians left the country; in 2007, the number went up to 38,000, and in 2012, nearly 80,000 people went to live abroad.

The vast majority of emigrants are young (almost all of them are under forty years old) and highly educated. The favorite destinations are Germany, Austria and the United Kingdom. Recently, London became the fifth largest "Hungarian" city: about 150,000 Hungarians live there. Beyond work, more and more Hungarian youngsters are choosing to get a degree at a foreign university. No one knows whether these young people will ever return to live in Hungary. Those people who stay in the country have decided to show their dissatisfaction with the regime.

The places of resistance – demonstrations

After 2010, two major movements were able to bring thousands of people to the streets. The first series of demonstrations was organized by a civil organization called Milla (One Million for the Free Press). As the name suggests, they started protesting against the new media regulations. Later, Milla's demonstrations became general anti-government protests, which attracted tens of thousands of people. At Milla's demonstration Gordon Bajnai in October 2012, the former Prime Minister announced his return to politics. Together with some other organizations, Milla became a party called Együtt (Together). As a result, Milla lost a lot of its popularity. In the elections of 2014, Együtt joined the Leftist Electoral Alliance, which included the unpopular MSZP, and practically disbanded.

The other – and more successful – movement was HaHa (Students' Network). Founded in 2011, the Students' Network held demonstrations and public panels against educational reform. In the winter of 2012-2013, HaHa's demonstrations attracted thousands of students. HaHa used many forms of protest. One method was interrupting speeches or conferences held by the representatives of the government. In early 2013, a group of students occupied the auditorium of a university for one and a half months. Some of their goals were achieved: the reduction of admissions was less radical than originally planned and the head of the state secretary for higher education was removed.

Another symbolic but important protest occurred against the fourth amendment of the new "Fundamental Law." This amendment restricted political campaigns, criminalized homelessness and deprived the rights of the Constitutional Court. Consequently, about seventy people – mostly university students – staged a sit-down protest at the entrance of the Fidesz headquarters. It was a peaceful protest, but after a few hours, Fidesz ordered the party's

318

own security guards – one of whom was convicted for murder and spent ten years in jail – to bring the protesters out of building's yard. The party tried to sue some of the protesters but the jury absolved all of them.

Following HaHa and the protest at the Fidesz headquarters, a wide network of young civil rights activists emerged in Budapest. Some activists were organizing demonstrations, some were hosting public panels on political issues, and others were working on one specific issue, for example, empowering Roma or homeless people. All of the activists were working tirelessly in the hope of positive change for Hungary.

In autumn of 2014, there was a new wave of mass demonstrations in Hungary. A proposed tax on Internet usage brought thousands to the streets, not only in Budapest but also across Hungary. The protests were successful: Orbán dropped the proposal. Even after the tax on Internet was removed, the demonstrations continued. The corruption scandals of the tax authority fueled the growing discontent. As polls suggested, a major problem was that people were disillusioned not only with Fidesz, but also with politics in general. However, it was extremely difficult to transform these movements into real political power. Even though some parties (e.g. Milla-Együtt, or LMP – Politics Can Be Different) tried to incorporate the movements, they did not succeed.

The two monuments of Szabadság tér

Orbán's willingness to reinterpret Hungary's history received a very concrete form in early 2014. The government announced the plan of a new monument to commemorate the 70th anniversary of World War II. The bronze monument placed on Szabadság tér (Freedom Square) portrays an eagle violently attacking an archangel. The fierce bird represents Germany while the innocent angel represents Hungary. Its inscription reads, "A monument to the victims of the German Occupation." This portrays a very specific view on Hungary's role in World War II and the Holocaust.

Hungary was the first country in Europe after World War I to adopt an anti-Semitic law – more than a decade before Germany. By the German occupation of Hungary in 1944, the Hungarian Jews were already deprived of equal rights and sent to forced labor camps. More than ten thousand Hungarian Jews were killed prior to the Holocaust. After 1944, in the last months of World War II, over half a million Hungarian Jews were exterminated, most of them in the camps of Auschwitz-Birkenau. The deportation of Hungarian Jews was organized by the Nazi commander Adolf Eichmann. However, he couldn't have succeeded without the collaboration of the Hungarian gendarmes who transacted the deportations, or the non-Jewish citizens who were neutral during the deprivation, deportation and execution of their Jewish neighbors.

Right after the plans of the Szabadság tér monument emerged, harsh criticism from Jewish organizations and the German and Israeli embassies ensued, claiming that the monument was falsifying history. A group of middle-aged individuals initiated a civil disobedience movement to prevent the execution of the monument plan. Seeing the resistance, the U.S. embassy asked the Hungarian government to respect democratic rules and to not build the monument. However, Orbán stated that the monument would be built, as it was "spotless." Two days after winning the elections, in April 2014, construction initiated and the protesters were removed by the police. By July, the monument was ready and armed with strong police presence. Protesters not only stood in front of the government's memorial, but they also improvised a memorial of their own: the "Living Memorial." They surrounded the monument with painted stones, photos, personal belongings and names of the victims of the Holocaust. The group gathered at Szabadság tér every day, organizing sit-ins about the Holocaust, personal stories, and other daily political issues.

The two monuments of Szabadság tér – one "official" monument ordered by the government and the other "living" monument built from the bottom up by individuals – represent the divided state of the Hungarian society.

Hope for the Future

Despite its current political and economic circumstances, Hungary is not lost. The abundance of creative and talented youngsters brings fame and pride to Hungary in fields of sports, science and the arts. Budapest is a capital of startups (for example, Prezi and Ustream are from Hungary) and the city's life is flourishing. The cultural life of Budapest offers endless opportunities from theaters, concerts and exhibitions to new high-quality restaurants opening across the city, bringing the first Michelin stars to Hungary. A new generation of designers has reached great success, mixing Hungarian tradition with the latest trends in their work. Summers in Hungary are full of music and cultural festivals, including one of the greatest European festivals, the Sziget festival. Not only have young tourists discovered Budapest, populating the streets and pubs, but Hungarians are also re-discovering their capital. Several agencies are offering special guided tours for locals.

The historical Jewish District, located in the center of the capital in the 7th District, is the heart of the night and cultural life of Budapest. Despite the horrors of the Holocaust, Jewish life in Hungary is flourishing. The Hungarian Jewish community is the largest in Eastern and Central Europe with its 100,000 members, mostly concentrated in Budapest. Young Jews are re-discovering and enjoying their identity. After World War II, many survivors left the country; others who stayed tried to forget what happened. The Communist Regime encouraged the silence, because in a communist society, there was no place for churches or religion. Most parents didn't mention their religious origins to their children at all.

This changed with the fall of communism, when young adults began discovering their faith. Young adults learning about their Jewish origins tend to express their identity in a positive way through religion and culture, not in relation to the Holocaust. Luckily, they have the opportunity to experience their Jewish identity. After the fall of communism, numerous organizations were established to assist in the identity formation of the new generation. Jewish communities sprouted not only in Budapest, but also in twenty-eight other cities. In the capital, there are thirty-one working synagogues with communities from orthodox, Neolog (comparable to conservative), and reform traditions. Jewish educational institutions range from schools to student camps to Jewish Universities. Several youth organizations offer informal education and Jewish cultural events.

Despite the anti-Semitism in Hungary, in the city center it is cool to be a Jew. Jewish festivals run with a full house and kosher and Jewish restaurants, pastry shops, and bars draw a magnificent young, social scene.

Hungary, including its Jewish communities, will overcome its obstacles to become a successful country that everyone can be proud of. The progressive Budapest and the active and energetic youngsters ensure it.

JEWISH BUDAPEST

Encyclopedia of Jewish Community Organizations,
Festivals, Food, Media, Memorials, Mikvah, Schools, Social
Services, Synagogues

Community Organization	Website
A.K.K.E.Z.D.E.T.P.H.A.I.	www.facebook.com/akkezdet
Alef Kids	www.alefkids.hu
Auróra	www.facebook.com/auroraunofficial
Bálint Ház	web.balinthaz.hu
B'nai B'rith	www.bnaibrith.hu
BZSH Budapesti Zsido Hitkozseg	www.bzsh.hu
Centropa	www.centropa.org
Eleven Emlékmü	www.facebook.com/
(The Living Monument)	ElevenEmlekmu
Mazsihisz (The Federation of the Hungarian	www.mazsihisz.hu/
Jewish Communities)	about-mazsihisz-37.html
Gólem Theatre	golemszinhaz.hu/english/about-golem
Hanna Női Klub	www.zsido.com/szoveg/
	29/Hanna_Noi_Klub
Hanoar Hatzioni Magyarország	hanoar.hu
Haver Foundation	haver.hu/english
Hungarian Jewish Archives	www.milev.hu
Israeli Cultural Institute (ICI)	izraelikultura.hu
Israeli Student Organization of Hungary	www.facebook.com/
(ISOH)	groups/5512707405
Jewish Meeting Point	jmpoint.hu
Kidma	www.kidma.hu
Kozma Street Jewish Cemetery	en.wikipedia.org/
	wiki/Kozma_Street_Cemetery
Lativ Kollel	lativ.hu
Limmud Hungary	limmud.hu
Maccabi Sports	www.maccabi.hu
MAROM	www.marom.hu
Memento70	www.memento70.hu/home-2

Mensch Foundation	www.mensch/hu/en/foundation.html
MiNYanim	izraelikultura.hu/minyanim
Moishe House	www.facebook.com/mohobp
Narancs Liget	www.narancs-liget.hu/
	adomanykozpont/index.html
Shoah Foundation	sfi.usc.edu/international/hungarian
Somer	somer.hu
Szarvas	www.szarvas.hu
Szochnut	www.szochnut.hu
Taglit Birthright Israel	www.facebook.com/
Hungary/Magyarország	TaglitBirthrightIsraelHungary
Tikva Hungary	www.mazsihisz.hu/
	2013/09/23/tanulj-a-tikvaval-6464.html
Tom Lantos Institute	tomlantosinstitute/hu
WIZO (Women's International	www.wizo.org
Zionist Organization)	
Yellow-Star Houses	www.yellowstarhouses.org
Zachor	iremember.hu

Festivals and Special Events	Website
Bálint Ház Events	www.facebook.com/BalintHaz/events
Bánkitó Festivál	www.facebook.com/bankitofeszt
Jewish Cultural Festival Budapest	www.budapestbylocals.com/
	event/jewish-summer-festival-in-budapest
Judafest	www.judafest.org
Negyed7Negyed8	www.facebook.com/negyed7negyed8
Teleki Tér Events	www.facebook.com/groups/telekiter/events
Yom Haatzmaut Hungary	izionist.org/eng/tag/yom-haatzmaut-hungary
ZsiFi: Hungarian Jewish Film Festival	zsifi.org/english

Food	Website
BaMo Kosher Store	jewisheurope.org/detail.asp?ID=1074
Cari Mama (Kosher Dairy Pizza)	www.carimama.hu/en
Carmel – Glatt Kosher	www.carmel.hu

Dafke Deli	www.dafkedeli.com
Fröhlich Kosher Confectionary	www.frohlich.hu
Fülemüle Étterem	www.fulemule.hu
Hanna – Glatt Kosher	www.facebook.com/HannaKosherRestaurant
Hummusbar Budapest	www.hummusbar.hu
Kádár Étkezde	welovebudapest.com/cafes.and.restaurants.l/ cheap.dinner.l/kadar.etkezde
Köleves Vendéglö	www.kolevesvendeglo.hu
Macesz Huszár	maceszhuszar.hu
Mazel Tov	www.facebook.com/mazeltovbp
Kazimír Bisztró	plus.google.com/102169850728746460627/ about?gl=hu&hl=en
Szamos Marcipán	www.szamosmarcipan.hu/en
Raj Ráchel Tortazsalon	torta.hu/raj-rachel-tortatervezo
Rosenstein	rosenstein.hu
Yidisshe Mama Mia	ymmrestaurant.com

Media	Website
Új Élet *(New Life)*	www.mazsihisz.hu/ index.php?page=dm_list&dmcis=2
Szombat *(Saturday)*	www.szombat.org
Múlt és Jövő *(Past and Future)*	www.multesjovo.hu

Memorial	Learn More
Carl Lutz	www.greatsynagogue.hu/blog/?page_id=253
Hanna Szenes	www.jewish.hu/view.php?clabel=szenes_hanna
Holocaust Memorial Center	www.hdke.hu/en
House of Fates	hungarianspectrum.org/tag/house-of-fates
House of Terror	www.terrorhaza.hu/en/museum/about_us.html
Hungarian Jewish Museum	www.zsidomuzeum.hu/ index.php?set_lang_code=en
Mediaeval Jewish Chapel – Budapest History Museum	www.btm.hu/eng/?q=imahaz
Raoul Wallenberg Holocaust	en.wikipedia.org/wiki/Dohány_

Memorial Park	Street_Synagogue#Raoul_Wallenberg_ Holocaust_Memorial_Park
Szabadság Tér Monument	hungarianspectrum.org/2014/ 04/16/days-of-protest-but-the-nazi- monument-will-stand-in-budapest
Shoes on the Danube	en.wikipedia.org/wiki/shoes_on_the_danube_bank
"Tree of Life" in	haygenealogy.com/nagy/
Dohány Street Synagogue	images/ahmemorial.html
Wallenberg Memorial –	www.greatsynagogue.hu/
Wallenberg utca	gallery_raoul.html
Wallenberg Statue in Buda	www.budapest.com/city_guide/ sights/monuments_of_art/raoul_wallenbergs statue_in_buda.en.html

Mikvah	Website
Ohel Sarah	www.mikvah.org/mikvah410/mikvah_ohel_sarah

School	Website
Amerikai Alapítványi Iskola	www.aai.co.hu/wordpress)t/index.php
Bet Menachem School	jewisheurope.org/detail.asp?ID=1261
BZSH Anna Frank Kollégium	www.annafrankkollegium.hu
BZSH Benjámin Óvoda	www.benjaminovi.hu
Central European University	web.ceu.hu/jewishstudies/about.htm
ELTE Hebrew and Israeli Studies	www.elte.hu/en
Gán Menáchem óvoda	www.zsidoiskola.hu/index.php?lang=_eng
Jewish Theological Seminary – University of Jewish Studies	www.or-zse.hu
Lauder	www.lauder.hu
Radnoti	www.radnoti.hu
Scheiber Sándor	www.scheiber.hu
Trendeli Nursery	www.trendeli.hu/bolcsode

Social Services · Website

Alma Utca Orthodox Nursing Home	godaven.com/detail.asp?Id=7274
Amerikai út 53 Nursing Home	
Jaffe Csaladsegito Szolgalat (Families at Risk)	www.mazs.hu/ magyar_zsigo_szocialis_segely_alapitvan y/tevekenysegeink_programjaink_jaffe _zsido_csaladsegito_szolgalat.html
Mazsihisz Szeretetkorhaz Hospital	www.szeretetkorhaz.hu
Idösek Otthona	www.ujpest.hu/hir/6996/Idosek_Otthona

Synagogue · Website

Alma utca 2 (Orthodox)	godaven.com/detail.asp?Id=7274
Amerikai út 53 Nursing Home	
Dohány utca 2 (Neolog)	www.dohanyutcaizsinagoga.hu
Bét Orim	www.facebook.com/betorim
Berzeviczy utca 8 (Újpest)	budapestcity.org/05 templomok/04/Ujpesti-zsinagoga/ infex-hu.htm
Bét Sálom (Conservative, Orthodox)	www.facebook.com/betshalom
Budakeszi út 48	
Dessewffy utca 23 (Orthodox)	www.facebook.com/ orthodoxiamagyarorszagon/info
Dor Hadas	dorhadas.com/en/dor-hadas
Dózsa György út 55	hu.wikipedia.org/wiki/Dózsa_György_úti_zsinagóga
Frankel Leó út 49 (Neolog)	frankel.hu/language/en
Hegedûs Gyula utca 3 (Bét Smuél)	
Hunyadi tér 3	
István út 17 (Behlen téri)	www.bethlenter.com
József körút 27	
Kazinczy utca 27 (Orthodox)	www.greatsynagogue.hu/ gallery_Kazinczy.html
Klauzal Shul	
Köbányai Zsinagóga	
Lajos utca 163 (Óbudai) (Chabad)	obudaizsinagoga.zsido.com
Mediaeval Jewish Chapel	www.btm.hu/eng/?q=imahaz

Nagyfuvaros utca 4

Páva utca 39 (Bokréta u. 27)

Rumbach Sebestyén utca 11-13   www.rumbachutcaizsinagoga.hu

Szim Salom (Reform)   www.szimsalom.hu

Táncsics utca (Medieval Jewish   www.budapest.com/city_guide/
Prayer House)   culture/churches/mediaeval_
                                                   jewish_chapel.en.html

Teleki Tér 22 (Shtiebel) (Orthodox)   www.budapestshul.com

Thököly út 83 (Orthodox)   www.bpxv.hu/index/
                                                   php?page=egyhazak&id=13

(BZSH Zuglói Templomkörzet)

Vazvári Pál utca 5

Visegrádi utca 3 (Pesti Shul) (Orthodox)   pestishul.wordpress.com

90956690R00205

Made in the USA
Columbia, SC
10 March 2018